The LAW of CHRIST

The LAW of CHRIST

— CHARLES LEITER —

HANNIBAL, MISSOURI
WWW.GRANTEDMINISTRIES.ORG

THE LAW OF CHRIST:

Copyright © 2012 by Charles Leiter.
Published by Granted Ministries Press, *A Division of Granted Ministries*.

Cover design and interior layout by Scott Schaller.
All rights reserved.

For information or additional copies of *The Law of Christ*
and other resources write:
GRANTED MINISTRIES PRESS
120 N. Third St.
Hannibal, MO 63401 USA
www.grantedministries.org
orders@grantedministries.org

ISBN 978-0-9840318-0-1
Library of Congress Control Number: 2012939870

ALL RIGHTS RESERVED.
No part of this publication may be reproduced, stored in a retrieval system, or transmitted in any form by any means—electronic, mechanical, photocopy, recording, or otherwise—except for brief quotations in printed reviews, without the prior permission of the publisher. Subject to USA copyright law.

Unless otherwise noted all Scripture quotations taken from the New American Standard Bible®, Copyright © 1960, 1962, 1963, 1968, 1971, 1972, 1973, 1975, 1977, 1995 by The Lockman Foundation.
Used by permission.

Scripture references which are cited with NAS95 refer to the 1995 edition of the New American Standard Bible, copyrighted by The Lockman Foundation.

First Edition
Printed in the United States of America
2012

Contents

Acknowledgements 11
Foreword 13
Preface 15

THE FLOW OF REDEMPTIVE HISTORY 19

Chapter 1 Old and New 21
   Not the Law of Moses 22
   The Old Covenant 23
   The New Covenant 24

Chapter 2 Abraham and Christ 29
   The Promises—Initial Fulfillment 31
   The Promises—Ultimate Fulfillment 32
   Christ 38

Chapter 3 The Abrahamic Covenant: "Promise" 41
   Promise 42
   Immutable 42
   Unconditional 44
   Certain 47

Chapter 4 The Mosaic Covenant: "Law" 51
   Blessings and Curses 52
   Law vs. Promise 56
   Why the Law Then? 57
   Promise vs. Law 58
   "Shut Up Under Sin" 61

Chapter 5 The New Covenant: "Faith" 65
   Promise Fulfilled 66
   Law Fulfilled 67
   The Glorious Cross 68

Chapter 6 Principles of Interpretation 71
   Spiritual Realities 71
   New Interpreting Old 74
   Christ the Key 75
   Hidden to be Revealed 77

FREEDOM FROM THE LAW

Chapter 7 Not Under Law 83
    The Curse 83
    Blessing and Favor 84
    External Rules 86
    Supply and Demand 88

Chapter 8 Listen to Him 93
    A Prophet Like Moses 94
    Prophet, Priest, and King 96
    Listen to Him 97
    God's Final Word to Men 98
    But I Say Unto You 99
    Civil Nation vs. Spiritual Nation 100
    Slaves vs. Sons 103

Chapter 9 The Least of These Commandments 107
    Lessons from the Ox 110
    Applying the Old Testament 113
    Searching for Christ 115

THE LAW OF CHRIST

Chapter 10 The New Commandment 121
    New Covenant 122
    New Example 123
    New Creation 123
    The Law of Love 124

Chapter 11 The Essence of the Law 127
    The Law—Its Essence 128
    The Law—Wonderful and Terrifying 129
    The Law—Its Applications 130
    The Law Written on the Heart 131
    The Law of Moses 133
    The Law of Christ 134

Chapter 12 Love and Law 137
    Love's Essential Nature 138
    Specific Commandments 139
    "Non-essential" Commandments 141
    Conclusion 142

Chapter 13 The Centrality of Love	**145**
Chapter 14 As I Have Loved You	**159**
Christ Our Standard	160
Following Christ	161
Serving	161
Yielding Our Rights	162
Accepting One Another	162
Forgiving One Another	163
Giving	163
Loving Our Wives	164
Walking in Love	164
Laying Down Our Lives	164
Not Striking Back	165
Endurance	165
Humility	166
Chapter 15 "One Another" Verses	**169**
Love One Another	170
Serve One Another	171
Pray for One Another	172
Build Up One Another	172
Be Humble Toward One Another	173
Forgive and Forbear One Another	174
Do Not Judge One Another	174
Be Honest with One Another	175
Maintain Unity with One Another	175
Be at Peace with One Another	176
Show Affection to One Another	176
Chapter 16 The Law of Christ	**179**
No "List of Rules"	179
The Outworkings of Love	181
Proving the Will of God	182
Who Kissed Me?	184
Is Your Mother Still Living?	186
Life in the Spirit	187
"Copious Laws"	188
Chapter 17 The Superiority of the Law of Christ	**191**
Coveting	192
Lust	193
Giving	193
Conviction of Sin	194

Apostolic Preaching.. 196
Christ Crucified... 198
Conviction by the Law of Christ.. 200
The Second Mile... 200
"Ordinary" Christians.. 205

Chapter 18 The Ministry of the Spirit—Part I........................ 207
   Old vs. New.. 208
   Letter vs. Spirit... 209
   The Ministry of the Spirit... 211
   The Fruit of the Spirit.. 212

Chapter 19 The Ministry of the Spirit—Part II....................... 217
   The Vine and the Branches.. 217
   Beholding the Glory of Christ... 219
   Cultivating a Love Relationship.. 221
   "Striving"... 222
   "According to His Power".. 224
   Sarah Edwards... 226
   Dirk Willems... 226
   Howell Harris.. 228

Chapter 20 Conclusion.. 231

APPENDICES   235

Appendix A Key Concepts... 237
   The Flow of Redemptive History.. 237
   Freedom from the Law.. 237
   The Law of Christ.. 238

Appendix B "God is Love".. 241

Appendix C "Civil, Ceremonial, and Moral"........................ 245
   The Law—A Unit... 245
   Civil, or Ceremonial, or Moral?.. 247
   "The Unchanging Moral Law".. 248
   Conclusion... 252

Appendix D The Lawful Use of the Law............................... 255
   Love is the Goal... 255
   To Convict the Jews of Sin.. 256
   To Testify of Christ.. 257
   To Instruct Believers... 258

    Using the Law Today 260
    The Ten Commandments 261

Appendix E   Frequently Asked Questions 265
    1. Are we obligated to keep the Sabbath Day? 265
    2. How are we to observe the Lord's Day? 266
    3. Is the Law "not too difficult" to obey? 274
    4. Is New Testament "law" made for a righteous man? 275
    5. Is the law of Christ a "higher" standard than the Law of Moses? 277
    6. Was the Abrahamic Covenant conditional or unconditional? 278
    7. Wasn't the Old Covenant actually a covenant of grace? 281
    8. Is the Law a "tutor" to Gentiles as well as Jews? 287
    9. Should we teach our children the Ten Commandments? 289
    10. What is the definition of sin, if not the Ten Commandments? 289
    11. What does it mean to have the "law written on the heart"? 290
    12. Were true believers in Old Testament times "born again"? 291
    13. Why is the term "in-lawed to Christ" significant? 293
    14. Why would Jews think Jesus came to "abolish" the Law? 294
    15. What does it mean that "the Law is spiritual"? 294
    16. Did Jesus only correct Jewish distortions of the Law? 296
    17. How can love tell us that homosexuality is wrong? 297
    18. Is it wrong to eat foods containing blood? 298
    19. Is it wrong to get tattoos? 299
    20. How does the New Covenant relate to infant baptism? 301
    21. What is the relationship between the church and Israel? ... 303
    22. Should Christians have as many children as possible? 306
    23. Were "ceremonial" laws meant as rules of good hygiene? 307
    24. How does the "law of Christ" relate to "theonomy"? 308
    25. Is the present-day teaching of "patriarchy" Biblical? 309
    26. How does "the law of Christ" relate to "pacifism"? 310
    27. Is it right for Christians to fight in "just" wars, etc.? 311

Appendix F   Legalism vs. Lawlessness 315
    Opposing Errors 315
    Characteristics of Legalism 316
    Characteristics of Lawlessness 324

Appendix G   Love in the New Testament 329
    God's Love 329
    Our Love for God 334
    Our Love for Others 338

ACKNOWLEDGEMENTS

I want to express my special gratitude to Garrett Holthaus of Kirksville, Missouri, for his helpful theological research and many valuable suggestions regarding this book's content, as well as his faithful friendship over the years that it was being written. I am also indebted to Paul Washer of HeartCry Missionary Society for consenting to write a foreword for the book and for taking the time to read and reread it before doing so. Most of all, I want to thank my wife, Mona—my best helper and greatest encourager—for her unfailing support during the production of this work.

FOREWORD

Since the first printing of Charles Leiter's earlier work, *Justification and Regeneration*, I have been amazed at the countless positive testimonies that I have received from believers around the world. What they all seem to have gained is a newfound freedom and joy established upon a clearer understanding of all that God has done for them in Christ. Any attempt to afford the believer a clearer understanding of the person and work of Christ is to be wholeheartedly commended. How much greater the commendation when the attempt is successful!

In his present work, *The Law of Christ*, Pastor Leiter carries on in the same tradition of making much of Christ and directing us to Him, not only for our justification, but also for our ultimate rule of ethics and our limitless source of life. From the preface to the final page, he draws our attention to Christ as the greatest revelation of the nature and will of God. Following the example of God the Father on the Mount of Transfiguration, Pastor Leiter points us to Christ and declares, "This is God's beloved Son, hear ye Him!"

Each chapter of this book is like the unfolding of a revelation. We are taken on a journey from the very beginning of God's redemptive work to its perfect fulfillment in the person of Christ. Along the way, we are pointed to the promises made to Abraham, the Law given to Moses, and the future hope of the Prophets. However, we are not allowed to tarry in any of these places too long. The one goal in view is that we be carried to Christ and left there.

Having established the supremacy of Christ in God's redemptive plan, Pastor Leiter goes on to expound the essence of what it really means to be and act Christian. For me, this is where the work truly shines. Over the years that he has been my friend, I have had the privilege of listening to Pastor Leiter teach these truths many times, and yet they have never lost their splendor. They are as marvelous to me now as they were the first time I heard them. I cannot communicate to you, the reader, how much my life has been blessed and transformed by these teachings. It is a most beautiful and empowering truth that the Christian life is just that: *It is life*, the very *life of Christ* in us. As stated in the preface, Christianity is not a system of philosophy or even a collection of timeless eternal truths; Christianity is the person of Christ!

It is a rare and wonderful blessing for me to recommend a book that not only honors the Scriptures, but also has been used by God as an instrument of transformation in my own life. Therefore, it is with great joy that I recommend this book to you. I have no doubt that every sincere believer who reads through it will find many pearls of great price that will lead them to a higher view of Christ, a greater appreciation for His work on their behalf, and greater power to live for His glory!

Paul David Washer

PREFACE

> And the Word became flesh, and dwelt among us, and we beheld His glory, glory as of the only begotten from the Father, full of grace and truth....For the Law was given through Moses; grace and truth were realized through Jesus Christ.   John 1:14, 17

Christianity is Christ! It is not a system of philosophy or a collection of timeless eternal truths. Rather, it is the story of how God Himself invaded this fallen world two thousand years ago in the glorious Person of Jesus Christ. The eternal "Word" who "was God"[1] "became flesh, and dwelt among us"—speaking words that had never before been spoken[2] and doing deeds that had never before been done.[3] In the presence of His unique divine glory—"glory as of the only begotten from the Father, full of grace and truth"— the apostles fell prostrate in awe and wonder. They then went forth proclaiming, not their own philosophies, but the glories of the One whom they had *seen and heard:* "What was from the beginning, what we have heard, what we have seen with our eyes, what we beheld and our hands handled, concerning the Word of Life—and the life was manifested, and we have seen and bear witness and proclaim to you the eternal life, which was with the Father and was manifested to us—what we have seen and heard we proclaim to you also, that you also may have fellowship with us; and indeed our fellowship is with the Father, and with His Son Jesus Christ."[4]

With the coming of Jesus Christ into the world, such a light of revelation shone among men that all former revelations now seem dark by comparison. He is the "Sunrise from on high" who has "visited" us.[5] He is the "true light which, coming into the world, enlightens every man."[6] He is God's final word to mankind,[7] "the radiance of His glory and the exact representation of His nature."[8] He is "the image of the invisible God"[9]; to see Him is to see the Father.[10] In Him "all the fulness of Deity dwells in bodily form."[11]

---

[1] John 1:1   [2] John 7:46   [3] John 9:32; 15:24   [4] 1 John 1:1-3   [5] Luke 1:78
[6] John 1:9   [7] Hebrews 1:1-2   [8] Hebrews 1:3   [9] Colossians 1:15   [10] John 14:9
[11] Colossians 2:9

In Him are hidden "all the treasures of wisdom and knowledge."[1] He is the goal toward which all history moves.[2]

It is in the context of this all-surpassing glory of Christ that John wrote the words quoted above: *"The Law was given through Moses; grace and truth were realized through Jesus Christ."* John does not mean that there was no grace or truth in the Law of Moses; indeed, there was. But in comparison with the absolute divine "fulness"[3] of grace and truth found in Jesus Christ, the grace and truth of the Old Covenant pale to insignificance. In the words of Paul, "For indeed what *had* glory, in this case has *no* glory on account of the glory that surpasses it."[4] Moses is to Christ as a candle is to the sun. It is this reality that we must ever bear in mind if we are to rightly understand the "law of Christ."

Like Christianity itself, the law of Christ is *Christ*. It is not a system of rules for men to follow. It is not the setting forth of a code of wise behavior as in Confucianism or the teaching of a "Noble Eight-Fold Path" as in Buddhism. Rather, it is Christ Himself, in all the wonder of His perfect divine humanity, calling His disciples to *follow Him*[5] and empowering them to do so by *His own resurrection life* "working within" them.[6] The high calling of every Christian is nothing less than to "put on the Lord Jesus Christ"![7]

This book, then, is an attempt to capture something of the unspeakable privilege of knowing and following Christ Jesus our Lord, while the very "life of Jesus" is being "manifested in our mortal flesh."[8] Its chapters explore what the Bible means when it describes Christians as those who "serve in newness of the Spirit and not in oldness of the letter,"[9] and they seek to set forth the tremendous liberties and great responsibilities given to us as mature sons of God.

What it means to "love as Christ loved" is an ocean with depths that no Christian will ever fathom during this lifetime. This book can only attempt to provide a basic understanding of what the law of Christ is and to point believers to Christ's resurrection

---

[1] Colossians 2:3   [2] Ephesians 1:9-10; Colossians 1:15-18   [3] John 1:14, 16
[4] 2 Corinthians 3:10 [Italics added for emphasis, here and throughout the book.]   [5] Matthew 9:9   [6] Ephesians 3:20; see also Ephesians 1:19-20; Philippians 3:10.   [7] Romans 13:14   [8] 2 Corinthians 4:11   [9] Romans 7:6

life, which alone can empower them to "fulfill" it. Those who adhere closely to certain forms of either "Covenant Theology" or "Dispensationalism" or "New Covenant Theology" may find some aspects of the book to be disappointing. Nevertheless, it is hoped that all true believers will hear in its pages the voice of their Shepherd calling them to follow Him more closely.

To aid readers in understanding the flow of thought, the book has been divided into three sections: Part One deals with the unfolding of redemptive history from creation to the coming of Christ, Part Two with the meaning of the Christian's freedom from the Law, and Part Three with the law of Christ itself. Throughout this book, many important Scriptures have been assigned to footnotes, and these are placed at the bottom of each page for easy reference. Several controversial issues are also considered in appendices, so as not to obscure unnecessarily the book's central theme. Some will strongly disagree with the positions I have taken in this book. If you are among those, I can only plead with you *to study these appendices carefully with an open mind* before discounting the book entirely. In the end, it is the Bible itself that must govern our theology, not the creeds and confessions of men, however worthy and revered they may be.

As I have approached this subject, I have been aware again and again of my unworthiness to deal with such a topic. How can we even speak of "loving as Christ loved" without hanging our heads in shame at the selfishness and coldness we still so often find within ourselves? In light of this, one cannot help but echo the words of Paul: "Who is adequate for these things?"[1] How thankful we can be that though we are *not* "adequate in ourselves to consider *anything* as coming from ourselves," yet "our adequacy *is* from God, who also made us adequate as servants of a new covenant, not of the letter, but of the Spirit; for the letter kills, but the Spirit gives life"![2]

> *Lord, it is my chief complaint*
> *That my love is weak and faint;*
> *Yet I love Thee, and adore;*
> *O for grace to love Thee more!*
>
> William Cowper

---

[1] 2 Corinthians 2:16   [2] 2 Corinthians 3:5-6

PART ONE

THE FLOW OF REDEMPTIVE HISTORY

If we are ever to catch a glimpse of the surpassing glories of the "law of Christ," we must first understand the flow of redemptive history. From the time of creation onwards, all of God's dealings with mankind converge on and find their meaning in Christ. From the very beginning, God was moving history towards its ultimate consummation in Him. His covenants with Noah, Abraham, Moses, and David were but stepping-stones leading to the Messiah. God spoke to the fathers through the prophets "in many portions and in many ways,"[1] but His revelation of Himself and of His will for mankind was always partial and incomplete. As a result, "many prophets and righteous men"[2] desired to hear the words that Christ would one day utter, but did not hear them. It was only when "the Word became flesh and dwelt among us" that God's final word to mankind was spoken, and it is in this final word that the "law of Christ" is made known to us.

Chapters 1-5 of Part One give a brief overview of the relationship between the Abrahamic, Mosaic, and New Covenants, showing that all Old Testament history finds its culmination and fulfillment in Christ. Chapter 6 then summarizes several basic principles of interpretation that have surfaced during this overview. This prepares the way for Part Two, where the meaning of the Christian's freedom from the Law of Moses is explored, followed by Part Three, where our attention will be focused on the law of Christ itself.

---

[1] Hebrews 1:1   [2] Matthew 13:17

– CHAPTER ONE –

OLD AND NEW

> For though I am free from all men, I have made myself a slave to all, that I might win the more. And to the Jews I became as a Jew, that I might win Jews; to those who are under the Law, as under the Law, though not being myself under the Law, that I might win those who are under the Law; to those who are without law, as without law, though not being without the law of God but under the law of Christ, that I might win those who are without law. To the weak I became weak, that I might win the weak; I have become all things to all men, that I may by all means save some. And I do all things for the sake of the gospel, that I may become a fellow partaker of it.
>
> 1 Corinthians 9:19-23

It is difficult for us to grasp just how radical these words were when they were first penned almost two thousand years ago. For every Jew of the first century, the human race consisted of two (and only two) categories: Jew and Gentile. But in these verses, Paul—who had grown up in the strictest sect of Judaism, a "Pharisee of the Pharisees"—separates himself from both groups. He speaks of "the Jews" as "those who are under the Law" and of the Gentiles as "those who are without law," but he makes it very clear that he belongs to neither group. As a Christian, he is neither "under the Law" nor "without law"; instead, he is "under the law of Christ." That is, Paul no longer thinks of godly living in terms of the Mosaic Covenant, nor does he give himself to ungodly license; rather, his heart and mind are now focused on Christ.

Paul's example in this regard provides us with an important test: If we as Christians were asked to summarize our standard for godly living, would our minds immediately turn, as Paul's did, to the "law of Christ"? Or would we think of some other standard? Do we even know what the law of Christ is? And if we do not, is there not something very wrong with the years of instruction we have received about what is important in the Christian life? Just what is this "law of Christ"? In seeking to answer this question, we will find ourselves drawn, as always, to the Person of Christ Himself. For the Christian, "to live is Christ."[1] But before we examine what the law of Christ is, we must first consider what it is not.

NOT THE LAW OF MOSES

Paul makes it very clear in these verses that the law of Christ is *not* the Law of Moses: "To the Jews I became as a Jew, that I might win Jews; to those who are under the Law, as under the Law, *though not being myself under the Law.*" Christians are not under the Law! This is the uniform teaching of the New Testament, and its meaning will be explored more fully in later chapters, but at this point, a few Scripture quotations will be sufficient to establish the fact:

- "Therefore, my brethren, you also were *made to die to the Law* through the body of Christ, that you might be joined to another, to Him who was raised from the dead, that we might bear fruit for God."[2]

- "But now *we have been released from the Law, having died to that by which we were bound*, so that we serve in newness of the Spirit and not in oldness of the letter."[3]

- "For He Himself is our peace, who made both groups into one, and broke down the barrier of the dividing wall, by *abolishing* in His flesh *the enmity, which is the Law of commandments contained in ordinances*, that in Himself He might make the two into one new man, thus establishing peace, and might reconcile them both in one body to God through the cross, *by it having put to death the enmity.*"[4]

- "For through the Law *I died to the Law*, that I might live to God."[5]

---

[1] Philippians 1:21 [2] Romans 7:4 [3] Romans 7:6 [4] Ephesians 2:14-16
[5] Galatians 2:19

- "Therefore the Law has become our tutor to lead us to Christ, that we may be justified by faith. But now that faith has come, *we are no longer under a tutor.*" [1]

Such statements regarding the Law would have appeared blasphemous to any Jew, and for good reason: *the Law had been given to Israel by God Himself!*

THE OLD COVENANT

When God established His covenant with Israel on Mount Sinai nearly fifteen hundred years before Christ, He set forth a visible display of His glory unlike any that had ever been seen in human history. We are told that the Lord "came down on Mount Sinai in the sight of all the people." [2] The entire mountain was so consecrated by God's presence that any man or beast that so much as "touched the border of it" was to be "surely put to death." [3] "There were thunder and lightning flashes and a thick cloud upon the mountain and a very loud trumpet sound, so that all the people who were in the camp trembled.... Mount Sinai was all in smoke because the LORD descended upon it in fire; and its smoke ascended like the smoke of a furnace, and the whole mountain quaked violently." [4] We are told that when Moses spoke, "God answered him with thunder." [5] God's audible voice was so terrifying that the people "begged no further word should be spoken to them" [6] lest they die.[7] The author to the Hebrews speaks of "blazing fire and darkness and gloom and whirlwind" and a sight "so terrible" that even Moses said, "I am full of fear and trembling." [8]

This was the context of God's giving of His holy and awful Law on Mount Sinai! It was at this time that He gave Israel the "words of the covenant, the Ten Commandments," [9] written by the very finger of God on tablets of stone,[10] as well as all the other laws pertaining

---

[1] Galatians 3:24-25   [2] Exodus 19:11   [3] Exodus 19:12   [4] Exodus 19:16, 18
[5] Exodus 19:19   [6] Hebrews 12:19   [7] Exodus 20:19   [8] Hebrews 12:18, 21
[9] Exodus 34:28; Deuteronomy 4:13   [10] Exodus 31:18; Deuteronomy 9:10

to their life as His covenant people. The wisdom and equity of these laws placed the nation of Israel far above all other nations: "What great nation is there that has statutes and judgments as righteous as this whole law which I am setting before you today?"[1] "So keep and do them, for that is your wisdom and your understanding in the sight of the peoples who will hear all these statutes and say, 'Surely this great nation is a wise and understanding people.'"[2]

Is it any wonder, then, that the Jews "relied upon the Law" and "boasted in the Law"?[3] After all, they had been "entrusted" with the very "oracles of God,"[4] the "form of knowledge and of the truth"![5] And is it any wonder that they would view a former Jew like Paul, who proclaimed every Christian's freedom from the Law, as an utter apostate? How could any Jew ever believe that the covenant made on Sinai with such visible displays of divine glory had now passed away? Yet God, through the prophets, had already foretold just such an event.

THE NEW COVENANT

Over eight hundred years after God established His covenant with Israel through Moses, He raised up the prophet Jeremiah to tell His people of a glorious new day that was coming:

> "Behold, days are coming," declares the LORD, "when I will make a new covenant with the house of Israel and with the house of Judah, not like the covenant which I made with their fathers in the day I took them by the hand to bring them out of the land of Egypt, My covenant which they broke, although I was a husband to them," declares the LORD. "But this is the covenant which I will make with the house of Israel after those days," declares the LORD, "I will put My law within them, and on their heart I will write it; and I will be their God, and they shall be My people.

---

[1] Deuteronomy 4:5-8; Psalm 147:19-20   [2] Deuteronomy 4:6   [3] Romans 2:17, 23
[4] Romans 3:2   [5] Romans 2:20

> And they shall not teach again, each man his neighbor and each man his brother, saying, 'Know the LORD,' for they shall all know Me, from the least of them to the greatest of them," declares the LORD, "for I will forgive their iniquity, and their sin I will remember no more."
>
> Jeremiah 31:31-34

We can only imagine the eager expectation with which every godly Jew awaited the coming of this "new covenant"—a covenant in which every participant "from the least to the greatest" would know the Lord personally. For one hundred years they waited, then two hundred, then four hundred, then six hundred. Finally, *after six hundred years*, not amidst terrifying peals of thunder and earthquakes and flashes of lightning, but in the quiet of an "upper room," the Lord Jesus Christ held forth a cup to His little band of disciples and announced, "This cup which is poured out for you is the *new covenant* in My blood."[1] With these simple words, a covenant was inaugurated that will last forever,[2] transforming human history and encompassing men from every tribe and tongue and nation on the face of the earth. Just as the covenant on Sinai was inaugurated with blood,[3] so this covenant would be inaugurated with blood—not with the blood of bulls and goats, which can never take away sins,[4] but with the "precious blood"[5] of God's own Son.

It is important for us to remember that when God made His covenant with Israel on Mount Sinai, He did not say, "I am going to make an *old* covenant with you." The Old Covenant is now called "old" for one reason only: it has been replaced by a "new" one. The writer to the Hebrews drives home the implications of this fact: "When He said, 'A new covenant,' He has made the first obsolete. But whatever is becoming obsolete and growing old is ready to disappear."[6] The covenant made on Sinai is *obsolete*; it is *old* and has now *disappeared*. It is for this reason that Paul adamantly maintains that Christians are no longer "under the Law."

---

[1] Luke 22:20 [2] Hebrews 13:20 [3] Hebrews 9:18-22 [4] Hebrews 10:4
[5] 1 Peter 1:19 [6] Hebrews 8:13; see also 2 Corinthians 3:6, 14 "new, old."

The Jews of Paul's day had a tremendous problem accepting such reasoning. Even those who were willing to profess faith in Christ sometimes insisted that it was necessary for Gentile converts to be circumcised and to observe the Law of Moses in order to be saved.[1] For any man who would thus "distort the gospel of Christ," Paul pronounced a resounding "Let him be accursed!"[2] Moreover, Paul was prepared to refute these "false brethren"[3] and "Judaizers" from the Bible itself. As we will see in the next chapter, he did this by unfolding the real meaning of the history recorded in the Old Testament Scriptures and especially of the covenant God had made with Abraham.

---

[1] Acts 15:1, 5   [2] Galatians 1:6-8   [3] Galatians 2:4

Chapter One Review

Paul describes the Christian's standard of conduct as "the law of Christ." He makes it clear that the law of Christ is not the Law of Moses.

The Law of Moses was given directly by God in an awesome display of glory on Mt. Sinai. The wisdom and equity of its statutes set the nation of Israel high above all other nations. But over 800 years after the Old Covenant was given on Mt. Sinai, God promised to one day establish a "new covenant" with "the house of Israel and the house of Judah."

This new covenant was inaugurated with the death and resurrection of the Lord Jesus Christ. Since the covenant established by Christ is described as "new" and is "not like" the covenant made on Mt. Sinai, it is obvious that the Mosaic Covenant has now become "old" and "obsolete." It has been superseded and replaced by the New Covenant.

The Jews of Paul's day had great difficulty accepting this fact. Some of them maintained that in order to be saved a person must not only believe on Christ, but also keep the Law of Moses. Paul viewed these people as "false brethren" who were preaching a "different gospel." As we will see in Chapter 2, he refuted them by unfolding the real meaning behind God's covenant with Abraham.

– Chapter Two –

Abraham and Christ

Several years ago, an article setting forth the basic tenets of Judaism was published in a widely read secular magazine. Not surprisingly, the rabbi who wrote that article asserted twice that the greatest Jew who had ever lived was Moses. This has been the conviction of Jews for many centuries, and it was the conviction of the Jews in Paul's day. But Paul realized from the Scriptures that the truth lay elsewhere. With the obvious exception of the Messiah Himself, the key player in Jewish history was not Moses, but Abraham. God revealed the foundational principles of salvation through His dealings with Abraham; His dealings with Moses only entered the main stream of redemptive history as a tributary—"from the side,"[1] as it were—in order to serve a subsidiary purpose in God's overall plan.

This explains why Paul repeatedly refers to God's dealings with Abraham in order to demonstrate the truths of his own gospel message. For instance, by appealing to the example of Abraham, "the father of believers," Paul is able to prove that justification has always involved the imputation of righteousness to undeserving sinners, by grace alone, through faith alone.[2] He is also able to prove that Abraham's circumcision had nothing to do with his justification[3] and that Abraham's faith provides a pattern for all who "follow in his steps," whether they are Jews or Gentiles.[4]

It should not surprise us then, that it is also in Abraham, and the covenant made with Abraham,[5] that Paul finds a more than adequate answer to those Jews who insisted that Gentiles must keep the Law of Moses in order to be saved. He sets forth this answer in the last half of Galatians 3. Paul's basic argument is simple: Because God's covenant with Abraham and his children ("seed") was ratified hundreds of years before the Mosaic Covenant was given,

---

[1] See Romans 5:20, where the word "entered" is literally "came in beside." See ASV.   [2] Romans 4:1-8   [3] Romans 4:9-12   [4] Romans 4:16-25
[5] Genesis 15:18; 17:1-21

the fulfillment of the Abrahamic Covenant cannot depend in any way on conditions established by the Law of Moses. Furthermore, it is *Christians* who are the true "children of Abraham" and heirs of the promises made to him. Therefore, Christians will receive the heavenly "inheritance" promised to Abraham and his "seed" entirely apart from keeping the Law.

Because the last half of Galatians 3 is so important for a proper understanding of redemptive history, it should be read and studied carefully:

> Brethren, I speak in terms of human relations: even though it is only a man's covenant, yet when it has been ratified, no one sets it aside or adds conditions to it. Now the promises were spoken to Abraham and to his seed. He does not say, "And to seeds," as referring to many, but rather to one, "And to your seed," that is, Christ. What I am saying is this: the Law, which came four hundred and thirty years later, does not invalidate a covenant previously ratified by God, so as to nullify the promise. For if the inheritance is based on law, it is no longer based on a promise; but God has granted it to Abraham by means of a promise.
>
> Why the Law then? It was added because of transgressions, having been ordained through angels by the agency of a mediator, until the seed should come to whom the promise had been made. Now a mediator is not for one party only; whereas God is only one. Is the Law then contrary to the promises of God? May it never be! For if a law had been given which was able to impart life, then righteousness would indeed have been based on law. But the Scripture has shut up all men under sin, that the promise by faith in Jesus Christ might be given to those who believe.
>
> But before faith came, we were kept in custody under the law, being shut up to the faith which was later to be revealed. Therefore the Law has become our tutor to lead us to Christ, that we may be justified by faith. But now that faith has come, we are no longer under a tutor. For you are all sons of God through faith in Christ Jesus. For

all of you who were baptized into Christ have clothed yourselves with Christ. There is neither Jew nor Greek, there is neither slave nor free man, there is neither male nor female; for you are all one in Christ Jesus. And if you belong to Christ, then you are Abraham's offspring, heirs according to promise. Galatians 3:15-29

Here we see that God's covenant with Abraham was based on *promises* that God made to Abraham and his "seed." Those promises were made and confirmed hundreds of years before the Law of Moses was ever given on Mount Sinai. But even in human relations, it is not possible to *add conditions to* or change a covenant that has already been ratified and settled. For example, when a person's "last will and testament" is being read after his death, no one has the right to draw a line through the name of someone listed as a beneficiary or deny the inheritance granted to that person. Even so, the inheritance God had promised to Abraham and his seed could not be conditioned upon or affected in any way by the Law of Moses, which came over four hundred and thirty years after God's promises had been made.

THE PROMISES—INITIAL FULFILLMENT

What, exactly, were the promises that God had made to Abraham? We will consider four of them: God promised Abraham a seed, a nation, a land, and a blessing.

Seed

The promised seed was Isaac, a "child of promise."[1] God promised Abraham, "Sarah your wife shall bear you a son, and you shall call his name Isaac."[2]

Nation

The promised nation was Israel, the physical descendants of Abraham. "I will make you a great nation."[3] "And He took him

---

[1] Galatians 4:28; Romans 9:8-9 [2] Genesis 17:19, 21 [3] Genesis 12:2

outside and said, 'Now look toward the heavens, and count the stars, if you are able to count them.' And He said to him, 'So shall your descendants be.'"[1]

Land

The promised land was Canaan, which God promised to Abraham and his seed as an inheritance. "And the LORD appeared to Abram and said, 'To your descendants [or "seed"] I will give this land.'"[2] "And the LORD said to Abram, after Lot had separated from him, 'Now lift up your eyes and look from the place where you are, northward and southward and eastward and westward; for all the land which you see, I will give it to you and to your descendants forever.'"[3]

Blessing

The promised blessing related to all kinds of material benefits: riches, protection, long life, etc. "And I will bless you, and make your name great; and so you shall be a blessing; and I will bless those who bless you, and the one who curses you I will curse. And in you all the families of the earth shall be blessed."[4] In keeping with these promises, God preserved Abraham for many years and made him rich. At the end of his long life, we read this: "Now Abraham was old, advanced in age; and the LORD had blessed Abraham in every way."[5]

THE PROMISES—ULTIMATE FULFILLMENT

If the Old Testament Scriptures were all we had to guide our understanding, we would likely conclude that these promises to Abraham were mostly physical in nature and found their fulfillment in the material realm. But when we come to the New Testament, we discover that the promises had a much deeper and more wonderful significance than at first appears. What was the full import of these promises to Abraham?

---

[1] Genesis 15:5 [2] Genesis 12:7 [3] Genesis 13:14-15 [4] Genesis 12:2-3
[5] Genesis 24:1

Seed

The real seed promised to Abraham was Christ. "Now the promises were spoken to Abraham and to his seed. He does not say, 'And to seeds,' as referring to many, but rather to one, 'And to your seed,' that is, Christ."[1] Christ was the true seed of Abraham, the One who would finally "inherit" all things, the One through whom "all the nations of the earth" would one day be "blessed."[2] *The promise to Abraham was ultimately made to Christ:* "[The Law] was added... until the seed should come *to whom the promise had been made.*"[3] God's promise to Christ becomes ours only because we are "in Christ." "For all of you who were baptized into Christ *have clothed yourselves with Christ.* There is neither Jew nor Greek, there is neither slave nor free man, there is neither male nor female; *for you are all one in Christ Jesus. And if you belong to Christ, then you are Abraham's offspring* [or "seed"], *heirs according to promise.*"[4] Christians are counted as Abraham's seed because they are "in" the one true Seed, Christ!

Christian, think of it! All of God's promises were made to Christ, and you have the unspeakable privilege of "being in" and "belonging to" Him! You have "clothed yourself with Christ," *and all of His inheritance is yours.* You are a "fellow heir"[5] with Christ!

Nation

When God "took Abraham outside" and instructed him to look toward the heavens and count the stars, promising him so many children that no man could number them, He had something far greater in mind for Abraham than just a large multitude of physical descendants. We learn from the New Testament that the true "children of Abraham" are those who put their faith in Christ: "Therefore, be sure that it is those who are of faith who are sons of Abraham."[6] "And if you belong to Christ, *then you are Abraham's offspring*, heirs according to promise."[7] *"For he is not a Jew who is one outwardly;* neither is circumcision that which is outward in

---

[1] Galatians 3:16 [2] Genesis 22:18 [3] Galatians 3:19 [4] Galatians 3:27-29
[5] Romans 8:17 [6] Galatians 3:7 [7] Galatians 3:29

the flesh. *But he is a Jew who is one inwardly;* and circumcision is that which is of the heart, by the Spirit, not by the letter; and his praise is not from men, but from God."[1] The true fulfillment of God's promise to Abraham that his descendants would be like the stars in number, and "like the sand which is on the seashore,"[2] is found in Revelation 7:9: "After these things I looked, and behold, *a great multitude, which no one could count,* from every nation and all tribes and peoples and tongues, standing before the throne and before the Lamb, clothed in white robes, and palm branches were in their hands."

Thus, the ultimate realization of God's promise to "make Abraham a great nation" was not Israel, but *the church*—the spiritual "nation" referred to by the Lord Jesus Christ in His parable of the vine-growers: "Therefore I say to you, the kingdom of God will be taken away from you, and be given to *a nation* producing the fruit of it."[3] (Notice that according to the Lord Jesus, the church produces "the fruit of the kingdom" without fail. If the institution we call "the church" is not producing fruit, we have a wrong definition and concept of the church!)

Peter, likewise, speaks of the church, not physical Israel, as the ultimate fulfillment of God's Old Testament desire for a "holy nation." Just before the giving of the Law on Mount Sinai, God had promised Israel, "Now then, if you will indeed obey My voice and keep My covenant, then you shall be My own possession among all the peoples... and you shall be to Me a kingdom of priests and a holy nation."[4] Even at its best, however, physical Israel's "holiness"[5] (separation from the rest of the nations) was in large measure external, and her "priests" offered sacrifices that "related only to food and drink and various washings, regulations for the body imposed until a time of reformation."[6] By contrast, Peter says that *Christians* are the true "holy priesthood," called "to offer up spiritual sacrifices acceptable to God through Jesus Christ,"[7]

---

[1] Romans 2:28-29; 9:6-8; Philippians 3:3   [2] Genesis 22:17   [3] Matthew 21:43
[4] Exodus 19:5-6   [5] Leviticus 20:24-26   [6] Hebrews 9:10   [7] 1 Peter 2:5

and *the church* is God's true "holy nation," a "people" for His own possession: "But you are *a chosen race*, a royal priesthood, *a holy nation, a people* for God's own possession, that you may proclaim the excellencies of Him who has called you out of darkness into His marvelous light; *for you once were not a people, but now you are the people of God*; you had not received mercy, but now you have received mercy." [1]

Christian, think of it! You are part of the most wonderful nation that has ever existed! It is a spiritual nation—made up solely of people who are chosen and holy—and it is a nation that will never decay or pass into oblivion—forever! [2]

Land

If we were to read only the Old Testament description of Abraham's wanderings, we might conclude that his main concern was with the physical land of Canaan. But, once again, when we come to the New Testament we learn that Abraham was looking for something far greater than a mere earthly inheritance:

> All these died in faith, without receiving the promises, but having seen them and having welcomed them from a distance, and having confessed that they were *strangers and exiles on the earth*. For those who say such things make it clear that they are *seeking a country of their own*. And indeed if they had been thinking of that country from which they went out, they would have had opportunity to return. But as it is, *they desire a better country, that is a heavenly one*. Therefore God is not ashamed to be called their God; for He has prepared a city for them.   Hebrews 11:13-16

As Abraham's true descendants, Christians will inherit much more than just the land of Canaan. According to Romans 4:13, "the promise to Abraham or to his descendants" was not merely that he would be heir of Canaan, but "that he would be *heir of the*

---

[1] 1 Peter 2:9-10   [2] Isaiah 9:6-7; Daniel 2:44; 7:13-14; Luke 1:32-33

world."[1] "Blessed are the gentle, for they shall *inherit the earth.*"[2] Christians may be persecuted and maligned in this present day, but the ground that now drinks their blood will one day belong to them! As Abraham's true seed, they will *"inherit* the land of their sojournings," just as God promised their father Abraham thousands of years ago.[3]

Christian, think of it! Though you are a "stranger and exile on the earth" at this present time, one day "the new heavens and the new earth" will belong to you! "You have made them to be *a kingdom and priests* to our God; *and they will reign upon the earth.*"[4]

Blessing

When God told Abraham that he would be "blessed" and that "all the nations of the earth" would be blessed in him, the blessing He had in mind was infinitely greater than any material blessing could ever be. Peter alludes to this in his sermon to the Jews after the notable healing of a lame man at the temple gate: "It is you who are the sons of the prophets and of the covenant which God made with your fathers, saying to Abraham, 'And in your seed all the families of the earth shall be *blessed.*' For you first, God raised up His Servant and sent Him *to bless you by turning every one of you from your wicked ways.*"[5] According to Peter, the "blessing" promised to Abraham had to do with men being turned away from their sins. Paul makes the meaning of this blessing even clearer: "The Scripture, foreseeing that God would *justify* the Gentiles by faith, preached the *gospel* beforehand to Abraham, saying, 'All the nations shall be *blessed* in you.'"[6]

The true blessing promised to Abraham and his seed was justification and its fruits. The blessing of justification is just the opposite of the curse and condemnation of the Law: "So then those who are of faith are *blessed* with Abraham, the believer. For as many as are of the works of the law are under a *curse*; for it is written, '*Cursed* is everyone who does not abide by all things written in the book of

---

[1] See also Psalm 2:8. [2] Matthew 5:5 [3] Genesis 17:8; 28:4
[4] Revelation 5:10 (NAS95) [5] Acts 3:25-26 [6] Galatians 3:8

the law, to perform them.'"[1] "Christ redeemed us from the *curse* of the law, having become a *curse* for us—for it is written, '*Cursed* is everyone who hangs on a tree'—in order that in Christ Jesus the *blessing* of Abraham might come to the Gentiles, so that we might receive *the promise of the Spirit* through faith."[2] "Just as David also speaks of the *blessing* upon the man to whom God *reckons righteousness* apart from works: '*Blessed* are those whose lawless deeds have been forgiven, and whose sins have been covered. *Blessed* is the man whose sin the Lord will not take into account.'"[3]

When God told Abraham that through his seed, "all the nations of the earth" would be "blessed,"[4] He was referring to Abraham's true seed, Christ, who would one day shed His blood so that men from "every tribe and tongue and people and nation"[5] could be redeemed, justified, and blessed in Him.

Christian, think of it! The "blessing of Abraham"[6] has come in fullest measure upon *you!* You are no longer *condemned and cursed;* instead, you are *justified and blessed* "with every spiritual blessing in the heavenly places in Christ."[7] Greatest of all these blessings is the "promised"[8] Holy Spirit Himself, given in New Covenant fulness to God's own "sons."[9] Hallelujah!

Once we understand the fuller meaning of God's promises to Abraham, Paul's argument that they cannot depend in any way upon the Law of Moses takes on tremendous significance. The inheritance promised to Christians as the true children of Abraham is glorious beyond measure, and it is bestowed on them *entirely apart from the Law.* It is in this way that Paul refutes the "false brethren" and Judaizers who insisted that Christians must keep the Law of Moses in order to be saved!

---

[1] Galatians 3:9-10 [2] Galatians 3:13-14 [3] Romans 4:6-8 [4] Genesis 22:18
[5] Revelation 5:9 [6] Genesis 28:4; Galatians 3:14 [7] Ephesians 1:3
[8] Galatians 3:14; see "Promise Fulfilled," p. 66. [9] Galatians 4:5-6; Romans 8:15-16

CHRIST

By this time, it should be clear that all the history of the Old Testament converges on Christ. From the very beginning, God was moving history towards its ultimate consummation in the Messiah. Before the foundation of the earth, He had purposed[1] to glorify Himself by saving "in Christ"—by grace alone, through faith alone—a multitude that no man can number. *It is this saving purpose that is the unifying principle behind all God's dealings in human history.* When Paul says that God has "saved us, and called us with a holy calling, not according to our works, but according to His own purpose and grace which was granted us in Christ Jesus from all eternity,"[2] his words apply to all who ever have been or ever will be saved.

We can see God's saving purpose in Christ unfolding from the time of the fall onwards. Immediately after man sinned, before God's curse had even been officially pronounced on the human race, He proclaimed the coming of One who as the "seed of the woman" would crush the serpent's head.[3] In Genesis 5, as a preparation for the coming of this Messiah, God raised up the line of Seth in the place of godly Abel, who was murdered by his brother Cain. As time passed, He made a succession of covenants with men. Each of these covenants was made with a view to the advancement of His one saving purpose. In Genesis 6-9, He preserved the lineage of the Messiah through Noah and made a covenant never again to destroy the earth by flood, thus ensuring that human history would continue until the promised Savior could be born and accomplish redemption. In Genesis 12, He called Abram out of idolatry and made His unconditional promises to him concerning the coming of Christ and the salvation of a great multitude through Him. As a step in this direction, He began to establish a physical nation—the nation later to be known as Israel—to be a recipient and preserver of divine revelation in preparation for the coming One. *Everything centered upon and led up to the coming of Christ.*

---

[1] Ephesians 3:11   [2] 2 Timothy 1:9   [3] Genesis 3:15

The same was true of the Law of Moses! Like the other covenants recorded in the Old Testament Scriptures, it was a stepping stone leading to Christ. It was never intended as a way of salvation or even as something permanent: "Why the Law then? It was *added* because of transgressions...*until* the seed should come to whom the promise had been made."[1] The Mosaic economy was what Paul calls a "tutor" or "child conductor" to lead the Jews to Christ. When Christ came and accomplished redemption, the work of the tutor was ended. "Therefore the Law has become our tutor to lead us to Christ, that we may be justified by faith. *But now that faith has come, we are no longer under a tutor.*"[2] The Law of Moses has found its fulfillment and culmination in Christ.

Paul makes it clear in the first chapter of Ephesians that *all* of God's purposes center on Christ:

> Blessed be the God and Father of our Lord Jesus Christ, who has blessed us with every spiritual blessing in the heavenly places *in Christ*, just as He *chose us in Him* before the foundation of the world, that we should be holy and blameless before Him. In love He predestined us to adoption as sons *through Jesus Christ* to Himself, according to the kind intention of His will, to the praise of the glory of His grace, which He freely bestowed on us *in the Beloved. In Him* we have redemption *through His blood*, the forgiveness of our trespasses, according to the riches of His grace, which He lavished upon us. In all wisdom and insight He made known to us the mystery of His will, according to His kind intention which He *purposed in Him* with a view to an administration suitable to *the fulness of the times, that is, the summing up of all things in Christ, things in the heavens and things upon the earth.*   Ephesians 1:3-10

Everything that God did during the Old Testament era, He did with a view to "the summing up of all things in Christ." *Christ is the focal point and goal of the entire Bible!*

---

[1] Galatians 3:19   [2] Galatians 3:24-25

CHAPTER TWO REVIEW

With the obvious exception of Christ Himself, the key player in Jewish history was not Moses, but Abraham. All of the foundational principles of salvation were revealed through God's dealings with him.

God's covenant with Abraham centered around promises that God freely gave him. These promises included a seed, a nation, a land, and a blessing. They had their initial fulfillment in Isaac (the promised seed), Israel (the promised nation), Canaan (the promised land), and material prosperity (the promised blessing). But God's promises to Abraham also had a deeper significance. They find their ultimate fulfillment in Christ (the promised Seed), the church (the promised nation), the new earth (the Promised Land), and justification and its fruits (the promised blessing).

God ratified His covenant with Abraham hundreds of years before Moses was even born; its fulfillment, therefore, cannot depend in any way on conditions established by the Law of Moses. Christians (the true children of Abraham) will receive their "inheritance" entirely apart from the Law. It is this teaching of Scripture that Paul used to refute the "Judaizers."

All the history of the Old Testament converges on Christ. Everything God did from the creation onwards, He did with a view to "the summing up of all things in Christ." Christ is the focal point and goal of the entire Bible!

– Chapter Three –

The Abrahamic Covenant: "Promise"

Brethren, I speak in terms of human relations: even though it is only a man's covenant, yet when it has been ratified, no one sets it aside or adds conditions to it. Now the promises were spoken to Abraham and to his seed. He does not say, "And to seeds," as referring to many, but rather to one, "And to your seed," that is, Christ. What I am saying is this: the Law, which came four hundred and thirty years later, does not invalidate a covenant previously ratified by God, so as to nullify the promise. For if the inheritance is based on law, it is no longer based on a promise; but God has granted it to Abraham by means of a promise.

Why the Law then? It was added because of transgressions, having been ordained through angels by the agency of a mediator, until the seed should come to whom the promise had been made. Now a mediator is not for one party only; whereas God is only one. Is the Law then contrary to the promises of God? May it never be! For if a law had been given which was able to impart life, then righteousness would indeed have been based on law. But the Scripture has shut up all men under sin, that the promise by faith in Jesus Christ might be given to those who believe.

But before faith came, we were kept in custody under the law, being shut up to the faith which was later to be revealed. Therefore the Law has become our tutor to lead us to Christ, that we may be justified by faith. But now that faith has come, we are no longer under a tutor. For you are all sons of God through faith in Christ Jesus. For all of you who were baptized into Christ have clothed yourselves with Christ. There is neither Jew nor Greek, there is neither slave nor free man, there is neither male nor female; for you are all one in Christ Jesus. And if you belong to Christ, then you are Abraham's offspring, heirs according to promise.   Galatians 3:15-29

As we have already seen, this passage from Paul's letter to the Galatians has profound implications for a correct understanding of redemptive history as a whole. In these verses, Paul sets forth God's dealings with men since the days of Abraham in terms of three categories: *Promise, Law,* and *Faith.* These three categories are embodied in three covenants: the Abrahamic Covenant, the Mosaic Covenant, and the New Covenant. If we are ever to have a proper grasp of the historical unfolding of God's saving purpose in Christ, we must understand the relationship between these three covenants. In Chapters 3-5, we will explore this relationship more fully by considering briefly the nature of each covenant.

PROMISE

Paul thinks of God's covenant with Abraham in terms of *promise*. Throughout the Bible, the concept of "promise" is a very rich one, and the writers of the New Testament refer to it repeatedly.[1] What Paul wants us to grasp when we think of "promise" in the context of the Abrahamic Covenant is that promise is *immutable, unconditional,* and *certain* of fulfillment. Paul brings out these three qualities of promise by using a variety of arguments and illustrations.

IMMUTABLE

The promise God made to Abraham is *immutable*—it *cannot* change. As we noted in Chapter 2, when a person's "last will and testament" is read after his death, no one has the right to draw a line through the name of someone listed as a beneficiary or deny the inheritance granted to that person. Paul argues that if even

---

[1] Luke 24:49; Acts 1:4; 2:33, 39; 7:5, 17; 13:23, 32-33; 26:6-7; Romans 1:2; 4:13-14, 16, 20-21; 9:4, 8-9; 15:8; 2 Corinthians 1:20; Galatians 3:14, 16-22, 29; 4:23, 28; Ephesians 1:13; 2:12; 3:6; 2 Timothy 1:1; Titus 1:2; Hebrews 6:12-18; 7:6; 8:6; 9:15; 10:23, 36; 11:9, 11, 13, 17, 33, 39; 2 Peter 1:4; 3:4, 9, 13

such human covenants are unchangeable, how much more is God's divine covenant with Abraham unchangeable? "Brethren, I speak in terms of human relations: even though it is only a man's covenant, yet when it has been ratified, no one sets it aside or adds conditions to it....What I am saying is this: the Law, which came four hundred and thirty years later, does not invalidate a covenant previously ratified by God, so as to nullify the promise." The promise God made to Abraham is immutable; it cannot be altered or conditioned in any way by the Law of Moses, since the Law came over four hundred years after the promise had been made.

> For when God made the promise to Abraham, since He could swear by no one greater, He swore by Himself, saying, "I will surely bless you, and I will surely multiply you." And thus, having patiently waited, he obtained the promise. For men swear by one greater than themselves, and with them an oath given as confirmation is an end of every dispute. In the same way God, desiring even more to show to *the heirs of the promise* the *unchangeableness* of His purpose, interposed with an oath, in order that by two *unchangeable* things, in which it is impossible for God to lie, *we may have strong encouragement,* we who have fled for refuge in laying hold of the hope set before us. This hope we have as an anchor of the soul, a hope both sure and steadfast and one which enters within the veil, where Jesus has entered as a forerunner for us....
>
> Hebrews 6:13-20

According to these verses, God's promise to Abraham is unchangeable because it rests upon an unchangeable purpose and has been confirmed by an unchangeable oath. Since the promise is ultimately spiritual in nature and is made to *us* (the true "heirs of the promise") *as believers in Christ,* the fact of its immutability gives us "strong encouragement" to press on in "faith and patience" until we "inherit"[1] all that the promise entails.

---

[1] Hebrews 6:12

Unconditional

God's promise to Abraham is not only immutable; it is also *unconditional*—its fulfillment does not depend ultimately upon any conditions that must be met by man.[1] Paul makes this point in several ways throughout his writings. He does this, first of all, by his emphasis on the unilateral (i.e., one-sided) nature of the Abrahamic Covenant. God's covenant with Abraham was "one-sided" in that it was ratified by God Himself,[2] without the agency of a mediator. Mediators are necessary when two parties are involved in a legal transaction. "Now a mediator is not for one party only; whereas God is only one." The Abrahamic Covenant was a one-sided *promise* on God's part, based on His sovereign and gracious purpose in Christ to save a multitude of people. *It bestowed an "inheritance,"* and that inheritance was "granted" to Abraham "by means of a promise."[3] The assignment of an inheritance can take place even without the beneficiary's consent or prior knowledge. For example, when my grandfather's will was read shortly after his death, I was surprised to learn that I had been mentioned by name in that will and was now the possessor of certain of his personal belongings. This is the nature of an inheritance! Over and over, the New Testament emphasizes that Christians are "heirs"[4] of an "inheritance"[5] that is theirs by "promise."[6] Glory to God!

In contrast with the "one-sidedness" of the Abrahamic Covenant, the Mosaic Covenant was "ordained through angels by the agency of a mediator" (Moses) and involved the faithfulness of *two* contracting parties—God and man.[7] The blessings offered in the Law hinged upon man's obedience. God laid down *conditions* that men must meet: "Do this and you will live."[8]

---

[1] See Appendix E, Q.6.   [2] Genesis 15:1-21; Hebrews 6:13-14   [3] Galatians 3:18
[4] Romans 4:13-14; 8:17; Galatians 3:29; 4:1, 7, 30; Ephesians 3:6; Titus 3:7
[5] Galatians 3:18; Ephesians 1:11, 14, 18; 5:5; Colossians 1:12; 3:24
[6] Romans 4:13-14; Galatians 3:18, 29; Ephesians 3:6; Hebrews 6:12, 17; 9:15
[7] Exodus 19:7-8; 24:3, 7-8; see Deuteronomy 5:5   [8] Leviticus 18:5; Luke 10:28; Galatians 3:12; Leviticus 26; Deuteronomy 28

THE ABRAHAMIC COVENANT: "PROMISE"

The fact that the Law is conditioned on human faithfulness and performance means that it is certain to fail. It also means that if Promise is in any way dependent on the Law, Promise will also be certain to fail: "For if those who are of the Law are heirs, faith is made void and *the promise is nullified; for the Law brings about wrath* ...."[1] According to Paul, Promise is "nullified" by the Law because men invariably break the Law and thus incur the "wrath" of God for their sins.

"Promise" and "Law" are seen here to embody two diametrically opposing principles. Law *always* nullifies Promise because Law depends on human faithfulness, and fallen men *always* fail. There is not *even one* of the sinful sons of Adam who, in his natural state, has *any* faithfulness or spiritual understanding or desire to seek for God.[2] There is not *one* who is capable of fulfilling even the minimal "condition" of trusting Christ for salvation, unless it is first granted to him by the Father.[3] If the fulfillment of Promise depends ultimately on *anything* in man, it will surely come to nothing. Promise, therefore, *cannot* depend on Law *in any sense*. Not only is the Law of Moses ruled out, but law (i.e., "conditions") of any kind. "For the Law brings about wrath, *but where there is no law* [as is actually the case in the realm of promise], *neither is there violation* [human failure]."[4]

The unconditional nature of promise is emphasized in many other places in Paul's writings. For example, in Romans 9:6-13 Paul ascribes the distinction between Isaac and Ishmael to the sovereign and unconditional "word of promise" that preceded and resulted in Isaac's birth.

> For they are not all Israel who are descended from Israel; neither are they all children because they are Abraham's descendants, but: "Through Isaac your descendants will be named." That is, it is not the children of the flesh who are *children of God, but the children of the promise* are regarded as descendants. *For this is a word of promise: "At this time I will come, and Sarah shall have a son."* And not only this, but

---

[1] Romans 4:14-15 [2] Romans 3:11 [3] John 6:65 [4] Romans 4:15

there was Rebekah also, when she had conceived twins by one man, our father Isaac; for though the twins were not yet born, and had not done anything good or bad, in order that God's purpose according to His choice might stand, not because of works, but because of Him who calls, *it was said to her, "The older will serve the younger."* Just as it is written, "Jacob I loved, but Esau I hated."

Romans 9:6-13

Lest any of the Jews should argue that the distinction between Isaac and Ishmael was not a result of God's unconditional promise, but a result of their having different mothers, Paul immediately appeals in these verses to the case of Jacob and Esau. Jacob and Esau had the same mother; in fact, they were twins! Yet God's unconditional and distinguishing "word of promise" with regard to Jacob was given to Rebekah before either of the twins had "done anything good or bad." Furthermore, Paul makes it clear in this passage that not only Isaac and Jacob, but *all* who are "children of God," become such solely by virtue of the fact that they are "the children of the promise."[1]

This unbreakable connection between being a "child of promise" and becoming a child of God is made even more explicit in Galatians 4.

> For it is written that Abraham had two sons, one by the bondwoman and one by the free woman. But the son by the bondwoman was *born according to the flesh,* and the son by the free woman *through the promise.* This is allegorically speaking: for these women are two covenants, one proceeding from Mount Sinai bearing children who are to be slaves; she is Hagar. Now this Hagar is Mount Sinai in Arabia, and corresponds to the present Jerusalem, for she is in slavery with her children. But the Jerusalem above is free; she is our mother. For it is written, "Rejoice, barren woman who does not bear; break forth and shout,

---

[1] Romans 9:8

you who are not in labor; for more are the children of the desolate than of the one who has a husband." *And you brethren, like Isaac, are children of promise.* But as at that time he who was *born according to the flesh* persecuted him who was *born according to the Spirit,* so it is now also. But what does the Scripture say? "Cast out the bondwoman and her son, for the son of the bondwoman shall not be an heir with the son of the free woman." So then, brethren, we are not children of a bondwoman, but of the free woman.

Galatians 4:22-31

Here Paul specifically says that every Christian is born, *like Isaac was,* as a *result* of God's unconditional promise. Sarah (the New Covenant, "the Jerusalem above," the church) is utterly unable of herself to produce seed. If Sarah is ever to have children (i.e., if the church is ever to have true converts), they must be born supernaturally, by the power of the Spirit. This God does through the miracle of the new birth!

Are you a Christian? Then you owe your very being, spiritually speaking, to a sovereign and miraculous birth "according to the Spirit." You are a "child of promise," born *"through* the promise." It is the promise of God made thousands of years ago to Abraham that *called you into existence* as a child of God! Every time *anyone* becomes a Christian, it is a result of the mighty outworking of this ancient promise. Hallelujah!

CERTAIN

Thirdly, God's promise to Abraham is *certain—nothing* can prevent its fulfillment. This certainty rests, first of all, upon the fact that the promise is not conditioned in any way by law; it is all of grace: "But where there is no law, neither is there violation. For this reason it is by faith, that it might be in accordance with *grace,* in order that the promise may be *certain* to all the descendants...."[1] God's promise is certain because its fulfillment rests solely upon His

---

[1] Romans 4:15-16

own faithfulness and power, and God cannot lie nor His purposes be overthrown. "I know that You can do all things, and that no purpose of Yours can be thwarted."[1] "I am God, and there is no other; I am God, and there is no one like Me, declaring the end from the beginning and from ancient times things which have not been done, saying, 'My purpose will be established, and I will accomplish all My good pleasure.'"[2]

Not only is the promise certain because its fulfillment depends on God alone; it is also certain because *it is ultimately made to Christ*. He is "the seed ... to whom the promise had been made."[3] Is there any possibility that God's promise to Christ will fail in its fulfillment? Will Christ "ask of the Father," yet the Father *not* "give Him the nations as His inheritance, and the very ends of the earth as His possession"?[4] It is unthinkable! The Lord Jesus Christ will certainly inherit all! *All* the promises of God find their fulfillment in Him![5]

Think of it, beloved! Long before the Law of Moses was ever given, God *promised* in Christ to save from all the nations of the earth a vast multitude that no man can number. Their salvation was not conditioned in any way upon their own goodness or performance, but solely upon the grace and faithfulness of God. The promise is therefore "*certain* to *all* the descendants." They are all "children of promise" who, like Isaac, owe their existence to a supernatural birth of the Spirit. God has "raised up from the stones" children to Abraham![6]

If you are a Christian, you are part of this vast multitude! The "blessing" of God rests upon you in fullest measure. The day is coming when you will "possess the gate of your enemies,"[7] in accordance with God's ancient promise to Abraham. In Christ, you will one day inherit not only the earth, but "all things."[8] You will be a "fellow heir" *with Him!*[9]

---

[1] Job 42:2 (NAS95)　[2] Isaiah 46:9-10　[3] Galatians 3:19　[4] Psalm 2:8
[5] 2 Corinthians 1:20　[6] Luke 3:8　[7] Genesis 22:17　[8] Revelation 21:7 (KJV)
[9] Romans 8:17

Chapter Three Review

Paul views God's redemptive dealings with men since the time of Abraham in terms of three categories: *Promise, Law,* and *Faith.* These three categories are embodied in three covenants: the Abrahamic Covenant, the Mosaic Covenant, and the New Covenant.

God's covenant with Abraham belongs to the category of Promise. When we think of "promise" in the context of the Abrahamic Covenant, we should think of that which is immutable, unconditional, and certain of fulfillment.

God's promise to Abraham is *immutable* because it is a divine covenant that rests on God's unchangeable purpose and oath.

God's promise to Abraham is *unconditional* because it involves an *inheritance* that is *bestowed* on undeserving sinners by *grace.* It depends solely on God's sovereign and gracious choice, not on anything good or evil that the "children of the promise" have done or ever will do.

God's promise to Abraham is *certain* of fulfillment because it is not dependent in any way on man's performance (Law), but rests solely upon God's own faithfulness and power. It is also certain because it is ultimately made to God's only begotten Son—the object of the Father's eternal good pleasure and delight.

– Chapter Four –

The Mosaic Covenant: "Law"

For the promise to Abraham or to his descendants that he would be heir of the world was not through the Law, but through the righteousness of faith. For if those who are of the Law are heirs, faith is made void and the promise is nullified; for the Law brings about wrath, but where there is no law, neither is there violation. For this reason it is by faith, that it might be in accordance with grace, in order that the promise may be certain to all the descendants, not only to those who are of the Law, but also to those who are of the faith of Abraham, who is the father of us all.

Romans 4:13-16

Now that no one is justified by the Law before God is evident; for, "The righteous man shall live by faith." However, the Law is not of faith; on the contrary, "He who practices them shall live by them."

Galatians 3:11-12

    In Chapter 3, we considered God's covenant with Abraham and his "seed"—a covenant that Paul describes by the term "Promise." In this chapter, we will consider God's covenant with Israel through Moses—a covenant that Paul describes by the term "Law." Then in Chapter 5, we will consider the New Covenant—a covenant that Paul describes by the term "Faith." It is clear that Paul views Law as fundamentally different from both Promise[1] and Faith.[2] He repeatedly speaks of the Mosaic Covenant in terms of "works," in contrast with "faith." "For as many as are of the *works of the Law* are under a curse; for it is written, 'Cursed is everyone who does not

---

[1] Galatians 3:18 [2] Galatians 3:12

abide by all things written in the book of the Law, to *perform* them.' Now that no one is justified by the Law before God is evident; for, 'The righteous man shall live by faith.' However, the Law is not of faith; on the contrary, 'He who practices them shall live by them.'"[1]

Some have argued that when Paul says "the Law is not of faith," he is speaking of a Jewish *misunderstanding* or *distortion* of the Law. They maintain that, in reality, the Law was a covenant of grace based on faith, but the Jews misconstrued it to be a covenant of works based on human performance. It is evident, however, that Paul is not setting forth here a Jewish misunderstanding or distortion of the Law, but the basic principles that characterized the Mosaic Covenant itself.

Blessings and Curses

To understand why this is so, we must remember that the Law had both a positive and negative side, setting forth the dual possibilities of either life or death. These possibilities were conditioned upon human obedience or disobedience. This is well illustrated by the blessings and curses pronounced from Mt. Gerizim and Mt. Ebal. Though this important passage should be read in its entirety if we are to feel its full impact,[2] a few excerpts will be sufficient to demonstrate the fact that the Old Covenant was characterized by "conditions" and that its blessings (or curses) hinged upon human performance.

> Now it shall be, *if you will diligently obey the Lord your God, being careful to do all His commandments which I command you today,* the Lord your God will set you high above all the nations of the earth. And all these blessings shall come upon you and overtake you, *if you will obey the Lord your God.* Blessed shall you be in the city, and blessed shall you be in the country. Blessed shall be the offspring of your body and the produce of your ground and the offspring of your beasts, the increase of your herd and the young of

---

[1] Galatians 3:10-12   [2] Deuteronomy 27:11-28:68; see also Leviticus 26.

your flock. Blessed shall be your basket and your kneading bowl. Blessed shall you be when you come in, and blessed shall you be when you go out ....
Deuteronomy 28:1-6

But it shall come about, if you will not obey the Lord your God, to observe to do all His commandments and His statutes with which I charge you today, that all these curses shall come upon you and overtake you. Cursed shall you be in the city, and cursed shall you be in the country. Cursed shall be your basket and your kneading bowl. Cursed shall be the offspring of your body and the produce of your ground, the increase of your herd and the young of your flock. Cursed shall you be when you come in, and cursed shall you be when you go out. The Lord will send upon you curses, confusion, and rebuke, in all you undertake to do, until you are destroyed and until you perish quickly, on account of the evil of your deeds, because you have forsaken Me ....
Deuteronomy 28:15-20

All this is summarized, on the one hand, by the Law's warning that "the soul who *sins* will *die*,"[1] and on the other hand, by the Law's assurance that "he who *practices*" the commandments "shall *live* by them."[2] This assurance that those who "do" will "live" had a temporal application to the Jews—as long as they obeyed the commandments and requirements of the Law of Moses, they would "live" in the land that God had given them and experience His "blessings."[3] This held true even if their obedience was far from perfect and (in many cases) only external or "outward in the flesh."[4]

But the promise of "life" also represented a deeper and abiding legal principle—it had to do, not only with "life in the land," but with *eternal* life. And the obedience required for obtaining such life involved nothing less than *perfect* love to both God and man. The Lord Jesus made this clear on more than one occasion:

---

[1] Ezekiel 18:4 [2] Galatians 3:12; Leviticus 18:5 [3] See Appendix E, Q. 3.
[4] Romans 2:28-29

THE LAW OF CHRIST

And behold, a certain lawyer stood up and put Him to the test, saying, "Teacher, what shall I do to inherit eternal life?" And He said to him, "What is written in the Law? How does it read to you?" And he answered and said, "You shall love the Lord your God with all your heart, and with all your soul, and with all your strength, and with all your mind; and your neighbor as yourself." And He said to him, "You have answered correctly; *do this, and you will live.*" [1]

Luke 10:25-28

Likewise, when the "rich young ruler" asked Jesus, "What good thing shall I *do* that I may *obtain* eternal life?" His reply was, "If you wish to enter into life, keep the commandments." [2] This means that if anyone were to keep the law perfectly, he would *earn* or *merit* eternal *life* by working out his own [3] righteousness in the eyes of the law. "For Moses writes that the man who *practices* the righteousness which is based on law shall *live* by that righteousness." [4]

Not only did the promise of "life" that was set forth by the Law represent more than mere "life in the land"; the Law's "curse" also represented more than mere physical death or expulsion from Canaan. This is made clear by Paul's statement that "Christ redeemed us from the curse *of the Law*, having become a curse for us." [5] The "curse of the Law" from which Christ has redeemed us by drinking the cup of God's wrath, is none other than the *eternal* death that is the just "wages of sin." [6] Christ did not die to save us from a Jewish misunderstanding of the Law's curse, but from the actual curse of the Law itself!

In light of these clear teachings of Scripture, we must conclude that, whatever gracious provisions the Mosaic Covenant may have included, it nevertheless represented *a covenant of works*. (See Appendix E, Q. 7.) It was characterized by the principle that *life* is contingent on *doing*. It was not just another "gracious administration of the covenant of grace," essentially one piece with

---

[1] Compare Leviticus 18:5.   [2] Matthew 19:16-17   [3] Philippians 3:9
[4] Romans 10:5   [5] Galatians 3:13   [6] Romans 6:23

THE MOSAIC COVENANT: "LAW"

the New Covenant, as some have supposed. The Law served a gracious purpose in God's overall plan, as we shall see, but the Law itself was not based on the principle of grace! Instead, it was given to "increase transgression," [1] and its inevitable result was to "bring about wrath." [2] This is why Paul views *the Old Covenant as such* to be a "ministry of death" [3] and a "ministry of condemnation." [4] It was not a Jewish misunderstanding of the Old Covenant that represented a "ministry" of death and condemnation, but the very "tablets of stone" [5] themselves!

It is true that most of the Jews *did* in fact fail to understand the real purpose of the Law of Moses. But their misunderstanding related, not to the fact that the Law promised life on condition of obedience, but to the fact that men are too sinful in themselves to merit this life.[6] Rather than realizing that the Law had been given to "shut them up under sin" [7] and show them their desperate need to be justified by faith as their father Abraham had been,[8] they supposed instead that they could obtain a "righteousness of their own" [9] by keeping the Law. "For not knowing about God's righteousness, and seeking to establish their own, they did not subject themselves to the righteousness of God. For Christ is the end of the law for righteousness to everyone who believes." [10]

The stark contrast between the demands of the Old Covenant and the provisions of the New is seen even in the very manner in which the two covenants were inaugurated. The giving of the Law on Sinai was an event full of fear, foreboding, and darkness—as sinful men trembled before an unapproachably holy God and the "holy, righteous, and good" [11] law He was calling them to obey.

> For you have not come to ... a blazing fire, and to darkness and gloom and whirlwind, and to the blast of a trumpet and the sound of words which sound was such that those who heard begged that no further word should be spoken

---

[1] Romans 5:20 [2] Romans 4:15 [3] 2 Corinthians 3:7 [4] 2 Corinthians 3:9
[5] 2 Corinthians 3:3, 7 [6] Romans 7:10 [7] Galatians 3:22 [8] Romans 4:1-5; 11-12
[9] Philippians 3:9 [10] Romans 10:3-4 [11] Romans 7:12

to them. For they could not bear the command, "If even a beast touches the mountain, it will be stoned." And so terrible was the sight, that Moses said, "I am full of fear and trembling."   Hebrews 12:18-21

By contrast, the New Covenant was inaugurated in the quiet intimacy of the Upper Room, where Jesus, "having loved His own who were in the world, loved them to the uttermost"[1] and spoke to them words of comfort and assurance before laying down His life for them. The inauguration of the New Covenant did indeed involve darkness, earthquake, and terror, but it was the darkness that fell upon Christ Himself[2] as He redeemed His people from the curse of the Law and drank the bitter "cup"[3] of God's wrath reserved for them!

LAW VS. PROMISE

According to Paul, "the Law is not of faith,"[4] and it is only when salvation is by *faith* that it can be a matter of *grace:*

> For if those who are of the *Law* are heirs, *faith* is made void and the *promise* is nullified ….For this reason it is *by faith,* that it might be *in accordance with grace,* in order that the promise may be certain to all the descendants ….
>
> Romans 4:14-16

We see in these verses that Law, because it is characterized by the principle of "works," is opposed to both Promise and Faith. And it is precisely this opposition that leads to Paul's question, "Is the Law then contrary to the promises of God?"[5] If Paul were teaching that the Law is a covenant based on the principle of grace, this question would never have arisen. But as it is, God has done something apparently inexplicable: He has made unconditional promises to Abraham and then followed them with a covenant that

---

[1] John 13:1   [2] Matthew 27:45-46   [3] Luke 22:42-44   [4] Galatians 3:12
[5] Galatians 3:21

is conditioned on human performance! Does He really intend that men will earn their salvation by keeping the Law? Paul's answer is an emphatic, "May it never be!" "For if a law had been given which was able to impart life, then righteousness would indeed have been based on law."[1] God never intended the Law as an alternate method of salvation, because man's sinful condition renders the Law "unable" to impart life. The problem lies, not in the Law's promise of life, but in man's inability to keep the Law and thus obtain its "righteousness." For this reason, Paul speaks of "what the Law *could not do, weak as it was through the flesh.*"[2] Instead of bringing life to fallen men, the Law brings only death: "And I was once alive apart from the Law; but when the commandment came, sin became alive, and I died; and this commandment, *which was to result in life,* proved to result in *death* for me."[3] The commandment *did* indeed promise life, but it "proved to result" only in death.

WHY THE LAW THEN?

If God never intended that men should be saved by law keeping, the question naturally arises, "Why the Law then?"[4] Paul's answer is that "it was *added because of transgressions... until* the seed should come to whom the promise had been made." Notice that Paul describes the Law here as something "added." It is not the main entity, but an attachment; it "came in beside."[5] Not only was the Law added; it was also temporary. "It was added... *until* the seed [Christ] should come to whom the promise had been made." When Christ appeared, the time of the Mosaic Covenant was over. "Now that faith has come, we are no longer under a tutor."[6]

Paul says that the Law was added "because of transgressions." What he means by this statement is spelled out in considerable detail in his other writings. According to Paul, the Law "arouses sinful passions" in those who are unconverted.[7] Sin "takes opportunity through the commandment" to produce more sin, to "deceive" us,

---

[1] Galatians 3:21 [2] Romans 8:3 [3] Romans 7:9-10 [4] Galatians 3:19
[5] Romans 5:20 (ASV) [6] Galatians 3:25 [7] Romans 7:5

and "through the commandment" to "kill" us.[1] The Law awakens and stirs up sin; in fact, the Law is the very "power of sin"![2] Thus, Paul can actually say, "the Law came in that the transgression might increase."[3] By showing men more clearly their condemnation and horrible bondage to sin, "the Law has become our tutor to lead us to Christ, that we may be justified by faith."[4] The Law of Moses did its part to *"shut up all men under sin,* that the promise by faith in Jesus Christ might be given to those who believe."[5]

The Mosaic Covenant does indeed serve a gracious purpose in that it "leads us to Christ." Its laws reveal to us our sinfulness, and its sacrifices foreshadow our Savior. But the Mosaic Covenant itself is not characterized by the principle of grace, "for it is written, *'Cursed* is everyone who does not abide by *all* things written in the book of the law, to perform them.'"[6]

PROMISE VS. LAW

Since "as many as are of the works of the Law are under a curse,"[7] it is evident that those Jews who found eternal life while living under the Mosaic Covenant, found it not through the Law as such, but through the Promise. Unlike their fellow countrymen who imagined that they could succeed in establishing a "righteousness of their own" by keeping the Law,[8] they realized, instead, that the Law itself only condemned them. They knew that even their "righteous" deeds were but "a filthy garment"[9] in God's sight, and they understood that scrupulous observance of the sacrifices and offerings of the Mosaic system could not actually take away their sins.[10] Instead, they "followed in the steps of the faith of their father Abraham which he had while he was yet uncircumcised."[11] They, like Abraham, "believed God," trusting Him to "justify the ungodly" and to "reckon righteousness" to them "apart from

---

[1] Romans 7:8, 11, 13   [2] 1 Corinthians 15:56   [3] Romans 5:20   [4] See Appendix E, Q.8.   [5] Galatians 3:22   [6] Galatians 3:10   [7] Galatians 3:10   [8] Philippians 3:9; Romans 9:31-32; 10:3   [9] Isaiah 64:6   [10] Micah 6:6-7; Psalm 51:16; Hebrews 10:4   [11] Romans 4:12

THE MOSAIC COVENANT: "LAW"

works."[1] They, like Abraham, looked in faith to the promise and to the coming of the One to whom the promise had been made.[2] As a result, they experienced the "blessing" of Abraham, even though they lived under the Law of Moses:

> Just as David [a man who lived directly under the Mosaic Law] also speaks of the blessing upon the man to whom God *reckons righteousness apart from works:* "Blessed are those whose lawless deeds have been forgiven, and whose sins have been covered. Blessed is the man whose sin the Lord will not take into account." Romans 4:6-8

The same principle applied to the survival of the nation of Israel as a whole. Time after time, when the nation of Israel should have been utterly destroyed,[3] it was Promise, not Law, that preserved a remnant. Under the conditions of the Law,[4] the people of Israel richly deserved every judgment that came upon them,[5] and the fact that God did not "make an end of them or forsake them" is attributed to His grace and compassion,[6] not to His legal justice. When Israel sinned, no prophet ever interceded for the nation on the basis of Law, but solely on the basis of grace, imploring God for mercy and appealing to the covenant God had made with Abraham, Isaac, and Jacob.

> Turn from Your burning anger and change Your mind about doing harm to Your people. *Remember Abraham, Isaac, and Israel, Your servants to whom You swore by Yourself,* and said to them, "I will multiply your descendants as the stars of the heavens, and all this land of which I have spoken I will give to your descendants, and they shall inherit it forever." *So the Lord changed His mind about the harm which He said He would do to His people.*
> Exodus 32:12-14 (NAS95)

---

[1] Romans 4:3-6   [2] John 8:56; 12:41; Acts 2:30-31; 1 Peter 1:10-12
[3] Deuteronomy 28:45, 48, 51, 61 "until you are destroyed"
[4] Deuteronomy 28:15-68   [5] Nehemiah 9:26-37; Daniel 9:1-19
[6] Nehemiah 9:30-31; Deuteronomy 4:29-31

> You have been rebellious against the Lord from the day I knew you. So I fell down before the Lord the forty days and nights, which I did because the Lord had said He would destroy you. I prayed to the Lord, and said, "O Lord God, do not destroy Your people, even Your inheritance, whom You have redeemed through Your greatness, whom You have brought out of Egypt with a mighty hand. *Remember Your servants, Abraham, Isaac, and Jacob; do not look at the stubbornness of this people or at their wickedness or their sin.*"
>
> Deuteronomy 9:24-27 (NAS95)

> Now Hazael king of Aram had oppressed Israel all the days of Jehoahaz. But the Lord was *gracious* to them and had *compassion* on them and *turned* to them *because of His covenant with Abraham, Isaac, and Jacob, and would not destroy them or cast them from His presence until now.*
>
> 2 Kings 13:22-23

In this remnant preserved by grace lay the hope and future of God's people. Through the prophets, God assured the Jews that one day He would yet fulfill every promise made to Abraham by sending the Messiah, who would establish a New Covenant with the renewed "house of Israel and house of Judah." [1]

> "Listen to me, you who pursue righteousness, who seek the Lord: Look to the rock from which you were hewn, and to the quarry from which you were dug. *Look to Abraham your father,* and to Sarah who gave birth to you in pain; when he was one I called him, then I blessed him and multiplied him." *Indeed, the Lord will comfort Zion; He will comfort all her waste places. And her wilderness He will make like Eden, and her desert like the garden of the Lord. Joy and gladness will be found in her, thanksgiving and sound of a melody* ...."Lift up your eyes to the sky, then look to the earth beneath; for the sky will vanish like smoke, and the earth will wear out

---

[1] Jeremiah 31:31-37; 32:37-41; Hebrews 8:6-13

like a garment, and its inhabitants will die in like manner, but My salvation shall be forever, and My righteousness shall not wane."... *So the ransomed of the Lord will return, and come with joyful shouting to Zion, and everlasting joy will be on their heads. They will obtain gladness and joy, and sorrow and sighing will flee away.* Isaiah 51:1-3, 6, 11

"Shut Up Under Sin"

In answer to the question, "Why the Law then?" Paul says that it was "added because of transgressions." After considering something of what he means by this phrase, we have seen that God's ultimate purpose in giving the Law to fallen men was not that they might save themselves by keeping it, but that their utter need of a Savior might be established by their failing to keep it! In light of this truth, several questions immediately press upon each of us, even though we have never lived directly under the Mosaic Covenant[1]:

- Do I see God's demands as "holy, righteous, and good"[2] and His requirements as only good and right? Have I stopped blaming God for my sins by excusing them or by imagining that He expects too much of me?

- Do I realize that I have fallen infinitely short of living a life of perfect love to God and man, and that, in myself, I stand hopelessly condemned in God's sight? Can I see that I am condemned, not because of any fault on God's part, but because of my own selfish and wicked heart?

- Do I realize that I will never be able to establish any righteousness of my own before God or do anything that will obligate Him to love and save me? Have I given up on ever being able to "merit" the merits of Christ? Do I realize that unless salvation is *entirely* by grace, I will never be saved?

If my answer is "yes" to all of these questions, then the law of God has done its intended work in me! I have *nothing* to do but

---

[1] See Appendix E, Q.8.   [2] Romans 7:12

to look away from myself and put my trust in Christ alone for my righteousness and salvation!

"So the ransomed of the LORD will return, and come with joyful shouting to Zion, and everlasting joy will be on their heads." Hallelujah!

Chapter Four Review

Paul describes the Mosaic Covenant by the term "Law." The basic characteristic of the Law is that its blessings and curses are conditioned upon human obedience or disobedience. In other words, the Law represents a "covenant of works."

By giving the Law, God has done something that is apparently inexplicable. Why would He make unconditional promises to Abraham and then follow them with a covenant that is conditioned on human performance? Is the Law contrary to and working at cross-purposes with the promises of God? Did God actually intend men to earn their salvation by keeping the Law? Paul's answer is an emphatic, "May it never be!" God never intended the Law as an alternate method of salvation, because man's sinful condition renders the Law "unable" to impart life.

If this is the case, the question naturally arises, "Why the Law then?" Paul's answer is that it was "added because of transgressions" *until* Christ should come. God gave the Law in order that "the transgression might increase." By showing men more clearly their condemnation and horrible bondage to sin, "the Law has become our tutor to lead us to Christ, that we may be justified by faith."

Those Jews who found eternal life while living under the Mosaic Covenant, found it not through the Law as such, but through the promise. The same principle applied to the nation of Israel as a whole. Time after time, when the nation of Israel would otherwise have been utterly destroyed, it was Promise, not Law, that preserved a remnant. In this remnant preserved by grace lay the hope and future of God's people.

– Chapter Five –

THE NEW COVENANT: "FAITH"

> But *before faith came,* we were kept in custody under the law, being shut up to *the faith which was later to be revealed.*
>
> Galatians 3:23
>
> But *now that faith has come,* we are no longer under a tutor.
>
> Galatians 3:25
>
> But now ... *the righteousness of God has been manifested,* being witnessed by the Law and the Prophets, even the righteousness of God *through faith in Jesus Christ* ....
>
> Romans 3:21-22
>
> But *when the fulness of the time came,* God sent forth His Son ... that we might *receive the adoption as sons.*
>
> Galatians 4:4-5

In Galatians 3-4, Paul describes the events surrounding the coming of Christ and the inauguration of the New Covenant[1] by the term "Faith." He does this in order to contrast the gospel's central principle (faith) with the central principle of *works* that characterized the Old Covenant. As we have seen, this does not mean that there was no faith before the coming of Christ. In fact, everyone who has ever been saved has been saved through faith! (Before Christ's coming, this faith related to the promise yet future; after His coming, it relates to the promise as it is now realized in Him.) Justification has *always* been by faith![2] Nevertheless, the changes that have taken place with the coming of the New Covenant are so great that Paul can speak (in relative terms) of the *past* as the time "before faith came,"[3] in contrast with the *present,* "now that faith has come."[4]

---

[1] 2 Corinthians 3:6; cf. Galatians 4:24   [2] Romans 4:1-12   [3] Galatians 3:23
[4] Galatians 3:25

PROMISE FULFILLED

Though the Abrahamic Covenant and the New Covenant ultimately have to do with the same spiritual realities, they are not identical. In the first place, the Abrahamic Covenant had a prominent physical and national dimension.[1] This is entirely absent in the New Covenant. Furthermore, even in terms of its "spiritual" dimension, the Abrahamic Covenant referred to blessings that were *yet future* (e.g., the justification of "all the nations"[2] through faith in Christ). The New Covenant, on the other hand, speaks of these same blessings *now realized* "in the fulness of time." In the unfolding of the history of redemption, these two covenants are separated by some two thousand years.

With the coming of the New Covenant, Promise finds its culmination and fulfillment! It is fulfilled by the arrival of the One "to whom the promise had been made"—the Lord Jesus Christ. *"All the promises of God find their Yes in Him."*[3] These "promises" include Christ's death and resurrection[4] for the salvation of His people, the ingathering of the Gentiles[5] and their justification[6] by faith, personal "teaching" from God[7] for every true child of Abraham, and especially the "promised" gift of the Holy Spirit:

> Christ redeemed us from the curse of the Law, having become a curse for us...in order that in Christ Jesus the blessing of Abraham might come to the Gentiles, so that we might receive *the promise of the Spirit* through faith.
>
> Galatians 3:13-14

> And behold, I am sending forth *the promise of My Father* upon you; but you are to stay in the city until you are clothed with power from on high.   Luke 24:49

---

[1] See Chapter 2.   [2] Galatians 3:8   [3] 2 Corinthians 1:20 (ESV)   [4] Acts 13:23, 32-33; 26:6-8   [5] Matthew 12:17-21; Acts 13:47; 15:17; Romans 15:10-12
[6] Galatians 3:8   [7] John 6:45; Hebrews 8:11

THE NEW COVENANT: "FAITH"

> In Him, you also, after listening to the message of truth, the gospel of your salvation—having also believed, you were sealed in Him with *the Holy Spirit of promise* ....
> Ephesians 1:13

It is this New Testament outpouring and "coming" of the Holy Spirit "according to promise" that Paul sees as the central characteristic of the new age in which Christians now live.[1] In fact, he refers to the New Covenant in its entirety as "the ministry of the Spirit."[2] As with every other "spiritual blessing," the promise of the Spirit is ours only because we are "in Christ."[3] He alone is the "Seed" to whom the "promise of the Spirit" (like every other promise) had ultimately been made:

> Therefore having been exalted to the right hand of God, *and having received from the Father the promise of the Holy Spirit,* He has poured forth this which you both see and hear.
> Acts 2:33

The age of Promise is swallowed up and fulfilled by the age of Faith! Every promise made to Abraham is realized in Christ. "All the promises of God find their Yes in Him."

LAW FULFILLED

But not only is Promise fulfilled by the coming of Christ and the arrival of the New Covenant; equally glorious is the fact that Law, too, is fulfilled by His coming! This is true of every aspect of the Law, down to its smallest letter or stroke.[4] In the first place, *every one of the prophecies, sacrifices, types, and shadows of the Mosaic Covenant* finds its fulfillment and consummation in Christ. Christ is the promised Messiah, the high priest who carries the people of God continually on His shoulders and on His heart.[5] He is the sacrifice whose blood atones for their sins and the scapegoat who

---

[1] See Chapters 18-19. [2] 2 Corinthians 3:6, 8 [3] Ephesians 1:3
[4] Matthew 5:17-18 [5] Exodus 28:12, 29

carries those sins away from the presence of God into a solitary land.[1] He is the true manna,[2] the Passover lamb,[3] the smitten rock.[4] His flesh is the veil which, when torn, opens the way into the very presence of God.[5]

But Christ does more than fulfill the Law's types and shadows; *every righteous principle of moral conduct embodied in the Law* is swallowed up, incorporated, and consummated in Christ's teachings as well. By His perfect example and lofty precepts, Christ sets forth a standard of behavior for His people that fulfills all the righteous and abiding moral principles of the Law of Moses.[6]

But there is yet another (and even more foundational) way in which Christ fulfills the Law of Moses. Not only the types and shadows, and not only the righteous principles, but also *all of the legal "conditions" of the Mosaic Law represented by its blessings and curses* are fulfilled in Christ as well! By His perfect life, He satisfies on our behalf the Law's positive demands[7] ("do this and you will live"), and by His perfect death, He satisfies on our behalf the Law's negative demands[8] ("the soul that sins shall die"). Every divine legal obligation embodied in and represented by the Law of Moses is satisfied in Christ!

The Glorious Cross

Because it represents the fulfillment of both Promise and Law simultaneously, the Cross of Christ is the supreme paradox of human history. It is both the greatest display of divine *grace* and, at the same time, the greatest display of divine *justice* ever seen among men. Promise and Law meet and find their fulfillment in one Person—the Lord Jesus Christ! Promise is swallowed up as *anticipation* gives way to *realization*, and Law is swallowed up as *demand* gives way to *satisfaction*. Oh, the wonder of wonders! God so loved the objects of His judicial wrath that He made a sovereign, unconditional Promise to save them, not by setting aside

---

[1] Leviticus 16:8-10   [2] John 6:31-35   [3] 1 Corinthians 5:7   [4] 1 Corinthians 10:4
[5] Hebrews 10:20   [6] See Chapter 9.   [7] Romans 5:19   [8] Galatians 3:13

the requirements of His holy Law, but by fulfilling them Himself, in the Person of His beloved Son! "Lovingkindness and truth have met together; righteousness and peace have kissed each other!"[1] To God be the glory, forever and ever!

> *Here is love, vast as the ocean,*
>   *Lovingkindness as the flood,*
> *When the Prince of life, our ransom,*
>   *Shed for us His precious blood.*
> *Who His love will not remember?*
>   *Who can cease to sing His praise?*
> *He can never be forgotten*
>   *Throughout heaven's eternal days.*
>
> *On the Mount of Crucifixion*
>   *Fountains opened deep and wide;*
> *Through the floodgates of God's mercy*
>   *Flowed a vast and gracious tide.*
> *Grace and love, like mighty rivers,*
>   *Poured incessant from above,*
> *And heaven's peace and perfect justice*
>   *Kissed a guilty world in love.*
>
>   William Rees

---

[1] Psalm 85:10

CHAPTER FIVE REVIEW

Paul describes the events surrounding the coming of Christ and the inauguration of the New Covenant by the term "Faith." He does this in order to contrast the gospel's central principle (faith) with the Old Covenant's central principle (works).

With the coming of Christ, Promise finds its culmination and fulfillment. "All the promises of God find their 'Yes' in Him." These promises include Christ's death and resurrection for the salvation of His people, the ingathering of the Gentiles and their justification by faith, personal "teaching" from God for every true child of Abraham, and especially the "promised" gift of the Holy Spirit.

With the coming of Christ, Law also finds its culmination and fulfillment. Christ fulfills every one of the Law's prophecies, sacrifices, types, and shadows. He also fulfills every righteous principle of moral conduct embodied in the Law. Not only this, but Christ fulfills all of the legal "conditions" of the Mosaic Law represented by its blessings and curses. By His perfect life, He satisfies on our behalf the Law's positive demands, and by His perfect death, He satisfies on our behalf the Law's negative demands.

Both Promise and Law find their culmination and fulfillment in the glorious Person and work of Christ. Promise is swallowed up as *anticipation* gives way to *realization*, and Law is swallowed up as *demand* gives way to *satisfaction*.

– CHAPTER SIX –

PRINCIPLES OF INTERPRETATION

> [These] things... are a mere shadow of what is to come; but the substance belongs to Christ.   Colossians 2:17
>
> For the Law... has only a shadow of the good things to come and not the very form of things ....   Hebrews 10:1

In the first five chapters, we have seen why the law of Christ cannot be identified with the Law of Moses. The Law of Moses served a temporary role as a "tutor" to the Jews until the time of Christ's coming, but now that Christ has come, we are "no longer under a tutor." Before we move on to explore more fully the implications of this fact, it may be helpful to summarize some principles of Biblical interpretation that have surfaced in the preceding overview. Three, in particular, stand out, and their relevance for a proper understanding of Scripture will be seen repeatedly in the chapters that follow.

SPIRITUAL REALITIES

It should be obvious by now that *even though many promises and prophecies of the Old Testament appear at first to be physical in nature, they often have to do finally with "spiritual"*[1] *realities*. Sometimes they will have an initial fulfillment that is physical and an ultimate fulfillment that is spiritual (as is the case with the promises made to Abraham); at other times, they will have a fulfillment that is solely spiritual. For example, when God speaks through Isaiah concerning the coming of Christ, "Clear the way for the LORD

---

[1] 1 Peter 2:5; 1 Corinthians 10:3-4; Ephesians 1:3

THE LAW OF CHRIST

in the wilderness; make smooth in the desert a highway for our God; let every valley be lifted up, and every mountain and hill be made low; and let the rough ground become a plain, and the rugged terrain a broad valley," [1] He is not referring to a building project in the deserts of Palestine. He is, instead, calling His people to repentance and humility.[2] Likewise, when Malachi foretells of the coming of "Elijah" to "restore the hearts of the fathers to their children, and the hearts of the children to their fathers," [3] his prophecy is actually referring to John the Baptist: "For all the prophets and the Law prophesied until John. And if you care to accept it, *he himself is Elijah, who was to come.*" [4] John the Baptist was not *literally* Elijah, but he came "in the *spirit and power* of Elijah." [5]

Again, Malachi 3:3 tells us that when the Messiah comes, "He will purify the sons of Levi and refine them like gold and silver, so that they may present to the LORD offerings in righteousness." But when we read the New Testament, we discover that literal blood sacrifices have been "fulfilled" and ended in Christ and that *every believer* has now become a priest to God.[6] In other words, the true "sons of Levi" who have been "purified" by the Messiah are simply *Christians*, who "offer up *spiritual* sacrifices acceptable to God through Jesus Christ." [7]

Another notable illustration of this principle is seen in God's covenant with David, in which He promises to establish David's descendants forever *"and his throne as the days of heaven."* (See especially Psalm 89:3-4, 28-37.) This covenant is repeated in Jeremiah: "Thus says the Lord, 'If you can break My covenant for the day, and My covenant for the night, so that day and night will not be at their appointed time, then My covenant may also be broken with David My servant *that he shall not have a son to reign on his throne ....*' " [8] If we had read only the Old Testament, we might understand these promises to refer to an endless physical succession

---

[1] Isaiah 40:3-4   [2] Luke 3:3-6   [3] Malachi 4:5-6   [4] Matthew 11:13-14   [5] Luke 1:17
[6] Revelation 1:6; 1 Peter 2:5, 9   [7] 1 Peter 2:5; Hebrews 13:15-16; Revelation 5:10
[8] Jeremiah 33:20-21

of David's sons.[1] When we come to the New Testament, however, we find these words ultimately fulfilled by the Lord Jesus Christ in a way that they could never have been fulfilled by any lineage of earthly kings. As the true "Son of David," His throne will literally last forever—"as the days of heaven." In the words of Gabriel to Mary, "He will be great, and will be called the Son of the Most High; and the Lord God will give Him the throne of His father David; and He will reign over the house of Jacob forever; and His kingdom will have no end."[2]

One more example will illustrate the way in which the apostles themselves understood Old Testament prophecy. In Acts 15:13-18 we find James addressing the official church council with these words: "Brethren, listen to me. Simeon has related how God first concerned Himself about *taking from among the Gentiles a people for His name*. And with this the words of the Prophets agree, just as it is written, ' "After these things I will return, *and I will rebuild the tabernacle of David which has fallen, and I will rebuild its ruins, and I will restore it, in order that the rest of mankind may seek the Lord, and all the Gentiles who are called by My name*," says the Lord, who makes these things known from of old.' " We learn here that the Apostle James understood Amos's prophecy about the "rebuilding" of the "ruins" of the "tabernacle of David"[3] to refer, not to the rebuilding of a physical structure, but to the spiritual restoration accomplished by Christ in His death, resurrection, and exaltation. It was this "rebuilding" that preceded God's "taking from among the Gentiles a people for His name."

In all these examples, we find that what at first seems to have reference only to that which is literal and physical, later proves to be "spiritual" in its ultimate fulfillment. These spiritual realities are *far more concrete and substantial* than their material counterparts, which were set forth only as temporary "shadows" of that which is lasting and eternal.[4]

---

[1] See Psalm 89:30-31; Jeremiah 33:17-18, 22.   [2] Luke 1:31-33; Isaiah 9:7
[3] Amos 9:11-12   [4] Colossians 2:17; 2 Corinthians 4:18-5:1; Hebrews 8:4-5; 9:23-24; 10:1

NEW INTERPRETING OLD

There is a second important lesson to learn from what we have considered thus far. By looking at the New Testament, we have discovered a fulness of meaning in the Old Testament that we could never have discovered by reading the Old Testament text alone. The principle is this: *We should always get our final understanding of the Old Testament by studying the way it is interpreted by our Lord and His apostles in the New Testament.* In particular, we should never study the Old Testament by itself, decide what the New Testament "ought" to teach in light of our understanding of the Old Testament, and then *impose* our ideas on the New Testament, forcing it to fit our theories. Throughout church history even godly men, in their commitment to a theological system, have often begun with a "logical" argument from the Old Testament and proceeded to pursue it relentlessly through the New Testament, not even realizing how far they are being carried away from what the apostles and early church actually taught and practiced.

Though the Anabaptists had some excesses and tended to be weak theologically (partly, perhaps, because many of their leaders were martyred before they could advance very far doctrinally), yet one thing can surely be said about them: they sensed something of the radical nature of New Testament Christianity and tried to live their lives accordingly. They breathed the celestial air of the New Covenant.[1] They did not try to join church and state in an unholy alliance, as other professing Christians did, nor did they use the example of Samuel's "hewing Agag to pieces"[2] as a justification for Christians burning "heretics" at the stake or drowning them in nearby rivers. When their enemies were sick and dying, they did not claim God's plagues upon Egypt as an excuse for rejoicing, but instead loved and prayed for their persecutors.

Every new Christian feels something of this reality when he first hears Christ's words in the Sermon on the Mount or reads the

---

[1] See Leonard Verduin, *The Reformers and Their Stepchildren* (Grand Rapids: Baker Book House, 1980). [2] 1 Samuel 15:33

early chapters of the book of Acts. It is only after he has listened to too many "theologians," softening and explaining away the radical teachings of Christ and His apostles, that the new convert finally settles down to living the "ordinary" life of a godly Old Testament Jew—*minus* the "ceremonial law," of course! Any teaching that causes us to weaken or distort the message of the New Testament by forcing it to fit the mold of the Old Testament is false. May God help us to let the New Testament say *what it actually says* and to interpret the Old Testament through the lens of the New—not vice-versa!

CHRIST THE KEY

A final important lesson to learn from what we have considered thus far is this: *The key to understanding the Bible is Christ.*[1] The Old Testament Scriptures point to Christ in their prophecies, types, covenants, sacrifices, and laws. As the Lord Jesus said to the Jews, "You search the Scriptures, because you think that in them you have eternal life; *and it is these that bear witness of Me.* If you believed Moses, you would believe Me, *for he wrote of Me.*"[2] "And *beginning with Moses and with all the prophets,* He explained to them *the things concerning Himself in all the Scriptures.*"[3]

As we have seen repeatedly, God's ultimate goal in history was and is the "summing up of all things in Christ."[4] This fact alone is sufficient to preserve us from many errors in our understanding of Biblical truth. Of the many examples that could be given, we will mention only one. It concerns the place of "Christ's body," the church,[5] in God's economy:

> To me, the very least of all saints, this grace was given, to preach to the Gentiles the unfathomable riches of Christ, and to bring to light what is the administration of the mystery *which for ages has been hidden in God,* who created

---

[1] Contrast both Dispensationalism (which has made national Israel the key to understanding Biblical revelation) and Covenant Theology (which has made the supposed "covenant of grace" the key).   [2] John 5:39, 46   [3] Luke 24:27
[4] Ephesians 1:8-10   [5] 1 Corinthians 12:12, 27; Ephesians 1:22-23; 5:28-32

all things; in order that *the manifold wisdom of God* might now be made known *through the church* to the rulers and the authorities in the heavenly places. *This was in accordance with the eternal purpose which He carried out in Christ Jesus our Lord* ....To Him be the glory *in the church and in Christ Jesus* to all generations forever and ever. Amen.

Ephesians 3:8-11, 21

We learn from these verses that God determined before the foundation of the world to glorify Himself in Christ and the church. The church is not an afterthought God had when His purposes for the covenant nation of Israel were thwarted by the Jews' rejection of Christ. Rather, God's covenant with national Israel was but a temporary step in His overall plan to ultimately establish the church! Just like the "nurse crop" of oats that is planted to protect the tender seedlings of alfalfa until they can become established in their first season of growth, so physical Israel served as a place where spiritual Israel[1] could be temporarily protected and nourished until the "fulness of time" had come. And just as the nurse crop is expected to die out after one growing season, so the "Old Covenant" made with Abraham's physical descendants was never intended to be permanent. When John the Baptist arrived on the scene, telling "covenant children" not to say, "we have Abraham for our father," [2] and calling them to individual and voluntary repentance, the time of the "nurse crop" was over.

It is true (according to Romans 11) that because of Israel's corporate election,[3] God will yet one day show "mercy" to Abraham's *physical* children.[4] But that mercy will be manifested by their being engrafted into the church[5]—a "nation" made up solely of Abraham's *spiritual* children. "But what does the Scripture say? 'Cast out the bondwoman [the Old Covenant] and her son [those who are merely physical children of Abraham, "born according to

---

[1] Romans 2:28-29; 9:6-8; Galatians 4:24-26; 6:15-16; Hebrews 12:22-24
[2] Luke 3:8-9 [3] Romans 11:28-29 [4] Romans 11:30-32 [5] Romans 11:23-27

the flesh"], for the son of the bondwoman shall not be an heir with the son of the free woman.' "[1]

The church is the highest pinnacle of God's gracious dealings with mankind! Every citizen of spiritual Israel is personally repentant—poor in spirit and pure in heart.[2] "For then I will remove from your midst your proud, exulting ones, and you will never again be haughty on My holy mountain. But I will leave among you a humble and lowly people, and they will take refuge in the name of the LORD."[3] *Every* individual in the New Covenant is regenerated,[4] has a personal knowledge of God,[5] and is justified![6] There is nothing greater than to be a member of the very body of Christ—flesh of His flesh and bone of His bone!

Christ and His heavenly kingdom are the ultimate fulfillment of Old Testament prophecy.[7] He is the promised "seed of the woman," the promised "seed of Abraham," and the promised "seed of David"! We may well say with Paul, "For as many as may be the promises of God, in Him they are yes; wherefore also by Him is our Amen to the glory of God through us."[8]

HIDDEN TO BE REVEALED

When we considered the true import of God's promises to Abraham in Chapter 2, we saw that the writers of the New Testament found meanings in the Old Testament Scriptures that are not at first apparent. For example, which of us would have discovered (as Paul did) a reference to *Christ* in God's use of the word "seed" in the book of Genesis?[9] How did Paul come to see this promise as having a deeper meaning? We know that he was inspired by the Holy Spirit in his understanding of the Old Testament, but surely there was a process of reasoning involved as well. It is important for us to keep in mind that Paul was not *importing* a meaning into the Old Testament text that is not really there; he was simply unfolding the

---

[1] Galatians 4:30-31; see vv. 21-31.   [2] Matthew 5:3, 8   [3] Zephaniah 3:11-12
[4] Hebrews 8:10   [5] Hebrews 8:11; John 6:45   [6] Hebrews 8:12   [7] Romans 15:8
[8] 2 Corinthians 1:20   [9] Galatians 3:16

true intent of what God had promised all along. But how did he come to an understanding of what that "true intent" was?

We do not have to search very far to understand something of what Paul's line of reasoning must have been. Before his conversion, Paul was a bitter enemy of Christ. Like all Jews, he found Christ—and especially *"Christ crucified"*—to be a great offence and "stumbling block."[1] To a Jew, the idea of a crucified Messiah was a contradiction in terms, and this for two reasons. First of all, most Jews were expecting a triumphant political Savior who would deliver them from their subjection to Rome. It was unthinkable that the Messiah would die in shame as a condemned criminal under Roman law—especially on a cross, the lowest form of Imperial punishment! But worse than that, the Mosaic Law itself plainly taught that "he who is hanged is *accursed"*—and not only "accursed," but *"accursed of God"!*[2] We can scarcely imagine how sacrilegious it must have sounded to the Jews to hear Christians preaching: *"The Messiah has come! He was hanged on a Roman cross and crucified!"* What intolerable blasphemy to a Jewish ear!

But all this changed when Paul met the risen Christ on the road to Damascus. He *knew* that he had encountered the Lord of glory; that much was absolutely certain. *But how was he to understand the cross?* As he pondered the prophecies of the Old Testament, perhaps the answer came to him in a flash: "Of course! The Messiah died hanging on a tree under the curse of God, *but the curse was not His! It was ours!"* Had Isaiah not said concerning the Coming One that we would "esteem Him stricken, smitten of God, and afflicted"?[3] Had he not also said that "the LORD has caused the iniquity of *us all* to fall on Him"?[4] "Surely *our* griefs He Himself bore, and *our* sorrows He carried.... He was pierced through for *our* transgressions, He was crushed for *our* iniquities. The chastening for *our* well-being fell upon Him, and by His scourging *we* are healed."[5] Christ indeed bore the curse, but He bore it for us!

---

[1] 1 Corinthians 1:23   [2] Deuteronomy 21:23   [3] Isaiah 53:4   [4] Isaiah 53:6
[5] Isaiah 53:4-5

But what is the opposite of the curse of God? The blessing of God! Christ bore the curse so that we might have the blessing. And just as the curse flows from our condemnation, so the *blessing* flows from our *justification*. Is it not suddenly clear that when God told Abraham that "in his *seed* all the *nations* would be *blessed*," He was actually "preaching the gospel beforehand" to him, telling him that in *Christ* the *Gentiles* would one day be *justified* by faith?[1] Glory to God!

---

[1] Galatians 3:8

PART TWO

FREEDOM FROM THE LAW

To rightly understand the law of Christ, we must first understand what the Bible means when it says that Christians have "died to" and "been freed from" the Law. Does freedom from the Law mean that Christians can now live in sin? What does it mean to be "not under law" but "under grace"? Are Christians free from the curse of the Law, but still "on probation" with regard to the Law's requirements for blessing and life? What is the relationship between the law of Christ and the Law of Moses? Is it a relationship of continuity or of discontinuity—or both? In what ways are the individual commandments of the Law of Moses still relevant to us as Christians?

In Chapter 7, the meaning of the Christian's death to the Law is explored, while Chapter 8 continues the theme of the Christian's release from the Law, showing Christ's superiority to Moses. As the long-awaited "prophet like Moses," Christ sets forth in the Sermon on the Mount principles of conduct for His spiritual kingdom. Finally, in Chapter 9, the Old Testament's abiding relevance for the Christian is considered. After thus establishing and explaining the Christian's freedom from the Law, we will be in a position to consider in Part Three the New Covenant believer's rule of life—the law of Christ.

Chapter Six Review

Three important principles of Biblical interpretation stand out from what has been considered in the preceding chapters.

First, it is clear that even though many promises and prophecies of the Old Testament appear at first to be physical in nature, they often have to do ultimately with "spiritual" realities. These spiritual realities are far more concrete and substantial than their material counterparts, which were set forth only as temporary "shadows" of that which is lasting and eternal.

Second, it is clear that we should always get our final understanding of the Old Testament by studying the way it is interpreted by our Lord and His apostles in the New Testament. We should never study the Old Testament by itself, decide what the New Testament "ought" to teach in light of our understanding of the Old Testament, and then impose our ideas on the New Testament, forcing it to fit our theories.

Third, it is clear that the key to understanding the Bible is Christ. The Old Testament Scriptures point to Christ in their prophecies, types, covenants, sacrifices, and laws. God's ultimate goal in history was and is the "summing up of all things in Christ."

This fact is sufficient in itself to preserve us from many errors in our understanding of Biblical truth. One example concerns the place of the church in God's overall plan of redemption. As Christ's very body, the church does not take second place to the physical nation of Israel in any way, but is the highest pinnacle of God's gracious dealings with mankind.

Finally, it is important for us to realize that when the New Testament writers found a "deeper" meaning in Old Testament promises and prophecies, they were not *importing* a meaning into the texts that was not really there. Rather, they were unfolding the true intent of what God had promised all along.

– CHAPTER SEVEN –

NOT UNDER LAW

> But now we have been released from the Law, having died to that by which we were bound, so that we serve in newness of the Spirit and not in oldness of the letter.
>
> Romans 7:6
>
> For through the Law I died to the Law, that I might live to God.   Galatians 2:19

In Chapter 1, several Scriptures were quoted to show that Christians are "not under the Law" but have "died to the Law." Likewise, in Chapters 3-5, the Law was seen to be a temporary "tutor," "added because of transgressions" until the time of Christ's coming. Christians have been "released from the Law," and are no longer "bound" by the Law, but have been "set free" by Christ from the Law's "yoke of slavery."[1] The lost man's relationship to God is one of law; for the Christian this is not the case. He dwells in a state of glorious "liberty" and "freedom."[2]

What does it mean that Christians have been "released from the Law"? Does it mean that Christians may now steal, commit adultery, and otherwise continue in sin? Paul's answer is a resolute, "May it never be!"[3] What exactly, then, does freedom from the Law entail? The answers to these questions are wonderful and far-reaching in their implications.[4]

THE CURSE

In what sense are Christians free from the Law? The first answer to this question is that Christians are free from the curse of the Law. All lost people live under a curse: "For as many as are of the works of the Law are under a curse; for it is written, 'Cursed

---

[1] Galatians 5:1   [2] Galatians 5:1, 13   [3] Romans 6:14-15   [4] This material has been adapted from Chapter 14 of my book, *Justification and Regeneration*.

is everyone who does not abide by all the things written in the book of the Law, to perform them.' "[1] No matter how well things may seem to be going in his life, the non-Christian lives continually under the curse of God. Though his children may be healthy, his garden thriving, and his flowers blooming beautifully, the wrath of God "abides" upon him at all times.[2] One day he will hear the awful words, "Depart from Me, *accursed* ones, into the eternal fire which has been prepared for the devil and his angels."[3]

The Christian, on the other hand, has been redeemed from the curse of the Law: "Christ redeemed us from the curse of the Law, having become a curse for us—for it is written, 'Cursed is everyone who hangs on a tree....' "[4] Glory to God! If you are a Christian, you are no longer under the curse! There is not the *least* bit of curse remaining upon you, for "there is *no* condemnation for those who are in Christ Jesus."[5] Furthermore, the curse will never come upon you again, for your sins are gone forever![6]

> *Free from the law, oh, happy condition,*
> *Jesus hath bled, and there is remission.*
> *Cursed by the law and bruised by the fall,*
> *Grace hath redeemed us, once for all.*
>
> *Once for all, oh, sinner receive it,*
> *Once for all, oh, brother believe it;*
> *Cling to the cross, the burden will fall,*
> *Christ hath redeemed us, once for all!*
>
> P. P. Bliss

BLESSING AND FAVOR

Not only are Christians free from the curse of the Law; they are free from the crushing burden[7] of having to keep the Law *as a means*

---

[1] Galatians 3:10 [2] John 3:36 [3] Matthew 25:41 [4] Galatians 3:13
[5] Romans 8:1 [6] Hebrews 8:12 [7] Perfect obedience represents a "crushing burden," not because the law is unreasonable in its demands, but because man's heart is so sinful—Romans 7:7-8, 12-13.

of obtaining righteousness and life. As we saw in Chapter 4, the Law holds out the promise of life and blessing to those who establish their own righteousness by keeping it.[1] Only one person in human history has ever done this; all others have failed completely. The Lord Jesus Christ alone has "fulfilled all righteousness."[2] He not only paid for our sins; He lived a life of perfect righteousness that is credited to us, and having received His *righteousness,* we are entitled to *life!* Not only did the curse due *us* fall on Him, but the blessing due *Him* fell on us.

Under the Law, men exhaust themselves (and fail miserably) trying to merit the favor of God and earn a title to eternal life. For the Christian, everything is different. Because of the perfect righteousness that has been given to him in justification, he *already has* eternal life; he already has the smile and favor of God—all because of the work of Christ on his behalf! God delights in him and rejoices over him like a groom rejoices over his bride: "And as the bridegroom rejoices over the bride, so your God will rejoice over you."[3] "In that day it will be said to Jerusalem: 'Do not be afraid, O Zion; do not let your hands fall limp. The LORD your God is in your midst, a victorious warrior. He will exult over you with joy, He will be quiet in His love, He will rejoice over you with shouts of joy!' "[4] Knowing as we do how sinful and unworthy of God's delight we still are, it is difficult for us to believe that He could really feel this way about us. But He does! He not only loves us; He loves us beyond our ability to comprehend—His love "surpasses knowledge"![5]

The Christian is free from the Law as a requirement for obtaining life. Christ has not only redeemed him from the curse of the Law; He has also obtained for him all the blessings of life and righteousness: "Christ redeemed us from the *curse* of the Law ... in order that in Christ Jesus the *blessing* of Abraham might come to the Gentiles, so that we might receive the promise of the Spirit through faith."[6] This means that instead of living under a curse, the Christian now lives under the perpetual blessing of God. Though his children may have sickness, his garden be scorched from

---

[1] Galatians 3:12; Luke 10:25-28; Philippians 3:9; Romans 10:5   [2] Matthew 3:15
[3] Isaiah 62:5   [4] Zephaniah 3:16-17   [5] Ephesians 3:19   [6] Galatians 3:13-14

drought, and his flowers wilted, he lives continually under God's loving care. This state of blessedness flows from his justification: "And the Scripture, foreseeing that God would *justify* the Gentiles by faith, preached the gospel beforehand to Abraham, saying, 'All the nations shall be *blessed* in you.' So then those who are of faith are *blessed* with Abraham, the believer."[1] "Just as David also speaks of the *blessing* upon the man to whom God reckons righteousness apart from works: '*Blessed* are those whose lawless deeds have been forgiven, and whose sins have been covered. *Blessed* is the man whose sin the Lord will not take into account.'"[2] It is infinitely better to waste away in a prison cell under the blessing of God, than to live in a palace under His curse! "Then the King will say to those on His right, 'Come, you who are *blessed* of My Father, inherit the kingdom prepared for you from the foundation of the world.'"[3]

The blessedness of God's children and the vastness of His love toward them is not negated by the fact that He sometimes has to "discipline" them. In fact, God's discipline is a further proof of His love![4] As a perfect Father, He insists that the children of His delight be prepared for the "inheritance" that will one day be theirs. He therefore disciplines us "for our good, that we may share His holiness."[5] This is but one more aspect of living under the continual favor of God.

Are you a Christian? Then the blessing of God rests upon you in ways too wonderful to imagine! "Things which eye has not seen and ear has not heard, and which have not entered the heart of man—all that God has prepared for those who love Him!"[6] "Surely goodness and lovingkindness will follow me all the days of my life, and I will dwell in the house of the LORD forever!"[7]

External Rules

It is clear from the sections above that some aspects of the Christian's "freedom from the Law" have to do with *justification*.

---

[1] Galatians 3:8-9 [2] Romans 4:6-8 [3] Matthew 25:34 [4] Hebrews 12:6-8
[5] Hebrews 12:10 [6] 1 Corinthians 2:9 [7] Psalm 23:6

He is free from the curse of the Law, and he is free from the Law as a means of obtaining life. But another aspect of the Christian's freedom from Law is a direct result of *regeneration*: The Christian is free from Law *as an external rule that contradicts his real nature and desires*. This freedom comes to him through the miracle of a new heart.

To understand what this means, we need only to consider the condition of every unbeliever: The Law imposes itself upon him from the outside and contradicts his true desires, keeping him in a state of continual bondage and frustration. It forbids the things that he loves and commands the things that he hates. When he reaches out his hand to steal, the Law says, "You shall not steal." When he looks on a woman to lust for her, the Law says, "You shall not commit adultery." The lost man's condition is thus summed up by the words of one popular bumper sticker: "Everything I like is either illegal, immoral, or fattening." The law constrains and directs the unregenerate man by fear and by threats, and he *hates* it: "The mind set on the flesh is hostile toward God; for it does not subject itself to the law of God, for it is not even able to do so."[1]

Every Christian has been freed from this state of bondage. For him the law is no longer an external rule that contradicts his true nature and desires. Rather, the law is internal; it has been "written on his heart" in the miracle of regeneration.[2] He is constrained by love, not law.[3] Though sin still tries to "reign" in the Christian's "mortal body,"[4] and his conflicts with sin are many and fierce, nevertheless, every believer has been given a new nature that loves righteousness. That which flows out of his innermost being conforms to the law and fulfills it naturally, for "love is the fulfilling of the law."[5] A Christian *being who he really is*[6] will never have to worry about coming into conflict with any law! "The fruit of the Spirit is love, joy, peace, patience, kindness, goodness, faithfulness,

---

[1] Romans 8:7 [2] Hebrews 8:10 [3] 2 Corinthians 5:14 [4] Romans 6:12; 8:13
[5] Romans 13:8-10; Galatians 5:14 [6] See my book, *Justification and Regeneration*, Chapters 4-13.

gentleness, self-control; *against such things there is no law.*[1] "If you are led by the Spirit, you are not under the Law."[2]

In keeping with this reality, Paul says that *"law is not made for a righteous man,* but for those who are lawless and rebellious, for the ungodly and sinners, for the unholy and profane, for those who kill their fathers or mothers, for murderers and immoral men and homosexuals and kidnappers and liars and perjurers, and whatever else is contrary to sound teaching."[3] The righteous man has no need of such external restrictions, since his own holy nature restrains him from such gross immorality. Even the commands and exhortations of the New Testament are necessary only because believers have not yet completely "become who they are." Since we are yet in this "mortal body" and subject to the "deceitfulness of sin"[4] and the "wiles of the devil,"[5] we still need guideposts to help us sort out right and wrong.[6] However, as we grow in grace, our minds are progressively "renewed," and "because of practice, our senses are trained to discern good and evil."[7] In this way, we are enabled more and more to "prove what the will of God is, that which is good and acceptable and perfect."[8]

The Christian is not "under" law; he is "in-lawed to Christ."[9] If all men were Christians, there would be no need for locks on houses or signs in stores forbidding shoplifting. And this state of affairs will become a reality in heaven, where everyone will experience absolute liberty to do as he pleases! There will be no signs in heaven saying, "You shall not murder" or "You shall love the Lord your God with all your heart"—there will be no need for them!

Supply and Demand

A fourth way that Christians have "died to the Law" is found in Paul's statement that Christians are "not under law, but under

---

[1] Galatians 5:22-23 [2] Galatians 5:18 [3] 1 Timothy 1:8-10 [4] Hebrews 3:13
[5] Ephesians 6:11 [6] See "Specific Commandments," p. 139 [7] Hebrews 5:14
[8] Romans 12:2 [9] 1 Corinthians 9:21 (Gk. *ennomos Christou*); see Appendix E, Q. 13.

grace."[1] They have died to the Law in that *they no longer live in the realm of "demand" but in the realm of "supply."* They are "under" grace, not law, as a dominating power, and they live in the realm where grace "reigns."[2] Here *nothing* depends ultimately on man; everything depends on God. Every desire for goodness and every act of obedience is graciously worked in the believer by God! "For it is God who is at work in you, *both* to *will* and to *work* for His good pleasure."[3]

In the realm where grace reigns, God undertakes to work in me *in spite of my weaknesses and failings* until I am perfectly conformed to the image of Christ. Though *I* may be shocked by my failures as a Christian, *God* isn't! He already knew all my sins and faults before He ever set His love on me, and He actually controls and directs my failures for my own good—in order to expose my weaknesses and to deliver me from them.

This reality is clearly illustrated in Peter's denial of Christ recorded in the gospels.

> "Simon, Simon, behold, Satan has demanded permission to sift you like wheat; but I have prayed for you, that your faith may not fail; and you, when once you have turned again, strengthen your brothers." And he said to Him, "Lord, with You I am ready to go both to prison and to death!" And He said, "I say to you, Peter, the cock will not crow today until you have denied three times that you know Me." Luke 22:31-34

It is apparent from these verses that even though Peter does not know his own weaknesses, Christ knows them fully. He deliberately gives Satan "permission" to "sift" Peter so that through Peter's failure and temporary denial of his Lord, he will come to recognize his sinful self-reliance and repent of it. Sustained by the power of God through Jesus' prayer, Peter's faith will not fail, and after he has "turned again," he will be in a position to actually strengthen others!

---

[1] Romans 6:14 [2] Romans 5:21 [3] Philippians 2:13

THE LAW OF CHRIST

In the New Covenant, God mercifully undertakes to "cleanse us from *all* our filthiness and from *all* our idols,"[1] and He will never rest until that work is finally accomplished! Hallelujah!

> *Safe in Thy sanctifying grace,*
> *Almighty to restore—*
> *Borne onward—sin and death behind,*
> *And love and life before—*
> *O, let my soul abound in hope,*
> *And praise Thee more and more!*
>
> A. L. Waring

---

[1] Ezekiel 36:25

Chapter Seven Review

Christians have been "released from the Law," and are no longer "bound" by the Law, but have been "set free" by Christ from the Law's "yoke of slavery." What exactly does this freedom from the Law entail?

First, every Christian is free from the curse and condemnation of the Law. "There is *no* condemnation for those who are in Christ Jesus."

Second, every Christian is free from the crushing burden of having to keep the Law as a means of obtaining righteousness and life. Christ has obtained for us all the blessings of life and righteousness.

Third, every Christian is free from the Law as an external rule that contradicts his real nature and desires. This freedom comes to him through the miracle of a new heart.

Fourth, every Christian is free from the Law as a realm of "demand"; he now lives in the realm of "supply." Christians are "not under law, but under grace." Grace "reigns" in the life of every true believer.

– CHAPTER EIGHT –

LISTEN TO HIM

> Therefore, my brethren, you also were made to die to the Law through the body of Christ, that you might be joined to another, to Him who was raised from the dead, that we might bear fruit for God.   Romans 7:4
>
> Therefore the Law has become our tutor to lead us to Christ....But now that faith has come, we are no longer under a tutor.   Galatians 3:24-25
>
> And a voice came out of the cloud, saying, "This is My Son, My Chosen One; listen to Him!" And when the voice had spoken, Jesus was found alone.   Luke 9:35-36

Thus far, we have considered four ways in which the Christian has been "released from" the Law. Each of these has to do, not only with his release from the Law of Moses as such, but with his release from the legal bondage formally represented by that Law. The Christian has been released from the curse of the Law, he has been released from the Law as a requirement for obtaining favor and life, he has been released from the Law as an external rule that contradicts his real nature, and he has been released from the Law as a realm of demand as opposed to a realm of supply ("the reign of grace"). In this chapter, we will consider yet another way in which the Christian has been released from the Law: *The Christian has been released from the Law as a covenant rule of duty.* When God established His covenant with Israel through Moses, He gave various laws and commandments in connection with that covenant. As Christians we are not under that covenant and, therefore, not under that covenant's laws and commandments. No longer do those who want to follow God have to be concerned about keeping holy days, offering blood sacrifices, or observing distinctions between clean and unclean animals. In fact, the laws associated with the Old Covenant that Christians are not "under" *as a covenant rule of duty* consist of *all* of its 613 commandments (as traditionally identified by Jewish rabbis), including the Ten Commandments. This follows from the fact that, in the Bible, the Law is always viewed as a unit, and to be "under" one of its laws is to be under all of them.[1] The rule of duty for the Christian is not the Ten Commandments but the "law of Christ." This does not mean that it is no longer wrong to steal or commit adultery, or that the righteous principles underlying the Mosaic Law have changed in any way,[2] but that our allegiance now belongs to Christ and His "law," not to the laws of the Old Covenant.

The Christian is not under the Law as a covenant rule of duty; he is "in-lawed to Christ." And Christ gives him a much clearer and higher revelation of duty than the Law of Moses did. It is not that the law of Christ *overthrows* the "holy and righteous and good"[3] Law of Moses. God forbid! Rather, it fulfills and surpasses it!

A Prophet Like Moses

We have already seen the unique place Moses held in Jewish history as the mediator of the Old Covenant and the mouthpiece of God to Israel. But Moses foretold in Deuteronomy of another Prophet "like Moses" who would one day take his place:

> The Lord your God will raise up for you *a prophet like me* from among you, from your countrymen, you shall listen to him. This is according to all that you asked of the Lord your God in Horeb on the day of the assembly, saying, "Let me not hear again the voice of the Lord my God, let me not see this great fire anymore, lest I die." And the Lord said to me, "They have spoken well. *I will raise up a prophet from among their countrymen like you,* and I will put My words in his mouth, and he shall speak to them all that I command him. And it shall come about that whoever will not listen to My words which he shall speak in My name, I Myself will require it of him."   Deuteronomy 18:15-19

---

[1] Galatians 5:3; see Appendix C, "Civil, Ceremonial, and Moral."
[2] See Chapter 11.   [3] Romans 7:12

It is significant that the book of Deuteronomy closes some sixteen chapters after this prophecy with the following words:

> *Since then no prophet has risen in Israel like Moses,* whom the Lord knew face to face, for all the signs and wonders which the Lord sent him to perform in the land of Egypt against Pharaoh, all his servants, and all his land, and for all the mighty power and for all the great terror which Moses performed in the sight of all Israel.
>
> Deuteronomy 34:10-12

In fact, throughout the entire Old Testament period, no prophet arose in Israel "like Moses"! At the time of Christ, the Jews still waited expectantly for "the Prophet" who was to "come into the world."[1] And Peter makes it clear that it was only in Christ that Moses' prophecy was finally fulfilled:

> Moses said, "The Lord God shall raise up for you a prophet like me from your brethren; to Him you shall give heed in everything He says to you. And it shall be that every soul that does not heed that prophet shall be utterly destroyed from among the people." *And likewise, all the prophets who have spoken, from Samuel and his successors onward, also announced these days.*
>
> Acts 3:22-23

When Christ appeared, He fulfilled everything in Moses' prophecy in a way that went far beyond what even Moses himself had experienced: God knew Christ "face to face" in a way that He had never known Moses; Christ performed "signs and wonders and acts of mighty power" far beyond those performed by Moses; Christ spoke "all that God commanded Him" with such perfection that He alone was worthy of being heeded in literally "everything" that He said, and every soul who did not heed Him was "utterly destroyed" from among the people![2]

---

[1] John 6:14; see also 1:21, 25.   [2] Acts 13:46; Romans 11:17-20

Prophet, Priest, and King

The Lord Jesus Christ has swallowed up and replaced Moses as Prophet, just as He swallowed up and replaced Aaron as Priest and David as King. Is Christ a true priest? Yes, He is the only *real* priest who has ever lived, the only Man who has ever truly been able to represent men before God and actually offer a sacrifice that would put away their sins! Is Christ a true king? Yes, He is the only *real* king who has ever lived, an *actual* Sovereign who truly reigns over men with total authority, the King of kings and Lord of lords! Is Christ a true prophet? Yes, He is the only *real* prophet who has ever lived, speaking the very words[1] of the Father and representing Him perfectly.[2] "God, after He spoke long ago to the fathers in the prophets in many portions and in many ways, *in these last days has spoken to us in His Son.*"[3] The Lord Jesus Christ is a Prophet infinitely greater than Moses!

> Therefore, holy brethren, partakers of a heavenly calling, *consider Jesus, the Apostle and High Priest of our confession* .... For He has been counted *worthy of more glory than Moses, by just so much as the builder of the house has more honor than the house.* For every house is built by someone, but the builder of all things is God. Now Moses was faithful in all His house *as a servant, for a testimony of those things which were to be spoken later*; but Christ was faithful *as a Son* over His house—*whose house we are,* if we hold fast our confidence and the boast of our hope firm until the end.
>
> Hebrews 3:1, 3-6

Christ, as the divine Son, builds the house of His redeemed people, of which we (and Moses) are a part. Christ's glory is just as much greater than Moses' glory as the builder of the house is greater than the house! Moses' role was simply to serve as "a *testimony* of those things which were to be *spoken* later," when Christ, the one true Prophet, would come to take his place.

---

[1] John 3:34; 14:10, 24; 17:8 [2] John 14:9 [3] Hebrews 1:1-2

LISTEN TO HIM

When Moses prophesied of the coming of Christ, his instructions were as follows: "The LORD your God will raise up for you a prophet like me from among you, from your countrymen, *you shall listen to him.*" It is highly significant that these were the very words spoken by God to the disciples on the Mount of Transfiguration.

> And six days later Jesus took with Him Peter and James and John his brother, and brought them up to a high mountain by themselves. And He was transfigured before them; and His face shone like the sun, and His garments became as white as light. And behold, Moses and Elijah appeared to them, talking with Him. And Peter answered and said to Jesus, "Lord, it is good for us to be here; if You wish, I will make three tabernacles here, one for You, and one for Moses, and one for Elijah." While he was still speaking, behold, a bright cloud overshadowed them; and behold, a voice out of the cloud, saying, "This is My beloved Son, with whom I am well-pleased; *listen to Him!*" And when the disciples heard this, they fell on their faces and were much afraid. And Jesus came to them and touched them and said, "Arise, and do not be afraid." And lifting up their eyes, they saw no one, except Jesus Himself alone.
>
> Matthew 17:1-8

We should note well that Peter's proposal for three tabernacles to be built on the mountain, "one for Christ, and one for Moses, and one for Elijah," represented such a serious error that it was met by a direct intervention of God: "This is My beloved Son.... *listen to Him!*" Clearly, God is commanding us here to lay aside our preoccupation with the Law (Moses) and the Prophets (Elijah) and to fix our attention on His own "beloved Son"! The Lord Jesus Christ is unique in glory and authority; He does not stand in a conjunctive relationship with anyone, not even Moses and Elijah! "Lifting up their eyes, *they saw no one, except Jesus Himself alone.*"

GOD'S FINAL WORD TO MEN

This same glorious truth finds eloquent expression in the opening words of the Epistle to the Hebrews: "God, after He spoke long ago to the fathers in the prophets in many portions and in many ways, in these last days has spoken to us in His Son...." Throughout the Old Testament period, God spoke to His people "in many portions and in many ways." Sometimes He spoke through dreams, sometimes through visions, and sometimes directly, but always He spoke in parts and portions. No one prophet or prophecy ever fully expressed what God had to say to mankind. One portion of His truth was delivered through Abraham, another through Moses, another through Isaiah or Ezekiel. But now, in "these last days," something unique has happened. God has given His final Word to humanity; He has spoken to us in His Son.

Readers of the English Bible will notice that the word "His" in this verse is often placed in italics in order to show that it has been supplied by the translators. More literally, the verse would read as follows: "God, after He spoke long ago to the fathers in the prophets in many portions and in many ways, in these last days has spoken to us in [One who is] Son." As many commentators have pointed out, the absence here of any article in the Greek places emphasis on the quality or characteristic of "Son-ness." Great as the Old Testament prophets were, they were nothing in comparison to the One who is a Son. He alone is "the radiance of God's glory and the exact representation of His nature"; He alone "upholds all things by the word of His power."[1] His words are the very words of God,[2] and His deeds are the very deeds of God;[3] to see the Son is to see the Father![4] In His words and His works—in fact, *in His very Person*— *the Son is God's final word to mankind*.

---

[1] Hebrews 1:3   [2] John 3:34; 12:49-50   [3] John 5:19; 14:10   [4] John 14:7-9

But I Say Unto You

In an earlier chapter, we considered the awesome display of God's glory associated with the giving of the Law on Mount Sinai. We can only imagine what it would have been like to be present on that occasion! But for those with eyes to see, there was an even greater manifestation of God's glory that took place fifteen hundred years later on a different "mountain," when God Incarnate in the Person of Jesus Christ "went up on the mountain" and "opening His mouth... began to teach them, saying, 'Blessed are the poor in spirit....'"

It is in this "Sermon on the Mount"[1] that the Lord Jesus sets forth principles of conduct for His spiritual kingdom. Six times,[2] He begins with "the ancients were told" or "it was said" and ends with the contrasting statement, "but I say to you":

> You have heard that *the ancients were told*, "You shall not commit murder" and "Whoever commits murder shall be liable to the court." *But I say to you* that everyone who is angry with his brother shall be guilty before the court; and whoever shall say to his brother, "Raca," shall be guilty before the supreme court; and whoever shall say, "You fool," shall be guilty enough to go into the fiery hell.

> You have heard that *it was said*, "You shall not commit adultery"; *but I say to you*, that everyone who looks on a woman to lust for her has committed adultery with her already in his heart.

> And *it was said*, "Whoever sends his wife away, let him give her a certificate of divorce"; *but I say to you* that everyone who divorces his wife, except for the cause of unchastity, makes her commit adultery; and whoever marries a divorced woman commits adultery.

---

[1] Matthew 5-7 [2] Matthew 5:21-48

Again, you have heard that *the ancients were told,* "You shall not make false vows, but shall fulfill your vows to the Lord." *But I say to you,* make no oath at all....

You have heard that *it was said,* "An eye for an eye, and a tooth for a tooth." *But I say to you,* do not resist him who is evil; but whoever slaps you on your right cheek, turn to him the other also.

You have heard that *it was said,* "You shall love your neighbor, and hate your enemy." *But I say to you,* love your enemies, and pray for those who persecute you....

It is important for us to realize that the Lord Jesus Christ is not disparaging or overthrowing the revelation of God's law given in the Old Testament by His repeated use of the word, "but." Even though He contrasts His own teachings with those of Moses, He specifically warns us not to think that He "came to abolish the Law or the Prophets."[1] Neither is He, on the other hand, simply correcting current Jewish misinterpretations of the Law.[2] Nor is He creating a totally new or different law than the one set forth in the Old Testament.[3] Nor is He only bringing out the full implications of what was already originally intended by the Law of Moses when it was first given!

CIVIL NATION VS. SPIRITUAL NATION

To understand—at least in part—what is taking place here, we need to remind ourselves of the vast differences between the Old and New Covenants. God made the Old Covenant with a *physical* nation of mostly unregenerate people.[4] He makes the New Covenant with a *spiritual* nation of one hundred percent regenerate people.[5] The laws associated with the two covenants differ accordingly. For

---

[1] Matthew 5:17   [2] See Appendix E, Q. 16.   [3] See Chapter 9.   [4] Deuteronomy 29:4; Psalm 95:8-11; Hebrews 3:7-19; 8:8-9; 1 Corinthians 10:1-11; etc.
[5] John 6:45; Hebrews 8:8-12

example, when God commanded "an eye for an eye and a tooth for a tooth," He was establishing principles of strict justice and equity within a civil nation. These principles were vital for the preservation of society and also served to teach the impossibility of forgiveness without satisfaction of justice. In contrast with this, when Jesus says, "But I say to you, do not resist him who is evil; but whoever slaps you on your right cheek, turn to him the other also," He is *not* laying down rules for the governing of a civil nation, but outlining the type of life to be lived by His regenerate people in the midst of a hostile and anti-Christian world.

Likewise, when the Law said, "You shall not commit adultery," it was setting forth one of the statutes of a theocratic society where adultery was punishable by death. Since civil judges had no way to discern "adultery in the heart," it is clearly the actual physical act of adultery that was in view in this commandment. The same holds true for the Law's prohibition of murder, which had to do with actual murder, not a heart attitude of contempt. This does not mean that godly people in the Old Testament did not know that lustful thoughts[1] or hatred[2] were wrong, but it does illustrate the fact that many of the actual precepts of the Law of Moses dealt more with outward matters than with inward matters.[3]

By contrast, the Sermon on the Mount (and the New Testament in general) centers on that which is inward and spiritual, emphasizing hidden motives and heart attitudes. This is why the Lord *begins* the series of contrasts in Matthew 5 quoted above by warning us that "unless our righteousness surpasses that of the scribes and Pharisees, we shall not enter the kingdom of heaven."[4] The scribes and Pharisees had an external righteousness. They did not outwardly commit adultery, steal, or murder. "As to the righteousness which is in the Law," they (like the Pharisee, Saul) were "found blameless."[5] But our Lord says that they were like "whitewashed tombs *which on the outside appear beautiful*, but inside they are full of dead men's bones and all uncleanness." They, too,

---

[1] Job 31:1 [2] Leviticus 19:17 [3] Hebrews 9:8-14; Mark 7:18-23 [4] Matthew 5:20
[5] Philippians 3:5-6; see also Matthew 19:16-20

"*outwardly appeared righteous to men,*" but inwardly were "full of hypocrisy and lawlessness."[1]

In contrast with this external "righteousness which is in the Law," Christians have an internal righteousness. Through the miracle of regeneration, they have had the law internalized—"written on their hearts." They have been given new hearts that are characterized by the marks of "the blessed"—purity, gentleness, poverty of spirit, hunger and thirst for righteousness, etc.[2] Not only does the Christian not murder his enemies; he does not hate them either.[3] Instead, he loves and prays for them.[4] Not only does the Christian not physically practice adultery; he does not live in a dream world of adultery in his heart either.[5] Not only does the Christian fulfill his vows, but honesty so characterizes everything he says that he doesn't even need to take oaths in order to give weight to his words.[6] None of these things is possible apart from the regenerating and empowering work of the Holy Spirit. It should be obvious that lost men can no more "live by the Sermon on the Mount" than leopards can change their spots.[7]

In Matthew 5-7, the Lord Jesus Christ is outlining principles of conduct for those who belong to His kingdom. These principles are meant for a spiritual nation totally made up of regenerate individuals indwelt and empowered by the Holy Spirit; they could never have been given to a physical nation of mostly unregenerate Jews. In this sense, the difference between the "laws" of the two "nations" is vast. Under the Old Covenant, when a husband discovered, for example, that his wife had begun to embrace false teachings, he did not come to prayer meeting and say, "Please pray for my wife; she has begun to worship Moloch." He followed, instead, a different set of instructions:

> *If your brother, your mother's son, or your son or daughter, or the wife you cherish, or your friend who is as your own soul,* entice you secretly, saying, 'Let us go and serve other gods'

---

[1] Matthew 23:27-28 [2] Matthew 5:3-11 [3] Matthew 5:21-26; 1 John 2:9-11; 3:14-15 [4] Matthew 5:44-48 [5] Matthew 5:27-30 [6] Matthew 5:33-37
[7] Jeremiah 13:23

(whom neither you nor your fathers have known, of the gods of the peoples who are around you, near you or far from you, from one end of the earth to the other end), you shall not yield to him or listen to him; *and your eye shall not pity him, nor shall you spare or conceal him. But you shall surely kill him; your hand shall be first against him to put him to death,* and afterwards the hand of all the people. So you shall stone him to death because he has sought to seduce you from the Lord your God who brought you out from the land of Egypt, out of the house of slavery. Then all Israel will hear and be afraid, and will never again do such a wicked thing among you. Deuteronomy 13:6-11

This was one of God's *commandments* under the Old Covenant. It was not optional; it was *covenant law* for Israel. The great difference between this covenant law and our Lord's teachings in the Sermon on the Mount should be obvious. The one is the "law of the tutor," keeping the child under strict discipline (like a slave) for his own good. The other belongs to the realm of full and glorious sonship, with far greater *liberties* and far greater *responsibilities*.

SLAVES VS. SONS

But before faith came, we were kept in custody under the law, being shut up to the faith which was later to be revealed. Therefore the Law has become our tutor to lead us to Christ, that we may be justified by faith. But now that faith has come, we are no longer under a tutor. For you are all sons of God through faith in Christ Jesus.... Now I say, as long as the heir is a child, he does not differ at all from a slave although he is owner of everything, but he is under guardians and managers until the date set by the father. So also we, while we were children, were held in bondage under the elemental things of the world. But when the fulness of the time came, God sent forth His Son, born of a woman, born under the Law, in order that He might redeem those who were under the Law, that we might receive the adoption as sons. And because you are sons, God has sent forth the Spirit of His Son into our hearts, crying, 'Abba! Father!' Therefore you are no longer a slave, but a son; and if a son, then an heir through God.

Galatians 3:23-26; 4:1-7

Here Paul likens the condition of Israel under the Old Covenant to a state of slavery. He contrasts this with the state of the Christian who is "no longer a slave, but a son." *The law of Christ surpasses the Law of Moses as far as sonship surpasses slavery.* This is not because the Law of Moses was bad; it was *perfect* for what God intended it to accomplish. When God decreed that even a man's wife or best friend was to be stoned to death for enticing others to serve false gods, His commandment was perfectly suited to the general state of His Old Covenant people. Apart from such strict discipline, the whole nation would have quickly fallen into apostasy: "Then all Israel will hear and be afraid, and will never again do such a wicked thing among you."[1]

The law of Christ belongs to a different realm than the Law of Moses only because of *who Christ is* and *who we are in Christ*. As stated above, this is the realm of full and glorious sonship—a realm characterized by far greater liberties and far greater responsibilities than those envisioned by Moses. When my oldest son was a child, I told him when to go to bed, when to get up, when to brush his teeth, and when to put on his shoes. But as he entered into maturity, my list of detailed instructions and restrictions became unnecessary and obsolete. The Christian lives in a realm of glorious freedom, a freedom that brings with it the responsibility to serve others through love. "For you were called to freedom, brethren; only do not turn your freedom into an opportunity for the flesh, but through love serve one another."[2]

---

[1] Deuteronomy 13:11 [2] Galatians 5:13

CHAPTER EIGHT REVIEW

There is a fifth way that Christians are free from the Law, in addition to the four already considered: Christians have been released from the Law as a covenant rule of duty. Their allegiance now belongs to Christ and His "law"—the revelation of God's will made known through Christ's own Person, words, and works.

The Lord Jesus Christ is God's final word to mankind. He is the long-awaited Prophet "like Moses," whose glory infinitely surpasses that of Moses or any other prophet. Because He is God's own "beloved Son," we are to "listen to Him" in "everything He says to us."

In the Sermon on the Mount, Christ gives us a glimpse of the radical goodness that characterizes those who belong to the kingdom of heaven. Their righteousness far surpasses that of the scribes and Pharisees, because it flows from a heart renewed and indwelt by the Holy Spirit.

The law of Christ does not overthrow the Law of Moses; rather, it "fulfills" and brings it to completion. The Law of Moses was like a guardian that is assigned to keep a child under strict discipline (like a slave) for his own good. The law of Christ, on the other hand, belongs to the realm of full and glorious sonship—a realm characterized by far greater liberties and far greater responsibilities than those envisioned by Moses.

– CHAPTER NINE –

THE LEAST OF THESE COMMANDMENTS

> Do not think that I came to abolish the Law or the Prophets; I did not come to abolish, but to fulfill. For truly I say to you, until heaven and earth pass away, not the smallest letter or stroke shall pass away from the Law, until all is accomplished. Whoever then annuls one of the least of these commandments, and so teaches others, shall be called least in the kingdom of heaven; but whoever keeps and teaches them, he shall be called great in the kingdom of heaven. For I say to you, that unless your righteousness surpasses that of the scribes and Pharisees, you shall not enter the kingdom of heaven.   Matthew 5:17-20

In light of the preceding chapters, a pressing question arises: What are we to do with the Old Testament? If the Old Covenant is "obsolete" [1] and has been "abolished," [2] if we are "no longer under a tutor," [3] then what place could the Old Testament possibly play in our lives as Christians? To answer this question, we must begin by recognizing the difference between the *Old Covenant* and the Old Testament *Scriptures*. The Old Covenant that was made between God and Israel on Mount Sinai has indeed been abolished and replaced by a New Covenant, but the Old Testament Scriptures, including those that set forth the precepts of the Law of Moses, remain an authoritative revelation of God to mankind until "heaven and earth pass away." The commandments of the Old Covenant do not bind us directly *as covenant law*, but every one of them has indirect relevance to us as part of the Word of God. This fact is evident in Paul's words to Timothy: "From childhood you have known the sacred writings which are able to give you the wisdom

---

[1] Hebrews 8:13   [2] Ephesians 2:14-15   [3] Galatians 3:24

that leads to salvation through faith which is in Christ Jesus. All Scripture is inspired by God and profitable for teaching, for reproof, for correction, for training in righteousness; that the man of God may be adequate, equipped for every good work."[1] The "sacred writings" to which Paul refers are the Old Testament Scriptures; the New Testament (as such) was not yet in existence. Paul is saying, then, that the Old Testament Scriptures, when understood and applied properly, remain "profitable" to New Testament believers, not only as a prophetic witness to Christ, but "for reproof, for correction, and for training in righteousness." With God "there is no variation or shifting shadow."[2] He has not changed in the least since the days of Abraham and Moses, and all the things He revealed to us in the Old Testament concerning His character and ways remain as true today as they ever were. The whole Old Testament is still the Word of God to us.

This means that there is a basic continuity between the Law of Moses and the law of Christ. In fact, our Lord explicitly teaches this continuity in the verses quoted above: "Do not think that I came to abolish the Law or the Prophets; I did not come to *abolish*, but to *fulfill*." As we have seen, Christ "fulfills" the Law and the Prophets on every level. He fulfills the Old Testament's prophecies, types, and shadows by the entire course of His incarnation and exaltation—from His birth in Bethlehem[3] to His resurrection from the dead,[4] to His seating at the right hand of the Father.[5] He fulfills the Law's requirements for obtaining eternal life by His perfect obedience to the Father. Moreover, He fulfills the Law's just penalty against all our sins by His death on our behalf.

The "fulfilling" of the Law that Jesus speaks of in verse 17, however, involves something more. It has to do with the radical and shocking statements that He has already made and will continue to make throughout the remainder of the Sermon on the Mount: "You have heard ... *but I say unto you*." Lest any should get the impression that His teachings are meant to set aside the Law of Moses as

---

[1] 2 Timothy 3:15-17 [2] James 1:17 [3] Matthew 2:4-6 [4] Acts 2:29-32
[5] Matthew 22:43-44

THE LEAST OF THESE COMMANDMENTS

irrelevant,[1] our Lord makes it clear from the outset that they are, in fact, a fulfillment of every aspect of that Law. His teachings are that toward which every detail of the Law pointed, and they incorporate and bring to completion all of the Law's commandments. Not the "smallest letter or stroke" of the Law is unimportant or dispensable, and each of them must and will find its fulfillment in the standards and kingdom that He is about to establish. Those who enter into the realities described in the Sermon on the Mount will find themselves fulfilling, not only the "weightier" commandments of the Law, but also the "lighter" ones as well. They will find their righteousness not only equaling that of the scribes and Pharisees, but also far surpassing it! It is on this basis that the Lord goes on in verse 19 to make the remarkable deduction that "whoever *then* annuls *one of the least of these commandments,* and so teaches others, shall be called *least in the kingdom of heaven*; but whoever *keeps and teaches them,* he shall be called great in the kingdom of heaven."

What does the Lord Jesus mean when He refers to one of the least of "these commandments"? Some have said that He is speaking of *His own commandments,* which He will soon set forth in the remainder of the Sermon on the Mount. When we read verse 19 in its context, however, this interpretation becomes very difficult to maintain. Consider, once again, verses 17-20:

> Do not think that I came to *abolish* the Law or the Prophets; I did not come to *abolish,* but to fulfill. For truly I say to you, until heaven and earth pass away, not the *smallest letter or stroke* shall pass away from the *Law,* until all is accomplished. Whoever then *annuls* one of the *least* of *these commandments,* and so teaches others, shall be called least in the kingdom of heaven; but whoever keeps and teaches them, he shall be called great in the kingdom of heaven. For I say to you, that unless your righteousness surpasses that of the scribes and Pharisees, you shall not enter the kingdom of heaven.

---

[1] See Appendix E, Q. 15.

Jesus is speaking in verses 17-18 about the fact that He has not come to *abolish* even the *smallest letter or stroke* of "the Law." Drawing a *conclusion* from what He has just said, He begins verse 19 with the word "then" (or "therefore" [1]) and immediately warns His disciples not to *annul* one of the *least* of "these commandments." Surely, it is clear that Jesus' own commandments (which have not yet been given) cannot be directly in view in this warning! Neither can Jesus be referring only to the Ten Commandments, since they are assuredly not "the least" of the Old Covenant commandments.

LESSONS FROM THE OX

What are some of "the least" commandments of the Mosaic Law? Several examples could be cited, but we will consider one that is found in the midst of a series of such commands in Deuteronomy 22: "You shall not sow your vineyard with two kinds of seed, lest all the produce of the seed which you have sown and the increase of the vineyard become defiled. You shall not plow with an ox and a donkey together. You shall not wear a material mixed of wool and linen together." [2] According to the Lord Jesus, "whoever annuls one of the least of these commandments, and so teaches others, shall be called least in the kingdom of heaven"! How can this be, especially when we know from Jesus' teachings elsewhere[3] that it is just such commandments that Christians are no longer required to obey? How is it that those "in the kingdom of heaven" can be said to "keep and teach" these commandments?

Part of the answer to this question is found in Paul's second letter to the Corinthians: "Do not be bound together [lit. "unequally yoked" [4]] with unbelievers; for what partnership have righteousness and lawlessness, or what fellowship has light with darkness?" [5] When Paul speaks here of being "unequally yoked," he is making reference to God's commandment in Deuteronomy 22:10 against plowing with an ox and a donkey together. Notice what Paul has

---

[1] See ESV, ASV, and KJV.   [2] Deuteronomy 22:9-11   [3] See, e.g., Mark 7:18-19; cf. Acts 10:9-15, 28-29.   [4] See ESV and KJV.   [5] 2 Corinthians 6:14

done in this verse. He has taken an Old Covenant commandment about not plowing with an ox and a donkey together and has applied its principles to Christians! Why would God command the Jews not to plow with an ox and a donkey together? Because one was a clean beast and one was unclean! [1] Even so, Paul says, the Christian should not be "unequally yoked together" with anyone who is an unbeliever. We see, then, that as Christians we *do* keep Deuteronomy 22:10, and we keep it in a deeper and fuller way than the Jews ever did!

Another illustration of this principle is seen in 1 Corinthians 9:6-10.

> Or do only Barnabas and I not have a right to refrain from working? Who at any time serves as a soldier at his own expense? Who plants a vineyard, and does not eat the fruit of it? Or who tends a flock and does not use the milk of the flock? *I am not speaking these things according to human judgment, am I? Or does not the Law also say these things? For it is written in the Law of Moses, "You shall not muzzle the ox while he is threshing." God is not concerned about oxen, is He? Or is He speaking altogether for our sake? Yes, for our sake it was written,* because the plowman ought to plow in hope, and the thresher to thresh in hope of sharing the crops.

In these verses, Paul appeals to another of "the least" commandments of the Law of Moses, found in Deuteronomy 25:4: "You shall not muzzle the ox while he is threshing." According to Paul, this commandment is fulfilled by Christians as they financially support those who minister the gospel to them. God *is* indeed concerned about how we treat animals, but according to the apostle Paul, God's concern for animals is inconsequential compared to His concern for us: "God is not concerned about oxen, is He? *Or is He speaking altogether for our sake? Yes, for our sake it was written....*" In other words, the *spiritual application* of this commandment to us as Christians was *God's ultimate concern in giving it in the first place!*

---

[1] Leviticus 11:1-8 1

Here Paul has taken a truly remarkable position concerning the Law of Moses! On the one hand, he quotes this commandment as having divine authority: "I am not speaking these things *according to human judgment,* am I? Or does not *the Law* also say these things?" On the other hand, he makes it clear that this divine authority resides, not in the fact that the commandment was part of the *Mosaic Covenant* as such, but in the fact that it is part of God's revelation in *Scripture.* The original place this commandment occupied as part of the 613 commandments of the Mosaic Law is of no consequence to Paul. It holds *no* authority over him or any other Christian on that basis. Rather, Paul views it as part of God's Old Testament revelation, *spoken and written "altogether" for the sake of New Covenant believers,* who would one day profit from its *spiritual application* once the Old Covenant had passed away!

Still another notable illustration of how Christians "keep" even the least commandments of the Law is seen in the matter of circumcision. According to Paul, if a man has circumcision of the *heart* (the spiritual reality of which physical circumcision was but a shadow), his physical *un*circumcision will be "regarded as" circumcision![1] Thus, *all Christians,* by virtue of the inward reality of their hearts, do indeed "keep" and "teach" the commandment of circumcision, and they keep it more truly than it was kept by those who were only Jews "outwardly"!

As we might expect, many of the commandments of the Mosaic Law clearly foreshadow the Person and atoning work of Christ, and their meanings are unfolded in the writings of the New Testament. The book of Hebrews, for example, explains much of the typology behind the laws related to the design, service, and sacrifices of the tabernacle. The way we, as Christians, "keep the least" of these laws is by believing on Christ as our great High Priest and Sacrifice for sins. In fact, the way in which we may be certain to "keep and teach" *every* commandment of the Old Testament—whether "weighty" or "least"—is not only by reverencing the Old Testament as the Word of God, *but by believing on and following closely our Lord and Master,*

---

[1] Romans 2:26

who in His Person and teachings is the "fulfillment" of the "smallest letter and stroke" of the Law.

Is the Christian under the laws of the Old Covenant? He is under *none* of them directly as covenant law, but he "keeps and teaches" *all* of them indirectly as he lives in the realities of the New Covenant. This does not mean that we as Christians can always discern the spiritual truth, if any, that God was signifying by giving a particular commandment to the Jews. There are many laws about clean and unclean foods, rules concerning sacrifices, etc., of which we may never fully understand the true import until we get to heaven. The manner in which any particular command of the Old Testament is to be fulfilled by us, even in its spiritual principles, depends on how that command is interpreted and applied by the Lord Jesus Christ and His inspired apostles. If no inspired application of a specific commandment is given to us in the New Testament, we may still be able (through the guidance of the Holy Spirit) to glean many profitable lessons from it. It is important for us to remember, however, that when the Lord and His apostles have given us no authoritative application of an Old Covenant commandment, we have no right to impose *our interpretation* of that commandment on the consciences of other believers. *Christians do not "keep and teach" the least commandments of the Law and prophets by codifying a new "list of rules" from the (spiritually interpreted) laws of the Old Testament, but by walking in love*[1] *by the power of the Spirit!*[2]

Applying the Old Testament

As Christians, we are to read the Old Testament "through the eyes" of Christ and His apostles. Paul illustrates this approach when he finds an abiding principle embodied in the promise that was attached to the Fifth Commandment: "Children, obey your parents in the Lord, for this is right. Honor your father and mother (which is the first commandment with a promise), that it may be well with

---

[1] Romans 13:9-10; Galatians 5:14; see Chapter 16. [2] Romans 8:4

you, and that you may live long on the earth."[1] Here Paul quotes one of the Ten Commandments, then "Christianizes" its promise and applies it to Gentile children. God's original promise ("that your days may be prolonged, and that it may go well with you on the land which the LORD your God gives you"[2]) had to do with the "prolonging" of the "days" of the Jewish nation in the land of Canaan.[3] Paul's application of that promise to Christians relates to the general principle that children who honor and obey their parents will experience blessing—it will "be well" with them, and they will usually live longer "on the earth" than children who do not honor their parents. Many of the promises set forth in the book of Proverbs follow a somewhat similar pattern. Those that relate to "long life" and physical riches are notable examples.[4] Though Christians may experience "deep poverty"[5] or be martyred at an early age,[6] it is still true (in general) that a life of diligence, wisdom, and righteousness tends toward longevity and material prosperity.

If we follow the lead of the apostles in applying the teachings of the Old Testament to our lives, we will find many riches in "the Law and the Prophets." "For *whatever* was written in earlier times *was written for our instruction*, that through perseverance and the encouragement of the Scriptures we might have hope."[7] "Now these things happened to them as an example, *and they were written for our instruction*, upon whom the ends of the ages have come."[8] According to the Lord Jesus, even God's words to Moses at the burning bush were in reality *spoken to us!* "Have you not read that which was *spoken to you by God*, saying, 'I am the God of Abraham, and the God of Isaac, and the God of Jacob'?"[9] In light of this wonderful assurance, how diligent ought we to be in our study of the Old Testament Scriptures!

---

[1] Ephesians 6:1-3   [2] Deuteronomy 5:16   [3] See also Exodus 20:12.
[4] E.g., Proverbs 3:1-2, 16; 4:10; 9:11; 10:4, 27; 22:4; 24:3-4   [5] 2 Corinthians 8:2
[6] Acts 7:58-60   [7] Romans 15:4   [8] 1 Corinthians 10:11   [9] Matthew 22:31-32; Exodus 3:6

SEARCHING FOR CHRIST

Above all, we should search for Christ in the pages of the Old Testament. We can do this with absolute confidence, since we *know* that "Moses wrote of Him."[1] According to the Lord Jesus, "It is these [Old Testament Scriptures] that bear witness of Me."[2] Not only the *laws*, but also many of the *historical events* that took place in the Old Testament were meant by God to foreshadow the Person and work of Christ. Christ is the real "manna," the "true bread out of heaven" who "gives life to the world."[3] He is also "our Passover"[4] and the "spiritual rock" from which the Israelites drank in the wilderness![5] Christ is everywhere in the Old Testament!

Hudson Taylor (1832-1905), missionary to China, tells of an experience he had while traveling on one of his missionary tours that well illustrates this fact:

> I had to pass the night in a very wicked town. All the inns were dreadful places, and the people seemed to have their consciences seared and their hearts sealed against the Truth. My own heart was oppressed and could find no relief; and I awoke the next morning much cast down and feeling spiritually hungry and thirsty indeed.
>
> On opening my Bible at the seventh chapter of Numbers, I felt as though I could not then read that long chapter of repetitions; that I must turn to some chapter that would feed my soul. And yet I was not happy in leaving my regular portion [daily reading schedule], so after a little conflict I resolved to read it, praying to God to bless me, even through Numbers 7. I fear there was not much faith in the prayer, but oh, how abundantly it was answered, and what a feast God gave me![6]

The insights Hudson Taylor received that morning from this obscure passage in the Law were such a blessing to him that

---

[1] John 5:46 [2] John 5:39 [3] John 6:31-35 [4] 1 Corinthians 5:7
[5] 1 Corinthians 10:4 [6] Hudson Taylor, *Separation and Service* (London: Morgan & Scott, n.d.) 7-8.

they were later written down and published in book form! [1] Such testimonies ought to greatly encourage us to echo the prayer of the Psalmist: "Open my eyes, that I may behold wonderful things from Your law!" [2]

---

[1] *Separation and Service*   [2] Psalm 119:18 (NAS95)

PART THREE

THE LAW OF CHRIST

The law of Christ is superior to every other revelation of law because it flows from His "new commandment" that we are to "love as He loved." This *Christlike love* embodies and fulfills the essence of the law and gives us the highest revelation of man's duty imaginable. In keeping with this fact, *love* is the central emphasis of the New Testament regarding the Christian's life and conduct. Because Christ Himself is our "law," the "law of Christ" presents both a wonderful and an impossible standard. It can only be fulfilled in our lives as Christ Himself, in the Person of the Holy Spirit, lives His life through us.

Chapters 10-13 explore the meaning and centrality of Christ's "new commandment" and the "law of love." Chapter 14 then explains why true, Biblical love must always be defined in terms of Christ's own actions; the New Testament teaches ethics by appealing to the example of Christ Himself. In Chapter 15, the practical outworkings of Christ's new commandment to "love one another" are illustrated by the many "one another" exhortations of the New Testament. In Chapter 16, the simplicity of the law of Christ is considered—Christians do not live by a "list of rules." Chapter 17 then explores more fully the superiority of the law of Christ to the Law of Moses, while Chapters 18-19 attempt to set the law of Christ in its proper context as part of the overarching "ministry of the Spirit" in the New Covenant.

Chapter Nine Review

Even though the Old Covenant has been abolished, the Old Testament Scriptures continue to be an authoritative revelation of God's character and ways until "heaven and earth pass away." There is a basic continuity between the law of Christ and the Law of Moses. Christ's teachings in the Sermon on the Mount do not overthrow the Law of Moses, but are, in fact, a fulfillment of every aspect of it. Those who enter into the realities described in the Sermon on the Mount will find themselves fulfilling, not only the "weightier" commandments of the Law, but also the "lighter" ones as well.

Christians "keep and teach" even the "least" commandments of the Law, not only by reverencing the Old Testament as the Word of God, but by believing on and following closely their Lord and Master, who in His Person and teachings is the "fulfillment" of the "smallest letter and stroke" of the Law.

As Christians, we are to read the Old Testament "through the eyes" of Christ and His apostles, realizing that "whatever was written in earlier times was written for our instruction, that through perseverance and the encouragement of the Scriptures we might have hope."

Above all, we should search for Christ in the pages of the Old Testament, since we know that "Moses wrote of Him" and He is the Old Testament's central theme.

– Chapter Ten –

The New Commandment

> To those who are without law, as without law, though not being without the law of God but under the law of Christ....
> 1 Corinthians 9:21

> Bear one another's burdens, and thus fulfill the law of Christ.
> Galatians 6:2

We are now in a position to consider the Christian's rule of duty, "the law of Christ"! However, when Paul says to the Galatians, "Bear one another's burdens, and thus fulfill the law of Christ," he does not give a detailed explanation as to what the "law of Christ" is. In fact, he does not give *any* explanation! Evidently, the meaning of the law of Christ was so well known in the early church that no explanation of it was necessary. To "bear one another's burdens" is to display *love*, and to display love is to "fulfill the law of Christ." But how was it that the early church had come to the place of referring to love as the "law of Christ"? The answer is found in our Lord's words to the disciples in the Upper Room.

Each of us should enter the holy ground of the Upper Room discourse with reverence and awe. It is here that the Lord Jesus, on the very eve of His crucifixion, prepares His disciples for the trials, blessings, and responsibilities that will soon be theirs. It is here that He gives His parting instructions and emphasizes those things that are of utmost importance for the disciples to remember and follow. And it is here that He gives us His "new commandment."

> A new commandment I give to you, that you love one another, even as I have loved you, that you also love one another. By this all men will know that you are My disciples, if you have love for one another.
> John 13:34-35

THE LAW OF CHRIST

This is My commandment, that you love one another, just as I have loved you. Greater love has no one than this, that one lay down his life for his friends.   John 15:12-13

This I command you, that you love one another.
                                                                John 15:17

We may well imagine the disciples' surprise when they hear that "love" is the "new" commandment! Had not God already commanded men to love one another? Why would the Lord Jesus make a point of calling this a "new" commandment? There are at least three reasons why the new commandment can rightly be called "new."

NEW COVENANT

When we think of the "new" commandment, we must remember that it was not the only thing that was "new" that evening in the Upper Room: "And in the same way He took the cup after they had eaten, saying, 'This cup which is poured out for you is the new covenant in My blood.' "[1] The *new commandment* is called "new" because it accompanies a *new covenant*. When the Old Covenant was given, there was a covenant meal, the sprinkling of blood, and the setting forth of commandments for the people to obey.[2] Even so, when the New Covenant is given, there is a covenant meal (the first "Lord's Supper"), the shedding of the blood of Christ, and the giving of a "new commandment" for us to follow. This "new commandment" is not some kind of new legal code or list of rules to be observed, but a *reminder* of what is really important in the Christian life.

Think of it, beloved! Under the Old Covenant, there were all sorts of laws and regulations to be meticulously followed—in fact, six hundred and thirteen of them! Under the New Covenant, there is only *one* guidepost for us to keep central in our thinking! (See Chapter 16.) As was pointed out in an earlier chapter, this fact not only grants us tremendous liberty, it also involves us in tremendous responsibility.

---

[1] Luke 22:20   [2] Exodus 24:7-11

NEW EXAMPLE

The new commandment is "new" because it is associated with a new covenant. But it is also "new" because it gives an entirely new depth of meaning to the word "love." This is obvious from the fact that our Lord did not just say, "A new commandment I give to you, that you love one another." He said, instead, "A new commandment I give to you, that you love one another, *even as I have loved you.*" In other words, the Christian's standard is not just "love," but love *of the same quality and magnitude as Christ Himself manifested* in His incarnation and death on the cross! This is indeed a "new" commandment, because it is the highest, clearest, and brightest revelation of man's duty that ever has been or ever could be given to the human race. There *can be* nothing more *exacting*, or more *demanding*, or more *wonderful* than this—to love others in just the same way and to the same degree that Christ loved us! No one has ever fathomed the full import of these words, nor has anyone ever begun to fully live up to them. We will examine the implications of these words more extensively in a later chapter.

NEW CREATION

There is a third reason why the new commandment is "new." John brings this out in his first epistle: "Beloved, I am not writing a new commandment to you, but an old commandment which you have had from the beginning; the old commandment is the word which you have heard. On the other hand, I *am* writing a new commandment to you, *which is true in Him and in you, because the darkness is passing away, and the true light is already shining.*"[1] The commandment to love is, in one sense, nothing new. John's readers had heard it from the beginning of their Christian experience. Even when it was given in the Upper Room, it was already centuries old.[2] But, then again, John says it *is* a new commandment, in another sense, because of something that is now true "in Christ and in us."

---

[1] 1 John 2:7-8 [2] Leviticus 19:18

As Christians, we now belong to a new realm and a new age: "The darkness is passing away, and the true light is already shining." We are new creatures[1] with new hearts[2] and new natures,[3] born anew[4] by the Spirit of God and raised up to walk in newness[5] of life. The new commandment is new "in us" because *we* are new. We now have new hearts with God's new commandment of love written upon them: "Now as to the *love of the brethren,* you have *no need* for anyone to write to you, *for you yourselves are taught by God to love one another.*"[6] "We know that *we have passed out of death into life, because we love the brethren.* He who does not love abides in death."[7]

THE LAW OF LOVE

Love is the "law" that God "writes on the heart" of every new believer! This becomes obvious when we consider what happens in regeneration: "For this is the covenant that I will make with the house of Israel after those days, says the Lord: I will put My laws into their minds, and I will write them upon their hearts. And I will be their God, and they shall be my people."[8] What does it mean that God has written His laws upon our hearts? The new Christian does not find himself instinctively not wanting to light a fire in his dwelling from six o'clock Friday evening until six o'clock Saturday evening.[9] Nor does he suddenly find himself not wanting to wear shirts that contain both polyester and cotton.[10] But he *does* find himself possessed by a love for God and for his fellow men! *Every* Christian loves God,[11] and *every* Christian loves others.[12] *And love is the very heart and essence of the Law!*

---

[1] 2 Corinthians 5:17   [2] Ezekiel 36:26-27   [3] Matthew 12:33
[4] John 3:3-8   [5] Romans 6:4   [6] 1 Thessalonians 4:9   [7] 1 John 3:14
[8] Hebrews 8:10   [9] Exodus 35:3; Leviticus 23:32   [10] Deuteronomy 22:11
[11] Romans 8:28; 1 Corinthians 16:22; Ephesians 6:24; 1 Peter 1:8; etc.
[12] 1 John 3:10-15; 4:7-8; etc.

CHAPTER TEN REVIEW

Christians are said to "fulfill" the law of Christ whenever they show love to one another. We can learn how love came to be known as the "law of Christ" by considering the one "new commandment" that Christ gave His disciples in the Upper Room: "A new commandment I give to you, that you love one another, even as I have loved you, that you also love one another."

Christ's new commandment is "new" because it is given in connection with the inauguration of the "new" covenant. Instead of 613 commandments, Christians have *one* guidepost to keep central in their thinking.

Christ's new commandment is also "new" because it gives an entirely new depth of meaning to the word "love." As Christians, we are to love one another "even as Christ loved us." This is indeed a "new" commandment, because it presents the highest, clearest, and brightest revelation of man's duty that ever has been or ever could be given to the human race.

Christ's new commandment is also "new" because of what Christ has done in the hearts of all believers. Christians belong to a new realm—a realm where "the darkness is passing away, and the true light is already shining." The new commandment is new "in Christ and in us" because *we* are new. We now have new hearts with God's new commandment of love written upon them.

– CHAPTER ELEVEN –

THE ESSENCE OF THE LAW

> "You shall love the Lord your God with all your heart, and with all your soul, and with all your mind." This is the great and foremost commandment. The second is like it, "You shall love your neighbor as yourself." On these two commandments depend the whole Law and the Prophets.
>
> Matthew 22:37-40

When "a certain lawyer" asked Jesus "which is the great commandment in the Law," He answered with the verses quoted above, declaring to him not only "the great and foremost" commandment, but "the second" which is "like it." Though the lawyer had not asked which was the second greatest commandment, the Lord Jesus deliberately volunteered it in order to lay the groundwork for an extremely important teaching that He wanted to set forth. Having quoted the two great commandments, He then went on to make this remarkable statement: *"On these two commandments depend the whole Law and the Prophets."* It is significant that the word translated "depend" in this verse is a word that literally means "to hang or suspend." According to the Lord Jesus Christ, the "whole Law and Prophets" *hang upon and are suspended from* the two great love commandments. These two commands are more than just a *summary* of the Law; they are like pegs on which every other command in the Law hangs. In other words, the *essence* or *substance* of the Law is love to God and love to our fellow men; all other commands are simply the *outworking* and *application* of these two commandments to the various situations of life.

The fact that these two commandments *encompass and contain in themselves every aspect of man's essential duty to God* is seen very clearly in our Lord's discussion with a "certain lawyer":

> And behold, a certain lawyer stood up and put Him to the test, saying, "Teacher, what shall I do to inherit eternal

life?" And He said to him, "What is written in the Law? How does it read to you?" And he answered and said, "You shall love the Lord your God with all your heart, and with all your soul, and with all your strength, and with all your mind; and your neighbor as yourself." And He said to him, "You have answered correctly; do this, and you will live."

Luke 10:25-28[1]

Here we learn from the Lord Jesus Christ that keeping the two great commandments is sufficient of itself to merit eternal life. All of the most exacting moral requirements of the Law are evidently fulfilled in the keeping of these two! It is these two commandments that make up the essence of the Law.

THE LAW—ITS ESSENCE

Any discussion of the "essence of the law" must take as its starting point the very being and character of God Himself. *Apart from God, there is no law*—no right or wrong, no good or evil. Specifically, there is no standard of "goodness" outside of God to which He must submit in order to be good. God Himself, in the perfect freedom of His will and being, is the standard by which all goodness is defined. That which is like God is "good"; that which is not like God is "evil." When this principle is applied to the human race, it means that men must be morally *like God* in order to be good, and all men who are not like God are, by definition *and in fact*, evil.

"Law" in its essence, then, is not an arbitrary enactment, but a *necessity* grounded in the very being of God. Law is an expression of God's character as that character relates to the created order. Since God "is" love,[2] and God's rational and moral creatures must be like Him in order to be good, *men are necessarily obligated to love, simply because of who God is.* Any failure to love is *sin*.

"Sin" in the final analysis is therefore "sinful" simply because it contradicts the absolutes of God's being. And as a contradiction of

---

[1] Compare Leviticus 18:5. [2] 1 John 4:8, 16; see Appendix B.

God's being, sin *necessarily* involves *separation from God*. But God is the fountain of all that constitutes "life."[1] Sin therefore necessarily involves "death" because it involves separation from God. "The soul that sins shall—of necessity—die."[2]

Because law is, in its essence, an expression of God's character, it should be very clear to us that, *since God can never change, the essence of the law can never change*. The essence of the law is "you shall love the Lord your God with all your heart, and with all your soul, and with all your mind" and "you shall love your neighbor as yourself." It can never be *right* for a finite, created being to love his infinitely glorious Creator with *less* than all his heart, soul, mind, and strength. Likewise, it can never be right for a finite, created being to love his "neighbor" *less* than he loves himself or do things to his neighbor that he would not want his neighbor to do to him. *The two great commandments are the unchanging moral obligation resting upon all men in all places throughout all time and eternity.*

THE LAW—WONDERFUL AND TERRIFYING

As a necessary expression of God's own character, law is both *wonderful* and *terrifying*. It is wonderful in that it describes all that is morally beautiful, desirable, and Godlike—the pathways of love, righteousness, peace, and life. It is terrifying in that it spells certain doom and destruction—separation from God—for all whose lives are a contradiction of the God that law describes. The existence of God is therefore both the best news imaginable and the worst news imaginable for fallen humanity. Just as certainly as there is an all-glorious and all-righteous self-existent God, so certainly must all the sinful sons of Adam be consigned to eternal separation from Him.

The unspeakable glory of the gospel is that God, by and through the cross of Christ, has satisfied the justice demanded by His own being, so that sinful men can be restored to His smile and favor. Through the cross of Christ, we die to the law—not the wonderful

---

[1] Psalm 36:9   [2] Ezekiel 18:4

aspect of the law, but the terrifying and burdensome[1] aspect of the law. We move from the realm of condemnation and curse to the realm of justification and blessing, from the realm of sin and death to the realm of righteousness and life, from the realm of requirement to the realm of provision, from the realm of external demand to the realm of internal conformity.

THE LAW—ITS APPLICATIONS

As noted above, the *essential duty* of all men at all times is unchanging. It is important to understand, however, that the specific *applications* of this duty have *not* been made equally clear to all men at all times. In fact, the outworkings of what it means—in terms of concrete actions—to love God supremely and to love one's neighbor as oneself *have been revealed more and more clearly over time and have differed under varying circumstances:*

- For the *Gentile*—the man without the Bible—they have been revealed only by way of *nature and conscience*—"the work of the Law written in the heart."[2]

- For the *Jew*, they were spelled out in terms of the *Mosaic Covenant*. Because of the special circumstances of that covenant, love to God and man in the setting of the Mosaic Law involved obedience to commandments that we now recognize as typical, ceremonial, and civil, as well as those that were "weightier" and related directly to the essence of law. For example, "love to God" under the theocracy meant, among other things, strictly keeping the Jewish Sabbath and offering the prescribed sacrifices in their appointed times, whereas "love to man" meant literally stoning to death the dearest loved one who advocated departure from the Lord.

- For the *Christian*, the concrete applications of what it means to "love God with all our heart, soul, mind, and strength, and our neighbor as ourselves" have been revealed in the clearest

---

[1] Acts 15:10; 1 John 5:3   [2] Romans 2:14-16

and highest terms imaginable—*the very character, conduct, teaching, example, life and Person of our Lord Jesus Christ.* They are summarized by the "law of Christ": *"as I have loved you."* In the remainder of this chapter, we will consider briefly each of these three revelations of the one unchanging law of God—the twofold commandment *to love*. In doing this, we will see that the essence of the law indeed never changes, *but the revelation of law takes on clearer and clearer expression, until it finds its culmination in Christ.*

THE LAW WRITTEN ON THE HEART

When Paul describes Gentiles as "those who are without law,"[1] he does not mean this in an absolute sense. Though they have never seen a Bible or heard of the Ten Commandments, Gentiles nevertheless have an innate knowledge of God and of right and wrong. When a poisonous snake attached itself to Paul's hand on the island of Malta, the natives said, "Undoubtedly this man is a murderer, and though he has been saved from the sea, justice has not allowed him to live."[2] How did they know that murder was wrong, and how did they know that "justice" required murder to be punished by the death of the offender? According to Paul, they knew this because of "the work of the Law written in their hearts." "For when Gentiles who do not have the Law do instinctively the things of the Law, these, not having the Law, are a law to themselves, in that they show the work of the Law written in their hearts, their conscience bearing witness, and their thoughts alternately accusing or else defending them, on the day when, according to my gospel, God will judge the secrets of men through Christ Jesus."[3]

When Gentiles "do instinctively the things of the Law," it is the essence of the law that is being manifested as "written on their hearts." Men know by nature that they should not do things to their neighbors that they would not want done to themselves. They know, for example, that they should not deceive, steal from, and murder

---

[1] 1 Corinthians 9:21   [2] Acts 28:1-6   [3] Romans 2:14-16

THE LAW OF CHRIST

their neighbors—i.e., they know that they should *love* them.[1] This is why some form of the "Golden Rule"[2] is found in all of the major world religions. In the same way, men know by nature that they should love and glorify God, and they know in their consciences that they have fallen far short of this obligation. Eloquent testimony is borne to this inescapable knowledge every time the blood of a chicken is offered on a heathen altar to propitiate an angry "god."

Though it has been greatly defaced by sin, man's knowledge of right and wrong is one of the most indelible aspects of his having been made in "the image of God." Long after his conscience has been "seared as with a branding iron"[3] and he has come to the place of "calling evil good and good evil,"[4] man still retains this innate knowledge in the depths of his being. It is an inescapable part of his basic makeup. Paul makes this clear in the first chapter of his letter to the Romans, where he sets forth the condemnation of "the man without the Bible." After describing in verses 21-31 the corruption of those whom God has "given over"[5] to the lowest reaches of depravity, he concludes by saying that *even those who have sunk to this state* still "know the ordinance of God, that those who practice such things are worthy of death." This is a remarkable statement! Apart from *any* special revelation from God (e.g., the Bible), all men nevertheless "know the ordinance of God" that those who practice "such things" as sexual immorality, homosexuality, unrighteousness, wickedness, greed, envy, murder, strife, deceit, malice, gossip, slander, hatred of God, insolence, arrogance, boasting, invention of evil, disobedience to parents, untrustworthiness, and lack of love and mercy, are "worthy of death"![6]

Long before the Law of Moses was ever given, God held men accountable for sinning against the work of the Law written on their consciences. For example, God destroyed the entire earth in the days of Noah because "the wickedness of man was great on the earth, and...every intent of the thoughts of his heart was only evil

---

[1] Romans 13:9-10 [2] Matthew 7:12 [3] 1 Timothy 4:2 [4] Isaiah 5:20
[5] Romans 1:24, 26, 28 [6] Romans 1:32

continually."[1] The cities of Sodom and Gomorrah were likewise destroyed for sinning against nature[2] by practicing things that they *knew*[3] were wrong.

THE LAW OF MOSES

When the Law of Moses was given to the Jews, it did not set forth any "new law" as to essence (an impossibility, since the essence of God's law can never change). It *did* set forth in much clearer light (and in terms of specific concrete commandments) the duties that all men had formerly known only through the law of conscience. In the presence of this clearly written code, the "sinfulness" of sin became even more apparent.[4] In addition, the Law of Moses set forth various new commands related to the particular circumstances of the theocracy. As stated above, "love to God" under the theocracy involved obedience to many commandments that we would now recognize as ceremonial or civil, as well as those that were "weightier" and related directly to the character of God.[5] With rare exceptions for special cases,[6] *all* of these commandments were binding on the consciences of those who were "under" the Mosaic Law, because no man can truly love God without obeying the commandments that God has given directly to him. No Jew would have ever thought that he could love God while ignoring (for example) the commandment of circumcision. In fact, Moses himself almost lost his life for delaying the circumcision of his son.[7] Yet, circumcision had *no* direct connection with the character of God or the essence of the law, and when we come to the New Testament, we learn that (physical) circumcision is "nothing" and is no longer even one of "the commandments of God"![8]

These principles are well illustrated in one of the "woes" that Jesus pronounced on the scribes and Pharisees: "Woe to you, scribes and Pharisees, hypocrites! For you tithe mint and dill and cumin,

---

[1] Genesis 6:5   [2] Genesis 18:20-19:25; Romans 1:26-27   [3] Genesis 19:7
[4] Romans 5:20; 7:13   [5] See Appendix C.   [6] Cf. Matthew 12:3-4
[7] Exodus 4:24-26   [8] 1 Corinthians 7:19; Galatians 6:15

and have neglected the weightier provisions of the law: justice and mercy and faithfulness; but these are the things you should have done without neglecting the others."¹ It is clear from our Lord's words that under the Mosaic Law some commandments were "weightier" than others. "Justice, mercy, and faithfulness," for example, related directly to the essence of the law, and their neglect by the religious leaders was particularly inexcusable. Nevertheless, the Law was treated by our Lord as a unit. God's people were not allowed to pick and choose among its commandments. All the precepts of the Mosaic Law were to be obeyed; none were to be neglected: "These are the things you should have done *without neglecting the others.*"

THE LAW OF CHRIST

Just as the Law of Moses did not set forth any new law as to *essence* (an impossibility), but did set forth more clearly the law's *applications*, even so it is with the law of Christ. As to its essence, it is one with the Law of Moses and the law of conscience, but as to its applications, it is higher and clearer than either of these. For this reason, it is called by the Lord "a new commandment." The specific outworkings of what it means to love God supremely and to love others as ourselves find their highest, clearest, and final expression in the law of Christ.²

It should be noted once more that it is not the Law of Moses as such, but the essence of that law (and of all law) that is "written on the heart" in the New Covenant. All Christians *by nature* find themselves filled with love to God and love to their fellow men, through the miracle of regeneration and the indwelling of the Holy Spirit. *All Christians love God.* This is so invariably true that Christians are actually designated in the Scriptures as "those who love God."³ If anyone does not love the Lord Jesus Christ, he is "anathema."⁴ *Likewise, all Christians love their fellow men.* "You

---

¹ Matthew 23:23   ² See Chapter 14.   ³ Romans 8:28   ⁴ 1 Corinthians 16:22

yourselves are taught by God to love one another." [1] "We know that we have passed out of death into life, because we love the brethren. He who does not love abides in death." [2] To tell professing Christians (as some preachers do) that they "ought not to hate one another so much," is to betray a total ignorance of the nature of true conversion. Though their love is far from perfect, *all* Christians, according to the Apostle John, "love the brethren"! "The one who does not love does not know God." [3]

---

[1] 1 Thessalonians 4:9; 1 John 3:14; etc. [2] 1 John 3:14 [3] 1 John 4:8

Chapter Eleven Review

The one unchanging law of God consists of the twofold obligation *to love*, and is rooted in His very character, since God *is* love. The *applications* of this one unchanging law have been revealed with greater and greater clarity throughout the unfolding of redemptive history. From Adam to Moses they were made known primarily through the law written on the heart. At the time of Moses, they were spelled out much more clearly through the giving of a codified covenant to the physical nation of Israel. With the advent of Christ, they were revealed in the highest and clearest terms imaginable—the very words, deeds, and Person of Christ.

Christ replaces the Law of Moses, not by destroying it, but by swallowing it up in fulness. Though the essence of the Law of Moses was love to God and man, the national setting of that Law required a formulation far below New Covenant standards. When Christ came, the Mosaic Covenant (with all its attendant laws) was abolished, and a New Covenant with an entirely regenerate and spiritual nation was established. All who are part of this New Covenant have the essence of the law—love to God and man—written on their hearts through the miracle of the new birth.

– CHAPTER TWELVE –

LOVE AND LAW

> Owe nothing to anyone except to love one another; for he who loves his neighbor has fulfilled the law. For this, "You shall not commit adultery, You shall not murder, You shall not steal, You shall not covet," and if there is any other commandment, it is summed up in this saying, "You shall love your neighbor as yourself." Love does no wrong to a neighbor; love therefore is the fulfillment of the law.
>
> Romans 13:8-10
>
> For you were called to freedom, brethren; only do not turn your freedom into an opportunity for the flesh, but through love serve one another. For the whole Law is fulfilled in one word, in the statement, "You shall love your neighbor as yourself." Galatians 5:13-14

Since the obligation to love is the very essence and substance of the law, it should be evident from the preceding chapter that love and law are inseparably united. Many theologians, however, give the opposite impression. Because of their desire to guard the concept of "love" from the abuses that it is sure to encounter in a fallen world,[1] they often imply that *love* is one thing and *law* is something entirely different. Law is thought of primarily in terms of *specific commandments specially revealed by God*. Of these, the Ten Commandments of the Mosaic Covenant are often particularly in view. Love, on the other hand, is viewed primarily as a *motivating emotion* that is *dependent on law* (the specific commandments of the Bible) to inform it of its duty. It is said that even in the case of Christians, love may *want* to do what is best for others, but it has no idea *what* to do in the absence of concrete, revealed laws. Law (in the sense of objective commandments) is really at the center

---

[1] See Chapter 14.

of godly living, and love is little more than a motivating power necessary for proper commandment keeping. According to this view, it is law that provides the real substance of moral behavior; love merely provides its emotional impetus.

By contrast, the Bible itself puts love at the very heart and center of godliness. As we have seen, Jesus explicitly says that "the whole Law and the Prophets" hang on the two love commandments. In another place, He tells us that to "treat others as we want them to treat us" *is* "the Law and the Prophets"![1] Paul, likewise, exhorts us to *"serve* one another through *love...* for the *whole Law* is fulfilled in *one word*, in the statement, 'You shall love your neighbor as yourself.'"[2] And in Romans 13:8-10, Paul instructs us to "owe nothing to anyone *except to love one another;* for he who *loves* his neighbor *has fulfilled the law*....Love does no wrong to a neighbor; love *therefore* is the fulfillment of the law." Surely such verses are meant to convey more than just the idea that love is a necessary motivator or "springboard" for proper law keeping! The fact that some theologians must constantly remind us that these verses are not saying what they appear to be saying, and that *law*, not *love*, is central to godly living, ought to cause us to question the validity of their theological perspective.

LOVE'S ESSENTIAL NATURE

Is love really nothing more than a motivating power that enables us to keep the law as it should be kept? Or is law, instead, a description of love in action? From what the Scriptures tell us concerning the nature of love, it would seem that the second alternative is much closer to the truth. What law *demands*, love (by its very nature) *is!* Love does not look to a law outside itself in order to discover that it *should* be patient; love *is* patient. Not only is love patient; "love is kind, and is not jealous; love does not brag and is not arrogant, does not act unbecomingly; it does not seek its own, is not provoked, does not take into account a wrong suffered, does

---

[1] Matthew 7:12 [2] Galatians 5:13-14

not rejoice in unrighteousness, but rejoices with the truth; bears all things, believes all things, hopes all things, endures all things. Love never fails."[1]

Love itself tells me not to murder my neighbor or seduce his wife or steal his car or falsely accuse him.[2] Supreme love for God, by its very nature, causes me to give Him first place in all my affections, makes me abhor idols as an insult to His infinite glory, and prevents me from speaking irreverently of Him.[3] Love tells me in my conscience that I should not curse a deaf man or place a stumbling block before a blind man.[4] Love also tells me that in order to protect others from possible injury, I should build a guard rail around a dangerous roof,[5] confine a dangerous animal,[6] and cover an open pit.[7] Love causes me to share the good news of the gospel with others,[8] give to those in need,[9] and do nothing that would cause others to stumble.[10] Love also tells me not to do those things that even Gentiles (without *any* special revelation from God) know to be wrong! As we have seen,[11] this includes such things as sexual immorality, homosexuality, unrighteousness, wickedness, greed, envy, strife, deceit, malice, gossip, slander, insolence, arrogance, boasting, invention of evil, disobedience to parents, untrustworthiness, and lack of mercy![12] Examples such as these could be multiplied. In the words of Paul, *"If there is any other commandment*, it is summed up in this saying, 'You shall love your neighbor as yourself.'"[13] In short, love does more than impel me to keep the law; love *is* itself "the fulfillment of the law."[14]

SPECIFIC COMMANDMENTS

The fact that true love fulfills the law naturally, *just by acting according to what it is,* does not mean that Christians have no need for concrete commandments. The many instructions, admonitions,

---

[1] 1 Corinthians 13:4-8   [2] Exodus 20:13-16   [3] Exodus 20:3-7   [4] Leviticus 19:14
[5] Deuteronomy 22:8   [6] Exodus 21:29   [7] Exodus 21:33-34   [8] Mark 16:15
[9] 1 John 3:17   [10] Romans 14:15   [11] Chapter 11, p. 132.   [12] Romans 1:26-31
[13] Romans 13:9   [14] Romans 13:10

THE LAW OF CHRIST

and warnings found in the New Testament provide abundant proof that we do! These commandments are necessary because we have not yet fully "become" *in practice* who we already "are" *in our innermost beings.* Christians have not yet been fully conformed to the new nature that God has given them or the new desires that He has "written in their hearts." Because of the "deceitfulness"[1] of sin, the subtlety of Satan,[2] and the remaining corruption of their flesh,[3] they are still in desperate need of specific instruction, even in matters that relate directly to the essence of the law. For this guidance, the words and example of Christ Himself provide the supreme pattern for Christian behavior and define for us what true love is.[4]

Christ's commandments are not "burdensome"[5] to the believer. Because the "law of love" has been written on his heart, he finds the ways of his Master to be supremely beautiful, and his delight is in the "law" of his Lord. Christ's commandments are a joy to his heart, and he is thankful for every one of them as he seeks to grow in grace.

The Christian is also thankful for all the other exhortations and commands of the New Testament, as well as the revelation of God's character and ways given in the Old Testament. God's word is a lamp to his feet and a light to his path.[6] God's commandments make him wiser than his enemies, and His testimonies give him more insight than all his teachers.[7] He treasures God's word in his heart that he might not sin against Him.[8] He follows the example of His Lord by using the "sword of the Spirit" to overcome the wiles of the devil.[9] He studies the Bible diligently and tests every teaching and practice by it.[10] Because "the word of God is living and active and sharper than any two-edged sword, and piercing as far as the division of soul and spirit, of both joints and marrow, *and able to judge the thoughts and intentions of the heart,*"[11] the Christian relies on its teachings and commandments to test his motives and

---

[1] Hebrews 3:13   [2] Genesis 3:1; 2 Corinthians 11:3   [3] Galatians 5:16-21   [4] See Chapter 14.   [5] 1 John 5:3   [6] Psalm 119:105   [7] Psalm 119:98-99   [8] Psalm 119:11   [9] Matthew 4:4, 7, 10; Ephesians 6:17   [10] 1 Timothy 6:3   [11] Hebrews 4:12

conduct. In light of the remaining corruption of his flesh, he realizes that when the Bible says something is wrong, he dare not trust his subjective feelings about it. Instead, he asks God to "renew his mind"[1] to know and believe "the truth" that will "set him free"[2] from sin's power. In short, he realizes that "all Scripture is inspired by God and profitable for teaching, for reproof, for correction, for training in righteousness; that the man of God may be adequate, equipped for every good work,"[3] and he blesses God for the glorious instructions and encouragements contained in its pages.

"NON-ESSENTIAL" COMMANDMENTS

The fact that true love fulfills the law naturally, just by acting according to what it *is,* does not mean, then, that Christians have no need for concrete commandments. In the same way, the fact that all other commandments "hang" on love does not mean that every commandment (whether in the Old Testament or the New) can be *logically deduced from love.* Some commandments do not *directly* relate to love or to the essence of the law at all. Circumcision is one example from the Old Testament;[4] baptism is an example from the New. These "non-essential" commandments are given by God in His wisdom for particular circumstances and periods of time. Though they are "non-essential" (in the sense that they do not relate directly to the *essence* of the law), nevertheless, they provide some of the most "essential" tests of Christian obedience! For example, many a new Christian has lost his family, home, and employment as a result of obeying Christ's command regarding baptism. According to the Lord Jesus, it is obedience to just such commandments that is the *evidence* of true love for Him. "If you *love* Me, you will keep My commandments....He who has My commandments and keeps them, he it is who *loves* Me....If anyone *loves* Me, he will keep My word....He who does not *love* Me does not keep My words...."[5]

---

[1] Romans 12:1-2; Ephesians 4:20-24   [2] John 8:31-32   [3] 2 Timothy 3:16-17
[4] Galatians 5:6   [5] John 14:15, 21, 23-24; cf. 1 John 2:3-4

Conclusion

Love is not one commandment among many; love is *the* commandment. Or, to say it another way, *love is man's supreme duty.* Love is at the very center of godly living! *The goal of our instruction is love!*[1] Lost men who try to pattern their conduct around "love" will pervert it into something evil. In fact, "law" (in the form of specified prohibitions) was made for such men![2] But Christians who pattern their conduct around love will find themselves unconsciously "fulfilling" the law! Love is the Christian's *supreme duty,* encompassing and fulfilling all other duties. Love is also his *supreme delight,* because the "law of love" has been written within him and the Spirit of love has taken up residence in his heart!

Law, in its essence, is nothing more than *the obligation to love.* And *love*—acting according to its own nature in the created order where God has placed it[3]—is *the fulfillment of the law.*

---

[1] 1 Timothy 1:5   [2] 1 Timothy 1:8-11   [3] See Appendix E, Q. 17.

Chapter Twelve Review

Since the obligation to love is the very essence and substance of the law, it should be evident that love and law are inseparably united. Love is more than a motivating power that enables us to keep the law as it should be kept. Instead, true love fulfills the law naturally, just by acting according to what it *is*.

This does not mean that Christians have no need for concrete commandments. Because of the deceitfulness of sin, the subtlety of Satan, and the remaining corruption of their flesh, Christians are still in desperate need of specific instruction, even in matters that relate directly to the essence of the law.

There are also some commandments that do not directly relate to love or to the essence of the law at all. Circumcision is one example from the Old Testament; baptism is an example from the New. Though these commandments do not directly relate to the essence of the law, they nevertheless provide some of the most "essential" tests of Christian obedience.

Love is not one commandment among many; love is *the* commandment. Love is man's supreme duty. It is at the very center of godly living. The goal of our instruction is love.

Law, in its essence, is nothing more than the obligation to love. And love—acting according to its own nature in the created order where God has placed it—is the fulfillment of the law.

– Chapter Thirteen –

THE CENTRALITY OF LOVE

Let all that you do be done in love.

1 Corinthians 16:14

It should come as no surprise to us that Christ's "new commandment" to love one another "as He loved us" is at the very center of the New Testament's teaching regarding Christian conduct. Over and over, the centrality of love is emphasized by our Lord and His apostles. *The purpose of this chapter is to establish the fact of love's preeminence in the New Testament* by quoting one Scripture after another where love is set forth as the highest Christian virtue. This overarching purpose should be borne in mind throughout the reading of this chapter. Though this brief overview can do little more than give an introduction to the New Testament's emphasis on love, all of the individual Scriptures quoted below deserve careful study and prayerful meditation. To these, many more could be added.[1]

Matthew 7:12—"Therefore, however you want people to treat you, so treat them, for *this is the Law and the Prophets."*

In this profound and simple statement, we learn that love is the "Golden Rule" by which all Christians are to live. In a statement very similar to the one He later makes in Matthew 22 when speaking of the two great commandments, the Lord Jesus tells us here that *love* is the essence and summation of "the Law and the Prophets."

Matthew 9:11-13—"And when the Pharisees saw this, they said to His disciples, 'Why is your Teacher eating with the tax-gatherers and sinners?' But when He heard this, He said, 'It is not those who are healthy who need a physician, but those who are sick. But go and learn what this means, "I desire compassion, and not sacrifice," for I did not come to call the righteous, but sinners.'"

---
[1] See Appendix G.

Here our Lord teaches that compassion for despised, sin-sick souls means infinitely more to God than the strictest adherence to religious rules and ceremonies. True holiness has to do with *love* for sinners, not Pharisaical "separation" from them.

Matthew 12:1-8—"At that time Jesus went on the Sabbath through the grain fields, and His disciples became hungry and began to pick the heads of grain and eat. But when the Pharisees saw it, they said to Him, 'Behold, Your disciples do what is not lawful to do on a Sabbath.' But He said to them, 'Have you not read what David did, when he became hungry, he and his companions; how he entered the house of God, and they ate the consecrated bread, which was not lawful for him to eat, nor for those with him, but for the priests alone? Or have you not read in the Law, that on the Sabbath the priests in the temple break the Sabbath, and are innocent? But I say to you, that something greater than the temple is here. But if you had known what this means, "I desire compassion, and not a sacrifice," you would not have condemned the innocent. For the Son of Man is Lord of the Sabbath.'"

Again, the Lord Jesus Christ uses the great overarching principle that God "desires *compassion* and *not* sacrifice" to reprove those who would place a higher value on meticulous rule keeping than on the welfare of their fellow men. Those who would do this "strain out a gnat and swallow a camel"[1] with regard to the things that really matter to God. To love God and our fellow men is "much more than all burnt offerings and sacrifices."[2]

Luke 6:27-35—"But I say to you who hear, *love* your enemies, *do good* to those who hate you, *bless* those who curse you, *pray for* those who mistreat you. Whoever hits you on the cheek, offer him the other also; and whoever takes away your coat, do not withhold your shirt from him either. *Give* to everyone who asks of you, and whoever takes away what is yours, do not demand

---

[1] Matthew 23:24   [2] Mark 12:32-34

it back. *And just as you want people to treat you, treat them in the same way.* And if you love those who love you, what credit is that to you? For even sinners love those who love them. And if you do good to those who do good to you, what credit is that to you? For even sinners do the same. And if you lend to those from whom you expect to receive, what credit is that to you? Even sinners lend to sinners, in order to receive back the same amount. But *love your enemies,* and *do good,* and *lend, expecting nothing in return;* and your reward will be great, and you will be sons of the Most High; for He Himself is *kind to ungrateful and evil men.*"

In these verses, our Lord again sets the tone of the Christian life: love for all men, especially our enemies—doing good to them, blessing them, praying for them, and giving to them. In the midst of His instructions, the "Golden Rule" of love, which "is" the Law and the Prophets, appears once more.

John 13:34-35—"A new commandment I give to you, that you love one another, even as I have loved you, that you also love one another. *By this all men will know that you are My disciples,* if you have love for one another."

Not only does love take center stage as "the new commandment"; it is also the distinguishing mark of true Christianity. One of the most powerful apologies for the truth of the gospel is *love,* as many converted Muslims have testified. Other religions know nothing of the love taught by the Lord Jesus Christ in the Sermon on the Mount and manifested by true Christians toward one another and all men.

John 21:15-17—"So when they had finished breakfast, Jesus said to Simon Peter, 'Simon, son of John, do you love Me more than these?' He said to Him, 'Yes, Lord; You know that I love You.' He said to him, 'Tend My lambs.' He said to him again a second time, 'Simon, son of John, do you love Me?' He said to Him, 'Yes, Lord; You know that I love You.' He said to him, 'Shepherd My sheep.' He said to him the third time, 'Simon, son of John, do you love Me?' Peter was grieved because He said to him the third time, 'Do you love Me?' And he said to Him, 'Lord, You know all things; You know that I love You.' Jesus said to him, 'Tend My sheep.'"

Here Jesus makes it clear that *love* is the central issue between a disciple and his Lord. Three times, He asks Peter the searching question, "Do you love Me?" And three times, in response to Peter's answer, He makes it clear that all true love for Himself is manifested by loving service to His people: "Tend My sheep."

Romans 13:8-10—"Owe nothing to anyone except to love one another; for he who loves his neighbor has fulfilled the law. For this, 'You shall not commit adultery, you shall not murder, you shall not steal, you shall not covet,' and if there is any other commandment, it is summed up in this saying, 'You shall love your neighbor as yourself.' Love does no wrong to a neighbor; love therefore is the fulfillment of the law."

Once again, love is presented in this remarkable passage as the essence of the law. The statement that "love does no wrong to a neighbor" and is thus "the fulfillment of the law" is similar to our Lord's statement in Matthew 7 that to treat others as we would want them to treat us "is" the Law and the Prophets.

1 Corinthians 8:1—"Now concerning things sacrificed to idols, we know that we all have knowledge. Knowledge makes arrogant, but love edifies."

It is highly significant that when Paul deals with differences among believers regarding matters of conscience, his central principle is that of *love*. This relates not only to those "gray areas" where the Bible has no clear teaching, but also to those areas where we *"know and are convinced in the Lord Jesus"*[1] that our position is Biblical. Even in these cases, to do anything that "causes a brother

---

[1] Romans 14:14

to stumble" is not *loving;* therefore, Paul determines that (if need be) he "will never eat meat again," that he "might not cause his brother to stumble."[1] "For if because of food your brother is hurt, you are no longer walking according to *love.*"[2]

1 Corinthians 13:1-14:1—"If I speak with the tongues of men and of angels, but do not have love, I have become a noisy gong or a clanging cymbal. And if I have the gift of prophecy, and know all mysteries and all knowledge; and if I have all faith, so as to remove mountains, but do not have love, I am nothing. And if I give all my possessions to feed the poor, and if I deliver my body to be burned, but do not have love, it profits me nothing.

"Love is patient, love is kind, and is not jealous; love does not brag and is not arrogant, does not act unbecomingly; it does not seek its own, is not provoked, does not take into account a wrong suffered, does not rejoice in unrighteousness, but rejoices with the truth; bears all things, believes all things, hopes all things, endures all things.

"Love never fails; but if there are gifts of prophecy, they will be done away; if there are tongues, they will cease; if there is knowledge, it will be done away. For we know in part, and we prophesy in part; but when the perfect comes, the partial will be done away. When I was a child, I used to speak as a child, think as a child, reason as a child; when I became a man, I did away with childish things. For now we see in a mirror dimly, but then face to face; now I know in part, but then I shall know fully just as I also have been fully known. But now abide faith, hope, love, these three; but the greatest of these is love. Pursue love...."

Paul's chapter on love is so unique that many have been tempted to isolate it from its context and place it in a book of poems or essays. But these verses are all the more remarkable in that they occur unexpectedly *in a letter* to the church at Corinth and in the

---

[1] 1 Corinthians 8:13 [2] Romans 14:15

midst of a discussion about spiritual gifts! This glorious chapter, like John 3:16, has lost much of its impact on us because of our repeated but superficial exposure to it. To get a fresh sense of its power, we need only imagine ourselves having never read these verses and then coming across them for the first time while reading the New Testament. The fact that relatively few Christians have memorized or meditated deeply on this chapter, while multitudes have memorized the more "doctrinal" sections of Paul's epistles, tells us much about our need to "grow up" in the Christian life.

In this chapter, Paul sets forth the *necessity* of love (vv. 1-3), the *character* of love (vv. 4-7), and the *permanence* of love (vv. 8-13). For Paul, love is the highest virtue a man can possess. It is the one thing above all others that we are to "pursue." Supernatural giftedness in preaching, possession of great insight and knowledge in doctrinal matters, or even having "all faith, so as to remove mountains," means *nothing* if we do not have love. In fact, apart from love, *we ourselves are nothing*. We are merely "noisy gongs" or "clanging cymbals," destined to perish with other supernaturally "gifted" men like Balaam, who truly prophesied under the inspiration of the Spirit of God,[1] yet did not have love. Even the *greatest sacrifices* mean nothing apart from love. We can give away all our possessions to Christian charities and die in excruciating pain as martyrs "for Christ," yet it will profit us nothing if we do not have love.

Love never fails. It is the one thing that will enable us to bear up under impossible burdens, to believe and hope in God when all hope is gone, and to endure things that seem beyond endurance. Gifts and ministries are temporary, but love is eternal. It will abide forever, the greatest of all virtues, because *God Himself is love*.

Galatians 5:6—"For in Christ Jesus neither circumcision nor uncircumcision means anything, but faith working through love."

The Christian life is not a matter of religious rites and ceremonies, but of *faith* that produces *works* through an overflow

---

[1] Numbers 24:2; 2 Peter 2:15; Revelation 2:14; Matthew 7:22-23

of *love!* Circumcision, which was so important in the Old Covenant, is seen in the New Covenant as having no direct connection with the character of God or the essence of the law at all. It does not "mean anything." This must have come as a shock to many Jews, who certainly would not have thought of circumcision as a "light" commandment!

> **Galatians 5:13-14**—"For you were called to freedom, brethren; only do not turn your freedom into an opportunity for the *flesh*, but through *love* serve one another. For the whole Law is fulfilled in one word, in the statement, 'You shall love your neighbor as yourself.'"

In Paul's thinking, *flesh* can be contrasted, not only with *Spirit*, but also with *love*, since love is the foremost "fruit of the Spirit" and the deeds of love are the exact opposites of the deeds of the flesh. "The deeds of the flesh are evident, which are: immorality, impurity, sensuality, idolatry, sorcery, enmities, strife, jealousy, outbursts of anger, disputes, dissensions, factions, envying, drunkenness, carousing, and things like these."[1] By contrast, Christian "freedom" finds its expression in loving service: "Through love serve one another." Once again, we see from these verses that love is the fulfillment of "the whole Law"!

> **Galatians 5:22-23**—"But the fruit of the Spirit is love, joy, peace, patience, kindness, goodness, faithfulness, gentleness, self-control; against such things there is no law."

According to Paul, the foremost fruit of the Spirit is *love*. It should not surprise us, then, that the man who "walks in the Spirit" will never be at variance with any law! This is only what we would expect, since love is the "fulfilling of the whole law."

> **Galatians 6:1-2**—"Brethren, even if a man is caught in any trespass, you who are spiritual, restore such a one in a spirit of

---

[1] Galatians 5:19-21

gentleness; each one looking to yourself, lest you too be tempted. Bear one another's burdens, and thus fulfill the law of Christ."

To lovingly serve others and to "bear their burdens" when they fall is to "fulfill" the law of Christ! These instructions seem very simple in theory, but are very profound in practice!

Ephesians 4:14-16—"As a result, we are no longer to be children, tossed here and there by waves, and carried about by every wind of doctrine, by the trickery of men, by craftiness in deceitful scheming; *but speaking the truth in love, we are to grow up in all aspects into Him,* who is the head, even Christ, from whom the whole body, being fitted and held together by that which every joint supplies, according to the proper working of each individual part, causes the growth of the body *for the building up of itself in love.*"

In Paul's thinking, love is central in the "building up" of the church. No amount of activity or even sound teaching can make up for a lack of love in the body of believers. Apart from love, even our "speaking the truth" will only "puff up" with pride, not "build up" with grace.

Colossians 3:12-14—"And so, as those who have been chosen of God, holy and beloved, put on a heart of compassion, kindness, humility, gentleness and patience; bearing with one another, and forgiving each other, whoever has a complaint against anyone; just as the Lord forgave you, so also should you. *And beyond all these things put on love, which is the perfect bond of unity.*"

It is remarkable that Paul, having instructed us to "put on a heart of compassion, kindness, humility, gentleness and patience; bearing with one another and forgiving each other," nevertheless goes on to emphasize once more that "beyond all these things" we are to "put on love"!

1 Thessalonians 3:11-13—"Now may our God and Father Himself and Jesus our Lord direct our way to you; *and may*

THE CENTRALITY OF LOVE

the Lord cause you to increase and abound in love for one another, and for all men, just as we also do for you; so that He may establish your hearts unblamable in holiness before our God and Father at the coming of our Lord Jesus with all His saints."

In these verses we learn that the way our hearts are "established unblamable in holiness" is not by following a list of rules or merely by learning more "doctrine," but by "increasing and abounding in love for one another"!

1 Timothy 1:5-11—*"But the goal of our instruction is love from a pure heart and a good conscience and a sincere faith.* For some men, straying from *these things*, have turned aside to fruitless discussion, wanting to be teachers of the Law, even though they do not understand either what they are saying or the matters about which they make confident assertions. But we know that the Law is good, if one uses it lawfully, *realizing the fact that law is not made for a righteous man,* but for those who are lawless and rebellious, for the ungodly and sinners, for the unholy and profane, for those who kill their fathers or mothers, for murderers and immoral men and homosexuals and kidnappers and liars and perjurers, *and whatever else is contrary to sound teaching, according to the glorious gospel of the blessed God*, with which I have been entrusted."

Here Paul says that *the whole purpose of our instruction to believers is that they might learn to love!* This love "issues from"[1] or "flows from"[2] a pure heart, a good conscience, and a sincere faith. Paul contrasts such love with "fruitless discussions" about the Law. The first step toward "using the Law" rightly in a New Covenant setting is to "realize the fact" that law is not made for righteous men. Many of the crimes and sins defined by the Law are just as "contrary to ... the glorious gospel of the blessed God" as they were to the Law of Moses. However, those who are righteous (i.e., those who

---

[1] ESV   [2] ISV

walk in love) do not commit these crimes anyway. Against their actions, "there is no law."[1]

Titus 2:3-4—"Older women likewise are to be reverent in their behavior... *teaching what is good,* that they may encourage the young women *to love their husbands, to love their children*...."

We might think that of all the things young women do *not* need to be taught, *loving their husbands and children* would surely be at the top of the list! But Paul knows that to truly love others (especially our "loved ones") is the epitome of godliness and the "goal of our instruction." If an older woman has not learned to love her husband and children, she has nothing to teach younger women, regardless of how much homemaking skill or doctrinal understanding she may have.

Hebrews 10:23-25—"Let us hold fast the confession of our hope without wavering, for He who promised is faithful; *and let us consider how to stimulate one another to love and good deeds,* not forsaking our own assembling together, as is the habit of some, but encouraging one another; and all the more, as you see the day drawing near."

One of the surest ways that a Christian can "encourage" a fellow believer to persevere in the faith is to *consider how to stimulate him to love*. We have no idea how destructive it is to the steadfastness of another Christian to plant in his mind seeds of suspicion and division with other brethren. If, on the other hand, we are stimulating him to love others, he will find his heart being "established unblamable in holiness" as he fellowships and is knit together with other believers. The body of Christ is established and built up through love; it is weakened, scattered, and torn down through lack of it.

James 2:1-4, 8, 12-13—"My brethren, do not hold your faith in our glorious Lord Jesus Christ with an attitude of personal

---
[1] Galatians 5:23

THE CENTRALITY OF LOVE

favoritism. For if a man comes into your assembly with a gold ring and dressed in fine clothes, and there also comes in a poor man in dirty clothes, and you pay special attention to the one who is wearing the fine clothes, and say, 'You sit here in a good place,' and you say to the poor man, 'You stand over there, or sit down by my footstool,' have you not made distinctions among yourselves, and become judges with evil motives?...If, however, you are *fulfilling the royal law*, according to the Scripture, '*You shall love your neighbor as yourself*,' you are doing well ....So speak and so act, as those who are to be judged by *the law of liberty*. For judgment will be merciless to one who has *shown no mercy*; mercy triumphs over judgment."

Here James speaks of love as "fulfilling the royal law" [marg. "the law of our King"]. This "royal law" of love is also called the "law of liberty." James applies it directly to our obligation to show mercy and to treat the poor with the same respect as the rich. Favoritism is an infraction of the law of love and is therefore a sin. Judgment will be merciless for those who have shown no mercy (i.e., broken the law of love completely).[1]

1 Peter 1:22; 2:1; 4:8—"Since you have in obedience to the truth purified your souls for a sincere love of the brethren, *fervently love one another from the heart*....putting aside all malice and all guile and hypocrisy and envy and all slander....Above all, *keep fervent in your love for one another*, because love covers a multitude of sins."

According to Peter, obedience to the truth of the gospel "purifies our souls" *for sincere love*. In other words, the ultimate goal and end result of salvation is *sincere love!* In keeping with this goal, Peter exhorts us "above all" to *fervently love one another*. This love will "cover" one another's sins, not in the sense of "atoning for" them, but in the sense of patiently bearing with and overlooking them as we all grow in Christlikeness.[2]

---

[1] See Matthew 18:23-35. [2] Proverbs 10:12; 17:9

1 John 3:11, 23; 4:7-8, 11-12; 2 John 1:5—"For this is the message which you have heard from the beginning, *that we should love one another*....And this is His commandment, that we believe in the name of His Son Jesus Christ, and *love one another, just as He commanded us*....Beloved, *let us love one another,* for love is from God; and *everyone who loves* is born of God and knows God. The one who does not love does not know God, for God is love....Beloved, if God so loved us, *we also ought to love one another.* No one has beheld God at any time; *if we love one another,* God abides in us, and His love is perfected in us....And now I ask you, lady, not as writing to you a new commandment, but the one which we have had from the beginning, *that we love one another."*

Christ's "commandment" that we "love one another" is clearly central and preeminent in John's thinking regarding the Christian life and walk. John agrees with Paul that if a man does not have love, *he is nothing,* for "the one who does not love does not know God." Over and over throughout his epistles, John emphasizes *love* as both the supreme reality and the supreme duty of the Christian life.

This brief overview of love's centrality in the New Testament leaves us facing some searching questions. Do we as Christians place the same premium on love that the New Testament does? Do we view it as the very pinnacle and "goal of our instruction"? Do we realize that even supernatural gifts of the Spirit are merely "childish things" in comparison with love? Do we understand that a Christian can have a doctorate in theology and be regarded by others as "a great theologian," yet still be a mere novice in the things that matter most to God? Do we really comprehend the fact that no amount of sacrifice, knowledge, or even faith means *anything,* apart from love? Is love our highest priority, as it is God's? Or do we value Bible knowledge, preaching ability, "ministry," and "gifts" above love? These are the questions that confront us as we consider "the law of Christ."

Chapter Thirteen Review

Christ's "new commandment" to love one another "as He loved us" is at the very heart of the New Testament's teaching regarding Christian behavior. Over and over, the centrality of love is emphasized by our Lord and His apostles. Love is the "Golden Rule" by which Christians are to live; it is the essence and summation of the Law and the Prophets. To love God and our fellow men is "much more than all burnt offerings and sacrifices."

Love is the distinguishing mark of true Christianity by which "all men" will know that we are Christ's disciples. Love is central in the building up of the church; above all, we are to "keep fervent" in our love for one another. Love is "the perfect bond of unity."

The foremost fruit of the Holy Spirit is love. The way that Christians are "established unblamable in holiness" is by increasing and abounding in love for one another and for all men. It is by bearing one another's burdens that we "fulfill" the law of Christ!

These facts leave us facing some searching questions. Do we as Christians value love as highly as the New Testament does? Do we view it as the very pinnacle and "goal of our instruction"? Do we really comprehend the fact that no amount of sacrifice, knowledge, or even faith means anything, apart from love? Is love our highest priority?

– Chapter Fourteen –

As I Have Loved You

Love one another, even as I have loved you.
John 13:34

We have seen that Christ's new commandment of love is the central emphasis of the New Testament with regard to how we should live and conduct ourselves in this world. But at this point a question arises: How can we tell what real love is? Two college students living together in sin often justify their behavior by the fact that they "love" each other. Abortion advocates frequently claim "love" as their motivation, since they want to "help" those with unwanted pregnancies and "save" unborn children from the "life of misery" that supposedly lies ahead of them. Assisted suicides are performed by doctors in the name of compassion and "love," since those whom they are "assisting" are suffering and want to die. In the name of "love" lusts are gratified, lies are told, murders are committed, and criminals are set free. It seems that the Lord Jesus has left us with a very flexible and nearly worthless standard of conduct!

The problem with such reasoning is that it does not quote the new commandment in its entirety. Jesus did not simply say, "Love one another"; He said, "Love one another, *even as I have loved you.*" *In other words, our definition of "love" must come from the very conduct and teaching of the Lord Jesus Christ Himself!* We are called upon to "walk as He walked" [1] and to get our concepts of "love" from His own words and actions, not from the misguided and selfish ideas of fallen humanity. "If anyone advocates a different doctrine, and does not agree with *sound words, those of our Lord Jesus Christ, and with the doctrine conforming to godliness,* he is conceited and understands nothing." [2] When Paul says that the "goal of our instruction is *love,*"

---

[1] 1 John 2:6   [2] 1 Timothy 6:3-4

he goes on to make it clear that unholiness, profanity, murder, immorality, homosexuality, lying, and a host of other sins are "contrary to *sound teaching, according to the glorious gospel* of the blessed God." [1] And John reminds us that "this is the love of God, *that we keep His commandments.*" [2]

CHRIST OUR STANDARD

The Christian's standard is thus not just *any sort* of "love," but *Christlike love—love of the same quality and magnitude as Christ Himself demonstrated* in His incarnation and death on the cross! By rising to pray and commune with His Father, by walking through jostling crowds in perfect peace and tranquility of heart, by opening His mouth in wisdom and compassion, by washing His disciples' feet, by forgiving His enemies—by *everything* He ever said and did, the Lord Jesus gave us the pattern for our conduct. As we indicated earlier, it is the highest, clearest, and brightest revelation of man's duty that could ever be given to the human race. There *can be* nothing more *exacting*, or more *demanding*, or more *wonderful* than this—to love God and to love others in just the same way and to the same degree that Christ did! No one has ever fathomed the full import of these words, nor has anyone ever begun to fully live up to them.

In light of these facts, it is not surprising that the New Testament method of teaching ethics (principles of right conduct and moral judgment) is not primarily to appeal to any "law" or set of rules, but to appeal to the example of Christ Himself. The standard and rule of conduct for the Christian in every area of life is the Lord Jesus Christ! This truth is seen repeatedly in both the Gospels and the Epistles, as the following examples will show.

---

[1] 1 Timothy 1:5-11   [2] 1 John 5:3

Following Christ

Then Jesus said to His disciples, "If anyone wishes to come after Me, let him deny himself, and take up his cross, and follow Me." Matthew 16:24

One of the most comprehensive calls to Christlikeness that could ever be made is found in our Lord's appeal to His disciples to "follow" Him. Again and again this call appears in the gospel records,[1] from the beginning[2] of the Christian life to its end.[3] It is a call that takes on ever-deeper meaning as we progress in the walk of faith, encompassing all aspects of discipleship and obedience. Christ is our standard for Christian living.

Serving

And so when He had washed their feet, and taken His garments, and reclined at the table again, He said to them, "Do you know what I have done to you? You call Me Teacher and Lord; and you are right, for so I am. *If I then, the Lord and the Teacher, washed your feet, you also ought to wash one another's feet. For I gave you an example that you also should do as I did to you.*" John 13:12-15

Here the Lord Jesus specifically tells us that He is our pattern in serving others. What greater example of humble service could there ever be than the One who "knowing that the Father had given all things into His hands, and that He had come forth from God, and was going back to God," yet "laid aside His garments; and taking a towel...girded Himself about...and began to wash the disciples' feet, and to wipe them with the towel with which He was girded"?[4]

---

[1] Mark 1:17; John 1:43; Luke 5:27-28; 9:57-62; Mark 8:34; 10:21; John 10:4-5, 27; 12:26; 13:36-38; etc. [2] Matthew 4:18-19 [3] John 21:19-22 [4] John 13:3-5

Yielding Our Rights

Now we who are strong ought to bear the weaknesses of those without strength and not just please ourselves. Each of us is to please his neighbor for his good, to his edification. *For even Christ did not please Himself;* but as it is written, "The reproaches of those who reproached You fell upon Me." Romans 15:1-3 (NAS95)

What greater argument could Paul ever find for yielding up our "rights" and "not pleasing ourselves" than the fact that even the Lord of glory did not please Himself, but bore the reproaches of all those who hated and reproached God?

Accepting One Another

Now may the God who gives perseverance and encouragement grant you to be of the same mind with one another *according to Christ Jesus,* so that with one accord you may with one voice glorify the God and Father of our Lord Jesus Christ. *Therefore, accept one another, just as Christ also accepted us to the glory of God.* For I say that Christ has become a servant to the *circumcision* on behalf of the truth of God to confirm the promises given to the fathers, and for the *Gentiles* to glorify God for His mercy; as it is written, "Therefore I will give praise to You among the Gentiles, and I will sing to Your name." Romans 15:5-9 (NAS95)

Who in all of history has ever "accepted" people of diverse backgrounds with greater warmth and less disdain than Christ Himself? His example of open-armed welcome to men and women of every race, culture, education, and defect is the highest *standard* that we could ever have. Likewise, His love and acceptance of *us* is the highest *motivation* we could ever have to love and accept others.

Forgiving One Another

And so, as those who have been chosen of God, holy and beloved, put on a heart of compassion, kindness, humility, gentleness and patience; bearing with one another, and forgiving each other, whoever has a complaint against anyone; *just as the Lord forgave you, so also should you.*

Colossians 3:12-13

Who has ever manifested greater forbearance and forgiveness toward anyone than Christ Himself has manifested toward us? In light of the unspeakable mercy shown to us by Christ in the forgiveness of *our* vast indebtedness, how could we ever refuse to forgive the trifles owed to us by others?[1]

Giving

But just as you abound in everything, in faith and utterance and knowledge and in all earnestness and in the *love* we inspired in you, see that you abound in this gracious work also. *I am not speaking this as a command,* but as proving through the earnestness of others *the sincerity of your love also. For you know the grace of our Lord Jesus Christ, that though He was rich, yet for your sake He became poor, that you through His poverty might become rich.* 2 Corinthians 8:7-9

Here Paul urges the Corinthians in the matter of giving, not by pressing on them the duty of the Old Covenant "tithe," but by holding up to them the example of Christ Himself. Never could any depth of sacrifice compare with what Christ did for us in laying aside His infinite "riches" and becoming "poor" for our sakes, that we "through His poverty might be rich"! Paul knows that those with "sincere love" for the brethren will cheerfully[2] want to follow Christ's example.

---

[1] Matthew 18:21-35   [2] 2 Corinthians 9:7

THE LAW OF CHRIST

LOVING OUR WIVES

> Husbands, love your wives, *just as Christ also loved the church and gave Himself up for her;* that He might sanctify her, having cleansed her by the washing of water with the word....
> Ephesians 5:25-26

In calling husbands to love their wives sacrificially, what battery of commandments from the Law of Moses or what list of exemplary husbands from the Old Testament could begin to compare with the compelling sweetness of the example of Christ as our Heavenly Bridegroom? Just to mention the love and conduct of Christ toward His bride is to set the highest standard imaginable for Christian husbands. Notice again the echo of the "law of Christ" that is contained in these verses: "Love...*just as Christ* also loved."

WALKING IN LOVE

> Let all bitterness and wrath and anger and clamor and slander be put away from you, along with all malice. And be kind to one another, tender-hearted, forgiving each other, just as God in Christ also has forgiven you. Therefore be imitators of God, as beloved children; *and walk in love, just as Christ also loved you,* and gave Himself up for us, an offering and a sacrifice to God as a fragrant aroma.
> Ephesians 4:31-5:2

What example of kindness and tender-heartedness and walking in love could possibly compare with the example of Christ Himself? Again, we see the "law of Christ" in action: "Walk in love, *just as Christ* also loved."

LAYING DOWN OUR LIVES

> *We know love by this, that He laid down His life for us; and we ought to lay down our lives for the brethren.* But whoever has the world's goods, and beholds his brother in need and closes his heart against him, how does the love of God

abide in him? Little children, let us not love with word or with tongue, but in deed and truth. 1 John 3:16-18

Here John tells us that "we know love by this, that He laid down His life for us." In other words, the nature of true love is known and demonstrated by the actions of Christ. By His example, He defines what real love is and sets the standard for us to follow. In light of His great love for us, we *ought* to lay down our lives for the brethren.

Not Striking Back

For what credit is there if, when you sin and are harshly treated, you endure it with patience? But if when you do what is right and suffer for it you patiently endure it, this finds favor with God. For you have been called for this purpose, since Christ also suffered for you, *leaving you an example for you to follow in His steps,* who committed no sin, nor was any deceit found in His mouth; and while being reviled, He did not revile in return; while suffering, He uttered no threats, but kept entrusting Himself to Him who judges righteously.... 1 Peter 2:20-23

Has there ever been anyone in human history more innocent than Christ? Has there ever been anyone who suffered more for doing what is right or anyone who more perfectly entrusted himself to the One "who judges righteously"? Once again, there is no standard of conduct that can even compare with the example of Christ Himself! He left us this example that we should follow in His steps!

Endurance

Let us run with *endurance* the race that is set before us, *fixing our eyes on Jesus,* the author and perfecter of faith, *who for the joy set before Him endured the cross, despising the shame, and has sat down at the right hand of the throne of God.* For consider Him who has endured such hostility by sinners *against Himself,* so that you may not grow weary and lose heart. You have not yet resisted to the point of shedding blood in your striving against sin...   Hebrews 12:1-4

Who among men has ever endured what Christ endured? Has anyone else ever been such an object of Satan's enmity and contempt? Has anyone else ever sweat great drops of blood in anticipation of what lay ahead of him or endured such darkness as that which fell upon Calvary, when the wrath of God was poured out in full strength upon the One who suffered there? Clearly, Christ is the greatest example of endurance that could ever be set before us!

HUMILITY

Do nothing from selfishness or empty conceit, but with humility of mind let each of you regard one another as more important than himself; do not merely look out for your own personal interests, but also for the interests of others. *Have this attitude in yourselves which was also in Christ Jesus,* who, although He existed in the form of God, did not regard equality with God a thing to be grasped, but emptied Himself, taking the form of a bond-servant, and being made in the likeness of men. And being found in appearance as a man, He humbled Himself by becoming obedient to the point of death, even death on a cross.

Philippians 2:3-8

Paul wants to exhort the Philippians to have humility of mind and to regard others as more important than themselves. What example does he hold before them? Not the example of Moses, who in his time was more humble than any man on the face of the earth.[1] Why not? Because the humility of Moses is not worthy to be compared with the humility of Christ. Never could *any* humility compare with the humility of the One who laid aside *equality with God* and came down from infinite heights of glory—not in order to

---

[1] Numbers 12:3

be served, but in order to "take the form of a bond-servant" and die as a condemned criminal at the hands of His own sinful creatures! *Christ Himself is our "law"—our highest example and standard.* No one has ever fathomed the full import of Christ's words, "as I have loved you," nor has anyone ever begun to fully live up to them!

Chapter Fourteen Review

Jesus did not simply say, "Love one another"; He said, "Love one another, even as I have loved you." In other words, our definition of "love" must come from the very conduct and teaching of the Lord Jesus Christ Himself! We are called upon to "walk as He walked" and to get our concepts of "love" from His own words and actions, not from the misguided and selfish ideas of fallen humanity.

The New Testament method of teaching ethics is not primarily to appeal to any "law" or set of rules, but to appeal to the example of Christ Himself. The standard and rule of conduct for the Christian in every area of life is the Lord Jesus Christ! Christ is our example in serving, giving, loving our wives, forgiveness, endurance, humility, and all other Christian virtues. *Christ Himself is our "law"—our highest example and standard.*

No one has ever fathomed the full import of Christ's words, "as I have loved you," nor has anyone ever begun to fully live up to them!

– CHAPTER FIFTEEN –

"ONE ANOTHER" VERSES

> A new commandment I give to you, that you love one another, even as I have loved you, that you also love one another.   John 13:34

Since Christ Himself is our standard and His new commandment focuses directly on our duty to love "one another" as He loved us, it is not surprising that the New Testament has much to say about "one another" relationships. Some of the more important "one another" verses in the New Testament are listed below. Many of these are direct exhortations to *love* one another, while others apply the outworkings of this love to practical areas of Christian living. These verses have been separated into general categories for the sake of clarity. There is a certain degree of overlap between these categories, and they represent only one of the many possible ways these verses could be arranged.

In Chapter 14, we saw that the real meaning of Christ's new commandment to "love one another" must be determined by considering the teachings and conduct of Christ Himself. We are to love one another *as Christ loved us*. In this chapter, we will see that the real meaning of Christ's new commandment is further illustrated by the many "one another" passages of the New Testament. These "one another" verses deserve our careful consideration, and ultimately call for a lifetime of prayerful meditation and application. For this reason, they have been given a place of central prominence in this book.

The purpose of this chapter is to show that the commandment to "love one another" has very real and practical applications that are spelled out in the New Testament. The "one another" exhortations take the law of Christ out of the realm of theory and put it into the realm of sacrificial daily living. They show the radical nature of New Testament Christianity, where there is "no Greek and Jew, circumcised and uncircumcised, barbarian, Scythian, slave and freeman, but Christ is all, and in all."[1] In this realm, Jewish freemen embrace Gentile slaves as "beloved brothers," and former homosexuals "lay down their lives" for former Pharisees!

Even though these verses are listed almost without comment, it is hoped that their tremendous importance will be felt and that readers will return to this chapter repeatedly after the book has been read. If so, this chapter could be more life changing and revolutionary than any other. "If you *know* these things, you are blessed if you *do* them."[2]

LOVE ONE ANOTHER

Because Christ's new commandment to "love one another" is at the very center of New Covenant ethics, it is not surprising that we find it often repeated throughout the New Testament.

John 13:34-35 "A new commandment I give to you, that you *love one another,* even as I have loved you, that you also *love one another.* By this all men will know that you are My disciples, if you have *love for one another.*"

John 15:12 "This is My commandment, that you *love one another,* just as I have loved you."

John 15:17 "This I command you, that you *love one another.*"

Romans 12:10 "*Be devoted to one another in brotherly love;* give preference to one another in honor."

Romans 13:8 "Owe nothing to anyone except to *love one another;* for he who loves his neighbor has fulfilled the law."

1 Thessalonians 3:12 "and may the Lord cause you to *increase and abound in love for one another,* and for all men, just as we also do for you."

1 Thessalonians 4:9 "Now as to the love of the brethren, you have no need for anyone to write to you, for you yourselves are taught by God to *love one another.*"

---

[1] Colossians 3:11   [2] John 13:17; cf. vv.14-15

2 Thessalonians 1:3 "We ought always to give thanks to God for you, brethren, as is only fitting, because your faith is greatly enlarged, and *the love of each one of you toward one another grows ever greater.*"

1 Peter 1:22 "Since you have in obedience to the truth purified your souls for a sincere love of the brethren, *fervently love one another from the heart*...."

1 Peter 4:8 *"Above all, keep fervent in your love for one another,* because love covers a multitude of sins."

1 John 3:11 "For this is the message which you have heard from the beginning, that we should *love one another*...."

1 John 3:23 "And this is His commandment, that we believe in the name of His Son Jesus Christ, and *love one another,* just as He commanded us."

1 John 4:7 "Beloved, let us *love one another,* for love is from God; and everyone who loves is born of God and knows God."

1 John 4:11-12 "Beloved, if God so loved us, we also ought to *love one another.* No one has beheld God at any time; if we *love one another,* God abides in us, and His love is perfected in us."

2 John 1:5 "And now I ask you, lady, not as writing to you a new commandment, but the one which we have had from the beginning, that we *love one another.*"

Serve One Another

Love for one another finds its concrete expression through serving one another. It is as we "bear one another's burdens" that we "fulfill the law of Christ."

John 13:14 "If I then, the Lord and the Teacher, washed your feet, you also ought to *wash one another's feet.*"

Galatians 5:13 "For you were called to freedom, brethren; only do not turn your freedom into an opportunity for the flesh, but *through love serve one another.*"

Galatians 6:2 *"Bear one another's burdens,* and thus fulfill the law of Christ."

1 Peter 4:9-10 *"Be hospitable to one another* without complaint. As each one has received a special gift, *employ it in serving one another,* as good stewards of the manifold grace of God."

Pray for One Another

How can we serve one another any better than by praying for one another? Prayer is one of the greatest expressions of love.

James 5:16 "Therefore, confess your sins to one another, and *pray for one another,* so that you may be healed."

Build Up One Another

One of the great characteristics of hate is that it destroys and tears down others; even so, one of the great characteristics of love is that it blesses and builds up others. In fact, love actively seeks for ways in which it can do this. "Knowledge puffs up, but love builds up." [1]

Romans 14:19 "So then let us pursue the things which make for peace and *the building up of one another."*

Romans 15:14 "And concerning you, my brethren, I myself also am convinced that you yourselves are full of goodness, filled with all knowledge, and able also to *admonish one another."*

Ephesians 5:19 *"speaking to one another in psalms and hymns and spiritual songs,* singing and making melody with your heart to the Lord...."

Colossians 3:16 "Let the word of Christ richly dwell within you, with all wisdom *teaching and admonishing one another with psalms and hymns and spiritual songs,* singing with thankfulness in your hearts to God."

---

[1] 1 Corinthians 8:1 (ESV)

"ONE ANOTHER" VERSES

1 Thessalonians 4:18 "Therefore *comfort one another* with these words."

1 Thessalonians 5:11 "Therefore *encourage one another*, and *build up one another*, just as you also are doing."

1 Thessalonians 5:15 "See that no one repays another with evil for evil, but *always seek after that which is good for one another* and for all men."

Hebrews 3:13 "But *encourage one another* day after day, as long as it is still called "Today," lest any one of you be hardened by the deceitfulness of sin."

Hebrews 10:24-25 "and let us *consider how to stimulate one another to love and good deeds,* not forsaking our own assembling together, as is the habit of some, but *encouraging one another;* and all the more, as you see the day drawing near."

BE HUMBLE TOWARD ONE ANOTHER

Love for others is evidenced by our esteeming them as more important than ourselves. It always involves death to our own pride and selfish interests. Love is humble; it "does not brag and is not arrogant ... it does not seek its own." [1]

Romans 12:10 "Be devoted to one another in brotherly love; *give preference to one another in honor.*"

Romans 12:16 "*Be of the same mind toward one another;* do not be haughty in mind, but associate with the lowly. Do not be wise in your own estimation."

1 Corinthians 11:33 "So then, my brethren, when you come together to eat, *wait for one another.*"

Ephesians 5:21 "and *be subject to one another* in the fear of Christ."

---

[1] 1 Corinthians 13:4-5

THE LAW OF CHRIST

Philippians 2:3 "Do nothing from selfishness or empty conceit, but with humility of mind *let each of you regard one another as more important than himself.*"

James 5:16 "Therefore, *confess your sins to one another*, and pray for one another, so that you may be healed."

1 Peter 5:5 "You younger men, likewise, be subject to your elders; and all of you, *clothe yourselves with humility toward one another*, for God is opposed to the proud, but gives grace to the humble."

Forgive and Forbear One Another

If we are filled with love for others, we will find that we are able to bear with their offences, shortcomings, and eccentricities. Our love for them will "cover a multitude of sins."[1] "Love is patient, love is kind... it is not provoked; it does not take into account a wrong suffered."[2]

Ephesians 4:2 "with all humility and gentleness, with patience, *showing forbearance to one another in love.*"

Ephesians 4:32 "And *be kind to one another*, tender-hearted, *forgiving each other*, just as God in Christ also has forgiven you."

Colossians 3:13 "*bearing with one another*, and *forgiving each other*, whoever has a complaint against anyone; just as the Lord forgave you, so also should you."

Do Not Judge One Another

Love believes the best about others. It does not unnecessarily impute evil motives to brothers and sisters in Christ or presume to know all the circumstances that lie behind their decisions and actions.

---

[1] 1 Peter 4:8   [2] 1 Corinthians 13:4-5

Romans 14:13 "Therefore *let us not judge one another* anymore, but rather determine this—not to put an obstacle or a stumbling block in a brother's way."

Romans 15:7 "Wherefore, *accept one another,* just as Christ also accepted us to the glory of God."

James 4:11 "*Do not speak against one another,* brethren."

James 5:9 "*Do not complain,* brethren, *against one another,* that you yourselves may not be judged; behold, the Judge is standing right at the door."

BE HONEST WITH ONE ANOTHER

Love is straightforward and honest. It "does not rejoice in unrighteousness, but rejoices with the truth." [1] It "speaks the truth," but it always speaks it "in love." [2]

Ephesians 4:25 "Therefore, laying aside falsehood, *speak truth, each one of you, with his neighbor, for we are members of one another.*"

Colossians 3:9 "*Do not lie to one another,* since you laid aside the old self with its evil practices."

MAINTAIN UNITY WITH ONE ANOTHER

Because love causes us to "show forbearance to one another...with all humility and gentleness," it also makes us "diligent to preserve the unity of the Spirit in the bond of peace." [3] "Only by pride comes contention," [4] but love is humble and seeks for unity.

Romans 15:5 "Now may the God who gives perseverance and encouragement grant you to *be of the same mind with one another* according to Christ Jesus...."

---

[1] 1 Corinthians 13:6 [2] Ephesians 4:15 [3] Ephesians 4:2-3
[4] Proverbs 13:10 (KJV)

1 Corinthians 12:25 "that there should be *no division in the body, but that the members should have the same care for one another.*"

BE AT PEACE WITH ONE ANOTHER

Because love "does not seek its own" and "is not jealous,"[1] it is characterized, not by disorder and discord, but by peace. "For where jealousy and selfish ambition exist, there is disorder and every evil thing," but "the seed whose fruit is righteousness is sown in peace by those who make peace."[2]

Mark 9:50 "Salt is good; but if the salt becomes unsalty, with what will you make it salty again? Have salt in yourselves, and *be at peace with one another.*"

Romans 14:19 "So then let us *pursue the things which make for peace and the building up of one another.*"

1 Thessalonians 5:13 "and that you esteem them very highly in love because of their work. *Live in peace with one another.*"

SHOW AFFECTION TO ONE ANOTHER

Christians are to be known by their love for one another. This means that, if necessary, we must break through the natural coldness of our personalities or cultures to show warmth and affection to one another.

Romans 16:16 "*Greet one another* with a holy kiss. All the churches of Christ greet you."

1 Corinthians 16:20 "All the brethren greet you. *Greet one another* with a holy kiss."

2 Corinthians 13:12 "*Greet one another* with a holy kiss."

1 Peter 5:14 "*Greet one another with a kiss of love.* Peace be to you all who are in Christ."

---

[1] 1 Corinthians 13:4-5   [2] James 3:16, 18

Chapter Fifteen Review

In Chapter 14, we saw that the real meaning of Christ's new commandment to "love one another" must be determined by considering the teachings and conduct of Christ Himself. We are to love one another *as Christ loved us*. In Chapter 15, we have seen that the real meaning of Christ's new commandment is further illustrated by the many "one another" passages of the New Testament.

The commandment to "love one another" has many concrete and practical applications that are spelled out for us in the pages of the Bible. Among other things, Christians are called upon to serve one another, pray for one another, build up one another, show humility toward one another, forgive one another, not judge one another, be at peace with one another, and show affection toward one another. The "one another" exhortations take the law of Christ out of the realm of theory and put it into the realm of sacrificial daily living.

– CHAPTER SIXTEEN –

THE LAW OF CHRIST

> Behold, My Servant, whom I uphold; My chosen one in whom My soul delights. I have put My Spirit upon Him.... and the coastlands will wait expectantly for His law.
>
> Isaiah 42:1, 4

Under the Old Covenant, there were all sorts of laws and regulations to be meticulously followed—in fact, six hundred and thirteen of them! Under the New Covenant, there is only *one* guidepost for us to keep central in our thinking—to love as Christ loved! This involves not only following the example of Christ,[1] but also obeying the commandments and exhortations of the New Testament,[2] as well as submitting to the Old Testament's revelation of God's character and ways.[3] The fact that "the law of Christ" (and not, for example, the Ten Commandments) is our rule of duty under the New Covenant does not mean that Christians are awash in a sea of subjectivism, having no objectively revealed standards of right and wrong by which to live.

NO "LIST OF RULES"

Nevertheless, the emphasis of the New Testament is not on any written list of commandments and prohibitions as our standard of conduct, but on *Christlike love* that is empowered and directed by the Holy Spirit. This can be clearly seen by an examination of the New Testament itself. First of all, there is no evidence that when Paul referred to "the law of Christ," he meant anything more than the new commandment. He certainly did not have in mind "the

---

[1] See Chapter 14. [2] E.g., 1 Corinthians 14:37-38; 2 Thessalonians 3:12-15; etc.
[3] 2 Timothy 3:16-17; Matthew 5:17-19

whole New Testament canon," which was not yet in existence! Instead, Paul repeatedly affirms that "love" is, in fact, sufficient of itself to "fulfill" the Law. "Love one another; for he who loves his neighbor has fulfilled the law."[1]

Secondly, as to the Old Testament, the vast majority of its teachings and commandments have not been given an authoritative interpretation in the New Testament by Christ and the apostles. Does the commandment forbidding tattoos still apply directly to believers? What about the commandment that immediately precedes it, which instructs us not to "harm" the edges of our beard?[2] The ways in which such things may or may not pertain to us as Christians cannot be directly discovered by reading the Bible. Instead, they must be prayerfully considered (with the help of the Holy Spirit) *in light of the broad general principles of love* set forth in the New Testament.[3] It is clear, therefore, that we cannot look to the Law of Moses to complete our "list of rules."

Thirdly, even the commandments of the New Testament were never intended as a "new law" in the sense of a "new legal code" to replace the Law of Moses. The sayings of Christ in the Sermon on the Mount were certainly not given for that purpose, but were meant to give us a glimpse of the radical goodness that characterizes those who are the citizens of the kingdom of heaven. Likewise, all the other exhortations and commandments given throughout the New Testament come nowhere near to providing a complete and detailed code of behavior for every situation that might arise in the Christian life. We must remember that the New Testament is primarily an account of Christ's life, death, and resurrection, together with a collection of apostolic letters; it is not a legal corpus of commands and sanctions! Even the complete record of Christ's words and actions chronicled for us in the four gospels falls far short of displaying the infinite depths of His character. If we look to the New Testament for a "what would Jesus do" list that will mechanically cover the needs of every situation we may

---

[1] Romans 13:8-10; Galatians 5:14; See also Matthew 7:12 and Luke 10:25-28.
[2] Leviticus 19:27-28   [3] 1 Corinthians 6:12; see Appendix E, Q. 19.

encounter, we will be sorely disappointed. *The law of Christ is as inexhaustible as the Person of Christ Himself!* To love "as Christ loved" is too penetrating of a standard to be exhaustively conveyed by any finite list of rules.

THE OUTWORKINGS OF LOVE

As we have seen repeatedly, what it means to love as Christ loved must be defined by the example and teachings of Christ Himself. (This includes, of course, the teachings of the apostles that He appointed to be His inspired representatives.[1]) No valid application of the law of Christ will ever *contradict* any of the plain teachings of Scripture. For example, the law of Christ can never be invoked to overthrow the clear teachings of the New Testament with regard to homosexuality or women's roles in the church. Nevertheless, even the commands of the New Testament do not *fully convey* the outworkings of the law of Christ. This can be clearly seen in the matter of slavery. It is easy to see why those with an Old Covenant mindset would defend slavery, as did many theologians of the South at the time of the American Civil War. However, even those who look solely to the New Covenant in these matters will be misled if they view the New Testament as a mere "legal corpus." Paul instructs Christian "masters" to "give up threatening"[2] and to grant "their" slaves "justice and fairness,"[3] but says *nothing* about giving the slaves freedom. We must remember that these words were written in a context where over one fourth of the Roman Empire was made up of slaves. In such a setting, Paul's wisdom in undermining the practice of slavery[4] without openly attacking it was remarkable. Nevertheless, to read the New Testament's exhortations to slave owners in a "legal" fashion will certainly leave one with the impression that slavery itself is acceptable among believers. But when the principles of "the law of Christ" begin to work themselves out, it becomes obvious that in most cases

---

[1] John 14:25-26; 16:12-15 [2] Ephesians 6:9 [3] Colossians 4:1
[4] Philemon 15-17, 21

one cannot *love his slave as he loves himself* and still refuse him his freedom. After all, in Christ "there is neither slave nor free man,"[1] and any slave who is in Christ is "no longer a slave, *but more than a slave, a beloved brother."*[2] Slavery was such an integral part of society that no culture on earth questioned its existence until Christians questioned it, and they questioned it because of the law of Christ, not because of the individual commandments of the New Testament that relate to slavery!

Too often Christians have assumed that they are free to do anything that the New Testament does not expressly condemn. This is clearly not the case. For example, the drinking of alcoholic beverages (in moderation) is certainly not condemned in the New Testament, and is sometimes even celebrated in the Old.[3] Nevertheless, there are many situations where drinking alcohol, even in moderation, will cause others to stumble or hinder our testimony to them. In such cases, the higher principle of *love* comes into play, and the Christian who wishes to follow his Master in such a setting will "never drink alcohol again, that he might not cause his brother to stumble."[4] "For you were called to freedom, brethren; *only do not turn your freedom into an opportunity for the flesh, but through love serve one another."*[5]

Even if a particular practice does not cause others to stumble, Christians may find themselves led by the Holy Spirit to abstain from it.[6] Their standard of conduct is not set by what is acceptable to other Christians, but by what they perceive to be God's will for them personally.

PROVING THE WILL OF GOD

Again and again throughout the Christian life, believers find themselves utterly cast upon God to know what they should do in various situations. Parents often find themselves at a loss as to how

---

[1] Galatians 3:28 [2] Philemon 16 [3] Deuteronomy 14:26; Psalm 104:14-15; yet, see also Proverbs 31:3-7. [4] 1 Corinthians 8:13 [5] Galatians 5:13 [6] See, e.g., 1 Corinthians 9:3-18; especially vv. 12, 15, 18.

they should respond to their rebellious teenager—should they extend more grace or force their child to leave home? Similar situations abound in the church. Should a spiritually needy brother be given a rebuke or more encouragement? When exactly should church discipline be exercised in a particular situation? At what point in a marriage is separation right or divorce permissible? In matters of war, should a Christian soldier obey an order to "kill everyone and take no prisoners"? Is it right to lie to Nazi interrogators about the Jews hidden in your home? All these questions are *real, life altering*, and *acutely important*. Yet *none* of them has hard and fast rules upon which even godly believers can agree!

For the Jew, "knowing God's will" and "approving the things that are excellent" was a matter of "being instructed out of the Law."[1] For the Christian, things are not so easy. The mature son has far fewer commandments than the minor child has, but he faces much greater responsibility. Christians must shoulder this responsibility. They must search the word of God with all diligence to see if any of its principles give an answer to their present need for guidance. But in the end, they must often "prove what the will of God is, that which is good and acceptable and perfect," not by reference to an objective commandment, but by "presenting their bodies a living and holy sacrifice"—refusing to be "conformed to this world," and instead being "transformed by the renewing of their minds."[2] This is why Paul prays for the Philippians that their "*love* may abound still more and more in real knowledge and all discernment, *so that they may approve the things that are excellent.*"[3]

If you are a Christian, "approving the things that are excellent" and "proving what the will of God is," is a matter of being transformed by the renewing of your mind, presenting your body as a living sacrifice, and having your *love* "abound still more and more in real knowledge and all discernment." It is this renewing of your mind and presentation of your body (Romans 12:1-2) that is the prerequisite for obeying the clearly revealed imperatives of the

---

[1] Romans 2:18 Gk.; KJV; ESV   [2] Romans 12:1-2   [3] Philippians 1:9-10 (Notice the contrast with Romans 2:18!)

New Testament (Romans 12:3-21). *Moreover, it is this same renewing of your mind, presentation of your body, and abounding of your love "in real knowledge and all discernment" that will enable you to "prove the will of God" in those situations where no clearly revealed imperatives exist!*

WHO KISSED ME?

This reality is well illustrated by an account from the life of Evangeline Booth (1865-1950), daughter of William Booth, founder of the Salvation Army. As one who ministered often to the dregs of society, she found herself one morning outside the large iron gates of a local police court and temporary prison. Waiting for the gates to open, she heard the shuffling of heavy feet and loud, agitated voices. In her own words:

> The gates opened wide, and I witnessed a sight which, if eternity could wash away from my mind, time never can. It was a woman. Two policemen walked in front and two behind. One stalwart man firmly held the right arm and the other the left. Her hair was uncombed and matted and disheveled. Her right temple was blackened with bruises. Clots of dry blood stood upon her left temple. Her clothes were torn and bloodstained. She tried to wrench her arms from the grasp of the policemen. The very atmosphere of the morning was laden with her curses and oaths. She tossed her head wildly as the six policemen dragged her down the passageway.
>
> What could I do? One more moment, and the golden opportunity to be of help would be gone. Could I offer a prayer? No, there was not time. Could I sing? It would be absurd. Could I give her money? She could not take it. Could I quote a verse of Scripture? She would not heed it.
>
> *Whether it was a divine suggestion or not, I did not stop to think, but the impulse of a burning desire which filled my heart as she passed made me step forward and kiss her on the cheek.* Whether the police were taken off their guard by my extraordinary action and relaxed their grasp, I do not

THE LAW OF CHRIST

know, but with one wrench she freed her arms and clasped her hands as the wind spread her matted, disheveled hair, and she looked toward the gray skies and said, "My God!" She looked around wildly for a moment and then said, "My God, who kissed me? My God, who kissed me? Nobody has kissed me since my mother died." Lifting her tattered apron, she buried her face in her hands, and like a little lamb, she was led to the vehicle which took her to prison.

Later I went to the prison in the hope of seeing her, and at the door stood the warden. When I approached the warden, she said, "We think her mind is gone. She does nothing but pace up and down her cell asking me every time I go in if I know who kissed her." "Would you let me go in and speak to her?" I asked. "I am her only and best friend...."

The door was opened, and I slipped in. Her face was clean, her eyes were large and beautiful, and she said, "Do you know who kissed me?" And then she told me her story: "When I was a little girl seven years old my widowed mother died. She died very poor, although she was of genteel birth. She died in a back basement in the dark. When she was dying she called me to her, took my little face in her hands, and kissed it, and said to me, 'My poor little girl, my defenseless little girl. O God, have pity on my little girl, and when I am gone protect her and take care of her.' From that day to this, nobody ever put a kiss upon my face until recently."

Then again she asked me, "Do you know who kissed me?" I said, "It was I who kissed you." Then I told her of Him whose life was so much more tender than mine could ever be and how He went to the cross and bore our sins upon Himself and was wounded for our transgressions that He might put the kiss of pardon upon our brow.

In Him she found light, and joy, and comfort, and salvation and healing and love. Before she was released from the prison, the warden testified not only to the change in her life but to its beauty. She was made through Christ the means of salvation to numbers of others who were down as low as she had been and who were bound with fetters as heavy as those with which she herself had been bound.[1]

Is Your Mother Still Living?

An account from the life of Norwegian missionary Marie Monsen (1878-1962) provides a further illustration of how Christians are enabled to "approve the things that are excellent" through "offering their bodies as a living sacrifice." Held captive for twenty-three days by Chinese pirates, she faced many "impossible" situations, where only "the mind of Christ" could meet her desperate need for wisdom. On one such occasion, two pirates who wanted to use her for their own gratification accosted her in her cabin:

> I had seen a good many bandits in the interior of China, but never any more hideously repulsive than those two. The subject of their whispered conversation was not hard to guess. One of them pushed the other into my cabin, closed the door and tried to lock it, but the key had been broken.
>
> I felt as if the devil himself had come in. His face, neck and hands were covered with horrible, open, stinking sores. He sat down on my suitcase so close to me that I felt his warm breath on my face.
>
> I sat repeating to myself the promise that had become so precious to me in the bandit-ridden province of Honan: "The angel of the Lord encamps round about them that fear Him, *and delivers them.*"
>
> To my own amazement it was I who began the conversation. It came perfectly naturally, without reflection: "Is your mother still living?" *"Yes."* "How old is she?" *"Fifty-one."* "No, really! Then she and I are just the same age."
>
> He was then asked about his father, his brothers and sisters and other relatives. We had a long talk. At my

---

[1] Evangeline Booth, *Who Kissed Me?* (Tract, n.d.)

request he opened the door again—without fresh air the stench was unendurable. Having done so, he sat down again.

I soon found out that he had heard the Gospel. He knew a missionary too...one of the rare souls, a truly godly man.

He also knew some Christians in his home town. I think we talked to each other for a whole hour. He was told the truth about his life; and he heard too about the Savior who cared for so many lost robbers and made all things new for them. He had heard quite a lot before and he sighed, even groaned a couple of times, and his eyes were blinded by tears when he finally slipped quietly out of the cabin. I did not see him again.[1]

In both these accounts, we see that to love "as Christ loved" is too penetrating of a standard to be conveyed by any finite list of rules! Only as we have our minds renewed, our bodies offered as living sacrifices, and our hearts filled with Christlike love, will we ever be able to walk according to this New Testament pattern.

LIFE IN THE SPIRIT

In all of this, Christ has not left us as orphans, without any Helper or Teacher.[2] He has come to dwell within us in the Person of the Holy Spirit! Christ Himself lives in the heart of every believer,[3] and His Spirit "teaches us about all things."[4] *The law of Christ is fulfilled only as Christ Himself lives His life through us.*

To view the law of Christ as a new "list of rules" to be scrupulously followed is, therefore, to miss the whole emphasis of the New Testament regarding the nature of the Christian's new life "in the Spirit."[5] As fearful as it may seem to those who want an objective commandment for every situation, the New Testament

---

[1] Marie Monsen, *A Present Help* (London: China Inland Mission, 1960) 78-80. [2] John 14:16-18 [3] John 14:23; Romans 8:9-10 [4] 1 John 2:26-27; John 10:4-5 [5] See Chapters 18-19.

envisions "walking in the Spirit" as the key to doing the will of God. Those who "walk according to the Spirit" will "fulfill the requirement of the Law"[1] as a matter of course, for when the Spirit has free rein in a believer's life, he or she will manifest "the fruit of the Spirit," which is "love, joy, peace, patience, kindness, goodness, faithfulness, gentleness, and self-control," and "against such things there is no law."[2]

"COPIOUS LAWS"

Christ gave us *one* "new commandment." This means that Christians have only one guidepost to keep central in their thinking! In his *Paradise of the Heart*, Jan Comenius (1592-1670) captures something of this New Covenant reality in a section entitled "The True Christian Requires Not Copious Laws":

> To him who verily loves God with his whole heart, it is not necessary to give many commandments as to when, where, how and how often he should serve God, worship and honor Him; for his hearty union with God, and his readiness to obey Him is the fashion in which he honors God best, and it leads a man to ever and everywhere praise God in his mind, and to strive for His Glory in all his deeds.
>
> He also who loves his fellow-men as himself requires not copious commandments as to where, when and wherein he should serve them, how he should avoid to injure them, and return to them what is due to them. This love for his fellow-men will in itself tell him fully, and show him how he should bear himself towards them.
>
> It is the sign of the evil man that he always demands rules, and wishes to know only from the books of law what he should do; yet at home in our heart God's finger shows us that it is our duty to do unto our neighbors that which we wish that they should do unto us. But as the

---

[1] Romans 8:4   [2] Galatians 5:22-23

world cares not for this inward testimony of our own conscience, but heeds external laws only, therefore is there no true order in the world; there is but suspicion, distrust, misunderstanding, ill-will, discord, envy, theft, murder, and so forth. Those who are truly subject to God heed but their own conscience; what it forbids them they do not, but they do that which it tells them they may do; of gain, favor, and such things they take no care.[1]

---

[1] Jan Comenius, "The Paradise of the Heart," *Christian History Magazine*, Issue 13, 1987: 27. (This quote should be read in light of the section above entitled "Specific Commandments," p. 139.)

Chapter Sixteen Review

Under the New Covenant, there is only one guidepost for us to keep central in our thinking—to love as Christ loved! The emphasis of the New Testament, therefore, is not on any written list of commandments and prohibitions as our rule of duty, but on Christlike love that is empowered and directed by the Holy Spirit.

To love "as Christ loved" is too penetrating of a standard to be conveyed by any finite list of commandments. *The law of Christ is as inexhaustible as the Person of Christ Himself!* Even the imperatives of the New Testament do not fully convey the outworkings of the law of Christ. If you are a Christian, "approving the things that are excellent" and "proving what the will of God is," is a matter of being transformed by the renewing of your mind, presenting your body as a living sacrifice, and having your love "abound still more and more in real knowledge and all discernment."

To view the law of Christ as a new "list of rules" to be scrupulously followed is, therefore, to miss the whole emphasis of the New Testament regarding the nature of the Christian's new life "in the Spirit." As fearful as it may seem to those who want an objective commandment for every situation, the New Testament envisions the "walk in the Spirit" as the key to doing the will of God. Those who "walk according to the Spirit" will "fulfill the requirement of the Law" as a matter of course, for when the Spirit has free rein in a believer's life, he or she will manifest "the fruit of the Spirit," which is "love, joy, peace, patience, kindness, goodness, faithfulness, gentleness, and self-control," and "against such things there is no law."

– CHAPTER SEVENTEEN –

THE SUPERIORITY OF THE LAW OF CHRIST

[Christ] was patient, [Christ] was kind, and was not jealous; [Christ] did not brag and was not arrogant, [Christ] did not act unbecomingly; [He] did not seek His own, was not provoked, did not take into account a wrong suffered, did not rejoice in unrighteousness, but rejoiced with the truth; bore all things, believed all things, hoped all things, endured all things. [Christ] never failed....

1 Corinthians 13:4-8

It is no longer I who live, but Christ lives in me.

Galatians 2:20

Christ is the perfect and final revelation of God's character, and the "law of Christ" is the perfect and final revelation of God's law.

The life of Christ was a life of perfect love—perfect love to God and perfect love to man. *Christ Himself, in the depths of His divine Person, is the epitome and definition of what real love is.* Christ is Love Incarnate, for He is God Incarnate, and God is love. Christ fulfilled the most stringent requirements of the law naturally, just *by living out* in life's varied circumstances *the reality of who He was.* It was His *delight* to do God's will, even when its accomplishment was costly beyond measure: "Then I said, 'Behold, I come; in the scroll of the book it is written of me; *I delight to do Your will,* O my God; *Your Law is within my heart.*'" [1]

In light of these facts, it is glorious beyond imagination that according to the New Testament, *Christ Himself* (in the Person of the Holy Spirit) *now lives in every believer!* [2] It is His very life, flowing

---

[1] Psalm 40:7-8 (NAS95); Hebrews 10:5-10 [2] Galatians 2:20

from the vine to the branches, that enables the Christian to bear the fruit of Christlikeness.[1] The implications of this reality will be explored more fully in Chapters 18-19, but at this point it is only necessary to note that *to the degree Christ's life is manifested in us,*[2] *to that degree the superiority of the "law of Christ" to every other "law" will also be manifested.* For example, the one who is filled with Christ's love for others will find that it is not enough just to keep the Eighth Commandment *not* to steal. He lives by a higher standard; not only does he "steal no longer," but he goes on to "labor, performing with his own hands what is good, *in order that he may have something to share with him who has need."*[3] Many practical examples of this reality are seen daily in the Christian life and walk.

COVETING

Suppose one of my Christian brothers is given a new car by someone who is no longer physically able to drive it. He already has a car that is newer than the one I own, but this one is even better. Soon, I begin to feel sorry for myself, wishing that I could have been given such a car. But I know from the Law of Moses that coveting is forbidden: "You shall not covet your neighbor's house; you shall not covet your neighbor's wife or his male servant or his female servant or his ox or his donkey or anything that belongs to your neighbor."[4] Knowing the sinfulness of coveting, I then determine to "not covet" this brother's car. Try as I may *not to covet*, I must admit that I still struggle some with resentment and self-pity. This is one possible scenario.

Now suppose, on the other hand, that my heart is overflowing with Christlike *love* toward this brother. Because of my affection for him, I long to see him blessed in every way. I am grateful for his service in the body of Christ and would be delighted to see his usefulness grow. In other words, suppose that to some degree, the "law of Christ" is being fulfilled in my heart. What will the outcome be? When I learn that he has been given a new car, my

---

[1] John 15:5   [2] 2 Corinthians 4:10-11   [3] Ephesians 4:28   [4] Exodus 20:17

first response will be genuine *joy;* I will *delight* to see him blessed. Because of my love for him, I will have fulfilled spontaneously and unconsciously the commandment not to covet. And not only will I have *not* coveted; I will have actually *rejoiced* in the joy of another.[1] Isn't it obvious that walking in the reality of the law of Christ is much more wonderful than being governed by a list of prohibitions?

Lust

Suppose I am walking down the street and see an attractive but sensually dressed woman coming toward me. I know from the Law of Moses that adultery is a great sin and my mind goes to its prohibition: "You shall not commit adultery." This is certainly better than having *no* standard of conduct, but something far greater and more wonderful is possible in Christ. Suppose, instead, that when I meet this woman my heart is overflowing with love and compassion for her. I have just come from a prayer meeting where tears and supplications have been poured out for lost and needy souls, and I am on my way to witness on the streets. Will not my thoughts toward this woman be entirely different than they might otherwise have been? Will not the reality of love in my heart enable me to fulfill the commandment not to commit adultery in a much higher way than I could have ever fulfilled it before? The account is told of a nineteenth-century evangelist who, as a new Christian full of love for God and man, was approached one day on the streets of an eastern city by a young prostitute. When he finally realized what she was asking of him, his first response was to burst into tears. Seeing his response, she too burst into tears. This is the reality of the law of Christ in action!

Giving

The law of Christ finds wonderful application in the realm of giving as well. For the Christian, the "tithe" of the Old Testament is

---

[1] Romans 12:15

merely the starting point of giving. The Old Testament laws related to tithing tell us that it is not unreasonable or burdensome in most cases to expect ten families to support one pastor and his family in the full-time work of the ministry. Churches with twenty families should be able to support two pastors, and so forth. Such support is part of the regular and on-going responsibility of churches toward their shepherds.[1]

But this is only a starting point. If I have ten dollars in my billfold, the command to "love as Christ loved" may involve my giving away not just *one* of the dollars, but *all ten* of them... and the billfold, too! Some Christian businessmen have found themselves led to give away ninety percent of their income and live on ten percent. Others, like the "churches of Macedonia," have at times been led "of their own accord" to give even *"beyond their ability... begging* with *much entreaty* for the *favor* of participation in the support of the saints."[2] The Lord Jesus commended the poor widow who "out of her poverty, put in *all she owned, all she had to live on*,"[3] though normally such giving would not be prudent or even *right*. Again, we see that the law of love is too incisive to be codified as a "list of rules" that can be followed in every circumstance. The Christian relies on the Holy Spirit to lead him as to how much, if any, he should give in a particular situation. Sometimes he may be constrained to give everything, sometimes nothing! Once again, the law of Christ shows itself to be far superior to the Law of Moses.

CONVICTION OF SIN

Much has been said in recent years about the necessity of preaching the Ten Commandments in evangelism in order to convict men of sin as a preparation for the gospel. The Lord Jesus Himself sometimes used the Law in this way to point self-righteous Jews to their sinfulness and need for grace; the "rich young ruler" is one example.[4] The Apostle Paul also was convicted of the "sinfulness of

---

[1] 1 Corinthians 9:7-14   [2] 2 Corinthians 8:1-5   [3] Mark 12:44
[4] Matthew 19:16-19

sin" in his own life when the deeper implications of one of the Ten Commandments "came" to him and "sin came alive."[1] And Paul makes it clear that the restraint and conviction of wicked men is still one of the "lawful uses of the Law," even in a New Covenant setting.[2] (More is said about how Christians can "lawfully use the Law" in Appendix D.)

Having said this, however, we need to remember that it was not Peter's failure to keep the Decalogue, but *a glimpse of the surpassing glory, kindness, and grace of Christ* that caused him to cry out, "Depart from me, for *I am a sinful man*, O Lord!"[3] And even in the case of the "rich young ruler," it was not Christ's enumeration of Old Covenant commandments, but His call to "sell all" *in devotion to Himself* that exposed the young man's sinful state.[4] It is highly significant, then, that when our Lord *taught explicitly* concerning conviction of sin by the power of the Holy Spirit, He associated it not with the Ten Commandments, but with *His own Person*.

It is in the gospel of John that we find Christ's direct teaching with regard to conviction of sin:

> When the Helper comes, whom I will send to you from the Father, that is the Spirit of truth, who proceeds from the Father, He will bear witness *of Me*, and you will bear witness also, because you have been with Me from the beginning. John 15:26-27

> And He, when He comes, will convict the world concerning sin, and righteousness, and judgment; concerning sin, *because they do not believe in Me*; and concerning righteousness, *because I go to the Father, and you no longer behold Me*; and concerning judgment, because the ruler of this world has been judged. John 16:8-11

Here the Lord promises the Apostles that as they go forth proclaiming the gospel and "bearing witness of Christ," the Holy Spirit will come alongside them and "bear witness of Christ" as

---

[1] Romans 7:7-14   [2] 1 Timothy 1:3-11   [3] Luke 5:8   [4] Matthew 19:20-22

well. Such "witnessing" on the part of the Holy Spirit will *center on the Person of Christ Himself* and will be the means of advancing the gospel in the world. According to the Lord Jesus, the Holy Spirit will "convict the world concerning sin," not primarily because those who are "of the world" have broken the Ten Commandments, but because they have failed to *believe in Him*.

APOSTOLIC PREACHING

When we examine the actual preaching of the early church in the book of Acts, we find that it follows this very pattern. *Nothing* is said by way of "preparatory preaching of the Ten Commandments." Instead, we find the Apostles preaching the rejection, crucifixion, resurrection, and exaltation of Christ, setting Him forth as the promised Messiah and Lord of glory—the One who will judge all men on the Last Day.[1] The Holy Spirit takes this message and applies it in mighty convicting power to Jew and Gentile alike:

> "Men of Israel, listen to these words: Jesus the Nazarene, a man attested to you by God with miracles and wonders and signs which God performed through Him in your midst, just as you yourselves know—this Man, delivered over by the predetermined plan and foreknowledge of God, *you nailed to a cross by the hands of godless men and put Him to death…. This Jesus God raised up again*, to which we are all witnesses. Therefore *having been exalted to the right hand of God*, and having received from the Father the promise of the Holy Spirit, He has poured forth this which you both see and hear. For it was not David who *ascended into heaven*, but he himself says: 'The Lord said to my Lord, *"Sit at My right hand, until I make Your enemies a footstool for Your feet."*' Therefore let all the house of Israel know for certain that *God has made Him both Lord and Christ*—this Jesus whom you crucified." *Now when they heard this, they were pierced to*

---

[1] John 5:22-23; Acts 17:30-31; Romans 2:16

the heart, and said to Peter and the rest of the apostles, "Brethren, what shall we do?" And Peter said to them, *"Repent,* and let each of you be baptized in the name of Jesus Christ for the forgiveness of your sins; and you will receive the gift of the Holy Spirit." Acts 2:22-23, 32-38 (NAS95)

But Peter and the apostles answered and said, "We must obey God rather than men. *The God of our fathers raised up Jesus, whom you had put to death by hanging Him on a cross. He is the one whom God exalted to His right hand as a Prince and a Savior,* to grant repentance to Israel, and forgiveness of sins. *And we are witnesses of these things; and so is the Holy Spirit,* whom God has given to those who obey Him." But when they heard this, *they were cut to the quick* and were intending to slay them. Acts 5:29-33

And Philip went down to the city of Samaria and began *proclaiming Christ to them*.... And Philip opened his mouth, and beginning from this Scripture *he preached Jesus to him.*
Acts 8:5, 35

"You know of Jesus of Nazareth, *how God anointed Him with the Holy Spirit and with power, and how He went about doing good, and healing all who were oppressed by the devil; for God was with Him.* And we are witnesses of *all the things He did* both in the land of the Jews and in Jerusalem. And they also put Him to death by hanging Him on a cross. *God raised Him up on the third day.... And He ordered us to preach to the people, and solemnly to testify that this is the One who has been appointed by God as Judge of the living and the dead.* Of Him all the prophets bear witness that through His name everyone who believes in Him receives forgiveness of sins." *While Peter was still speaking these words, the Holy Spirit fell upon all those who were listening to the message.*
Acts 10:38-44

CHRIST CRUCIFIED

It is evident from these and other passages[1] in the Book of Acts that the Holy Spirit is well able to convict men of sin by preaching that is centered on Christ Himself. Wherever Christ—the rejected, crucified, risen, and exalted Lord of glory—is set before men, the Holy Spirit has no lack of resources to use in driving home to the sinner's heart his own depravity and lostness.

> And I will pour out on the house of David and on the inhabitants of Jerusalem, the Spirit of grace and of supplication, *so that they will look on Me whom they have pierced; and they will mourn for Him, as one mourns for an only son, and they will weep bitterly over Him, like the bitter weeping over a first-born.*   Zechariah 12:10

These words, which found their initial fulfillment on the Day of Pentecost,[2] describe what happens when God "pours out" His Holy Spirit in convicting power upon the lost, forcing them to "look on" the One whom they have pierced. The result is heart-wrenching sobs and groans, "like the bitter weeping over a first-born or only son"!

> *Behold the Man upon a cross,*
> *My sin upon His shoulders;*
> *Ashamed, I hear my mocking voice*
> *Call out among the scoffers.*
> *It was my sin that held Him there*
> *Until it was accomplished;*
> *His dying breath has brought me life—*
> *I know that it is finished.*
>
>   Stuart Townsend

Oh, the blackness and vileness of rejecting or ignoring the infinitely glorious Son of God, who was "pierced" for our transgressions and who paid the highest price imaginable that sinners might

---

[1] See also Acts 3:13-21; 4:8-12; 7:51-58; 13:23-43; 17:2-3; 17:22-34; 26:22-23; 28:23-24.   [2] Acts 2:37

not perish! Here is sin in its most wicked and horrible manifestation. Even the sin of Sodom and Gomorrah was not as great as the sin of those who reject "the light of the glorious gospel of Christ, who is the image of God." [1]

> And whoever does not receive you, nor heed your words, as you go out of that house or that city, shake off the dust of your feet. Truly I say to you, it will be more tolerable for the land of Sodom and Gomorrah in the day of judgment than for that city. Matthew 10:14-15

> Then He began to reproach the cities in which most of His miracles were done, because they did not repent. "Woe to you, Chorazin! Woe to you, Bethsaida! For if the miracles had occurred in Tyre and Sidon which occurred in you, they would have repented long ago in sackcloth and ashes. Nevertheless I say to you, it shall be more tolerable for Tyre and Sidon in the day of judgment, than for you. And you, Capernaum, will not be exalted to heaven, will you? You shall descend to Hades; for if the miracles had occurred in Sodom which occurred in you, it would have remained to this day. Nevertheless I say to you that it shall be more tolerable for the land of Sodom in the day of judgment, than for you." Matthew 11:20-24

Oh, the terrible guilt that rests upon the heads of all who hear the true gospel of Christ crucified and then turn away in apathy or contempt! This is sin far greater than any sin against the Law of Moses! "Anyone who has set aside the Law of Moses dies without mercy on the testimony of two or three witnesses. *How much severer punishment do you think he will deserve who has trampled underfoot the Son of God?*"[2] "This is the judgment, *that the light is come into the world, and men loved the darkness rather than the light;* for their deeds were evil."[3]

---

[1] 2 Corinthians 4:4   [2] Hebrews 10:28-29   [3] John 3:19

Conviction by the Law of Christ

All that has been said thus far does not mean that lost men should never be confronted with their sins of immorality,[1] excess,[2] idolatry,[3] and so on,[4] nor does it mean that the Holy Spirit does not use "law" to convict men of sin. Sin has no meaning apart from our failure to live up to some standard. But the most convicting standard that can ever be applied to the hearts of men is not the Law of Moses, but the law of Christ. Christ Himself is the embodiment of that law. Many are convicted by this "law" when they catch a glimpse of the glories of "Christ and Him crucified"[5] through the preaching of the gospel. (See the passages from Acts quoted above.) Others are convicted by the law of Christ as they begin to see how far short they fall of Christ's teachings throughout the gospels and especially in the Sermon on the Mount. Still others are convicted by the Christlike characteristics manifested in the lives of all true Christians.[6] In fact, church history is filled with accounts of those who have realized their lostness by encountering Christ in His people.

The Second Mile

> But whoever slaps you on your right cheek, turn to him the other also .... and whoever shall force you to go one mile, go with him two .... I say to you, love your enemies, and pray for those who persecute you.
>
> Matthew 5:39, 41, 44

Under Roman law, soldiers had the right to compel passers-by to carry their burdens for them from one stage of their journey to the next. We might think that to do this without grumbling and complaining would be accomplishment enough, but our Lord sets forth a higher standard: we are to go voluntarily, not *one* mile, but *two!* This standard will seem burdensome *unless* we are filled with

---

[1] John 4:16-18 [2] Acts 24:25 [3] Acts 17:22-30; Romans 1:18-32
[4] See Appendix D. [5] 1 Corinthians 1:23; 2:2 [6] Matthew 5:3-16

THE SUPERIORITY OF THE LAW OF CHRIST

Christlike love for the Roman soldier, in which case the "second mile" will be a delight to our hearts. During the second mile, we will have an opportunity to tell the soldier about the One who has made us so "different" from the others who have borne his burden. During the second mile, the life of Christ will be manifested "within our mortal bodies." And, during the second mile, the Holy Spirit will have occasion to use "the law of Christ" to convict the soldier of his sin.

Watchman Nee tells the story of a Christian in South China who had a rice field in the middle of the hill:

> In the time of drought he used a water-wheel, worked by a tread-mill, to lift water from the irrigation stream into his field. His neighbor had two fields below his, and one night made a breach in the dividing bank and drained off all his water. When the brother repaired the breach and pumped in more water his neighbor did the same thing again, and this was repeated three or four times. So he consulted his brethren, "I have tried to be patient and not to retaliate," he said, "but is it right?" After they had prayed together about it, one of them replied, "If we only try to do the right thing, surely we are very poor Christians. We have to do something more than what is right." The brother was much impressed. Next morning he pumped water for the two rice fields below, and in the afternoon pumped water for his own field. After that the water stayed in his field. His neighbor was so amazed at his action that he began to inquire the reason, and in course of time he too became a Christian.[1]

We see in this story the convicting power of the "law of Christ" when it is demonstrated in the lives of God's people.

Martyn Lloyd-Jones tells a similar account from the life of Billy Bray, who before his conversion was an excellent boxer:

---

[1] Watchman Nee, *Sit, Walk, Stand* (1957; reprint, Fort Washington: Christian Literature Crusade, 1970) 26.

One day, down in the mine, another man who used to live in mortal dread and terror of Billy Bray before Bray's conversion, knowing he was converted, thought he had at last found his opportunity. Without any provocation at all he struck Bray, who could very easily have revenged himself upon him and laid him down unconscious on the ground. But instead of doing that Billy Bray looked at him and said, "May God forgive you, even as I forgive you," and no more. The result was that that man endured for several days an agony of mind and spirit which led directly to his conversion.[1]

Another illustration of the convicting power of the "law of Christ" comes from the testimony of Corrie ten Boom. After she had successfully saved the lives of hundreds of Jews during the Nazi occupation of Holland, one day a fellow Dutchman approached Corrie asking for help. He told her that his wife had been arrested for rescuing Jews but that he had found a police officer who was willing (for the sum of 600 guilders) to take the risk of releasing her. Not knowing that this man's story was a fabrication designed to trap her, Corrie was able—by sacrificing the 200 guilders that she herself possessed and by asking for additional money from her friends—to gather the amount needed. A few hours after the man had received his money, the Gestapo arrived at Corrie's door to arrest everyone in the house and send them away to the horrors of the concentration camps.

While in prison, Corrie ten Boom learned the identity of her betrayer. At first she struggled with bitterness but soon found cleansing and forgiveness in Christ. In her own words, spoken with great power and conviction:

> When I had repented of that sin, the Lord cleansed my heart with His blood, and a heart cleansed by the blood of Jesus, He fills with the Holy Spirit, and the fruit of the

---

[1] Martyn Lloyd-Jones, *Studies in the Sermon on the Mount* (Grand Rapids: Wm. B. Eerdmans, 1977) 281.

Spirit is *love*—love even for enemies. And instead that I hated [i.e., "instead of hating"] that man, I loved him. And after the war that man was sentenced to death because he had caused the death of many Dutch people. When I heard that, I wrote him: "Your betrayal has meant the death of my old father (he was 84 years old when they brought him into prison; after 10 days he died), my sister (who died after 10 months [of] terrible suffering), my brother (he came out alive, but a sick man, and died through that sickness), and his son ([who] never came back). I myself have suffered terribly in three different prisons. But I have forgiven you, and that is because *Jesus* is in my heart. And when Jesus tells you to love your enemies, He gives you the love that He demands from you." And I sent that man a New Testament and underlined the way of salvation. And that man wrote me: "That you could forgive me is such a great miracle that I have said, 'Jesus, when you give such a love in the heart of your followers, there's hope for me.' And I have read in the Bible that you sent me that Jesus has died at the cross for the sins of the whole world, and I have brought my terrible sins to Jesus and I know that they are forgiven. Your forgiveness has shown me what it means that there is forgiveness through Jesus Christ." And that man was brought to death that same week, but he was reconciled with God, and God had used me—who had hated him—to bring him to the Lord!"[1]

A final example of the convicting power of the law of Christ is taken from Doug Nichols' account of his early days as an Operation Mobilization missionary in India in 1967.

> Doug had been on the mission field only a short time before he came down with tuberculosis. Because he had no money for better treatment, he found himself in a government-operated sanitarium. When he tried to hand out gospels of

---

[1] Corrie ten Boom, *The Greatest of These is Love*, 1972.

John and other literature in the language of the people, his fellow patients tore them up and threw them in his face. No one would accept his tracts, perhaps thinking that he was just another rich American.

That night Doug awoke at 2 A.M. coughing. Across the aisle, he noticed an old man trying to get out of bed. After trying repeatedly to stand up, the old man finally fell back into his bed and began to whimper. In the morning, a stench filled the ward and everyone was angry with him for not containing himself. One of the nurses who cleaned up the mess even cuffed him on the head for what he had done.

The next night a similar thing happened. Doug woke up coughing in the middle of the night. Once more, he saw the old man trying to get out of bed; again, the man was not able to stand and began to cry softly. Though he was very weak himself, Doug got out of bed and went over to the old man's bedside. Placing one arm under his skinny legs and the other under his back, Doug carried him to the dirty bathroom, which was just a hole in the floor, held him in position while he relieved himself, and then brought him back to his bed. As Doug leaned forward to put him down, the man kissed him on the cheek. Completely exhausted, Doug went back and fell into his own bed.

To his surprise, he was awakened at 4:30 A.M. by another patient with a steaming cup of tea. This man made motions to let him know that he wanted a copy of Doug's booklet—the gospel of John. Throughout that whole day, patients, nurses, and doctors kept coming to him and asking for his literature. By noon, all 350 of them had either a gospel of John, a gospel of Mark, or a gospel booklet. Over the weeks, many came to a saving knowledge of Christ.[1]

---

[1] Doug Nichols, *Let's Get On With It*, 1995 Desiring God Conference for Pastors, 1 Feb. 1995.

"Ordinary" Christians

While we should certainly draw encouragement and inspiration from such striking accounts, there is a danger that we may overlook and undervalue the many acts of Christlike love performed daily by "ordinary" Christians. From the student weeping in prayer for a lost roommate to the mother baking cookies for a next-door neighbor, the life and law of Christ is demonstrated daily in the lives of His people. This reality was impressed upon me in a fresh way recently, as I attended the funeral of one of these "ordinary" believers. When opportunity was given for those present to speak, I soon learned how extraordinary this ordinary Christian had been! I marveled as one coworker after another from his secular workplace stood and bore witness to the impact his love had made upon them personally. One Christian friend who had helped him cut firewood testified that as soon as the first truckload of wood was finished, it was taken immediately, not to the man's own home, but to an elderly neighbor who lived nearby. This is New Testament Christianity!

Many years ago, I lived for a time with a large family where Christlikeness was manifested daily in the home. One day, when the kitchen was filled with women busily preparing a meal for a large gathering of visitors, one of the children came into the midst of the activity and began to pour himself a glass of milk from the refrigerator. This unnecessary disturbance just a few minutes before lunch time would have been annoying enough in itself, but the child then proceeded to drop everything, scattering milk and glass all over the kitchen floor. His mother turned to him in disbelief and instantly responded by taking his face in her hands and warmly proclaiming, "Stephen, I love you!" That display of the law of Christ in action left an indelible impression on my mind and did more to convict a self-centered college student of his selfishness than a thousand "Thou shalt not" sermons ever could have!

Chapter Seventeen Review

Only eternity will tell how many times scenes like these have been reenacted down through church history. May God help us to "go and do likewise"!

Christ is the perfect and final revelation of God's character, and the "law of Christ" is the perfect and final revelation of God's law. To the degree that Christ's life is manifested in us, to that degree the superiority of the "law of Christ" to every other revelation of law will also be manifested.

This reality is illustrated daily in the lives of true Christians. A Christian who is filled with Christlike love will find himself fulfilling as a matter of course the Law's commandments against stealing, coveting, and adultery. Furthermore, he will do this in a positive way that far surpasses the negative stipulations of the Law of Moses. The same is true with regard to "tithing" and other such requirements of the Old Testament.

It is in relation to conviction of sin, however, that the superiority of the law of Christ is seen most clearly. No standard of righteousness compares to the standard of Christ's own life and Person. It was a glimpse of the surpassing glory, kindness, and grace of Christ that caused Peter to cry out, "Depart from me, for I am a sinful man, O Lord!" And it was the preaching of "Christ and Him crucified" that the Holy Spirit used to convict and convert thousands of both Jews and Gentiles in the earliest days of the church.

Aside from the *preaching of Christ*, the Holy Spirit has also used the *manifestation of the life of Christ* in the daily practice of true Christians to convict men of sin. This often happens during "the second mile," when Christians have the opportunity to demonstrate Christlike love, patience, and forgiveness in a way that lost men and women have never before seen or experienced.

– Chapter Eighteen –

The Ministry of the Spirit—Part I

> Not that we are adequate in ourselves to consider anything as coming from ourselves, but our adequacy is from God, who also made us adequate as servants of a new covenant, not of the letter, but of the Spirit; for the letter kills, but the Spirit gives life. But if the ministry of death, in letters engraved on stones, came with glory, so that the sons of Israel could not look intently at the face of Moses because of the glory of his face, fading as it was, how shall the ministry of the Spirit fail to be even more with glory? For if the ministry of condemnation has glory, much more does the ministry of righteousness abound in glory. For indeed what had glory, in this case has no glory on account of the glory that surpasses it. For if that which fades away was with glory, much more that which remains is in glory.... Now the Lord is the Spirit; and where the Spirit of the Lord is, there is liberty. But we all, with unveiled face beholding as in a mirror the glory of the Lord, are being transformed into the same image from glory to glory, just as from the Lord, the Spirit. 2 Corinthians 3:5-11, 17-18

As we have seen repeatedly throughout this study, the Christian's standard of conduct is none other than Christ Himself. He is the ultimate and final revelation of the invisible God and His will for us. It should be obvious, then, to anyone who has had even a glimpse of "the glory of God in the face of Jesus Christ," that "the law of Christ" is both a wonderful and an impossible standard. Apart from a miracle, none of us has any hope of fulfilling, even in principle, such a glorious pattern.

It is part of the incomparable "good news" of the gospel that just such a miracle has taken place in the life of every Christian. In Christ, we are new creatures, with new hearts, living in a new realm—the realm of grace. By the regenerating power of the Holy Spirit, God's law—the law of love—has been written within us. And that law is fulfilled, not by slavish obedience to an external code, but by the outworking of an inward Power—the very life of Christ in us. The depth and passion of the love we owe to God and to our fellow men is beyond the ability of any commandment to produce in us, but it is not beyond the ability of Christ! Christ Himself, in the person of the Holy Spirit, has taken up residence in our hearts and by His Spirit manifests "the life of Jesus" in our mortal bodies.[1]

OLD VS. NEW

It is in this context that Paul's words from 2 Corinthians quoted above are seen in their proper perspective. In these verses, Paul strikingly contrasts the New Covenant with the Old.

	Old Covenant	**New Covenant**
v.6	"the letter"	"the Spirit"
v.6	"the letter kills"	"the Spirit gives life"
v.7, 8	"the ministry of death"	"the ministry of the Spirit"
v.7, 3	"in letters engraved on stones"	"on tablets of human hearts"
v.9	"the ministry of condemnation"	"the ministry of righteousness"
v.10	"what had glory … has no glory"	"on account of the glory that surpasses"
v.11	"that which fades away"	"that which remains"
v.17	["slavery"[2]]	"liberty"

---

[1] 2 Corinthians 4:7-10   [2] Galatians 4:24-25; 5:1

It is vital for us to understand that when Paul contrasts "the letter" with "the Spirit," he is not talking about "dead" Bible studies or sermons as opposed to those that are "full of life." Nor is he talking about the "literal" meaning of the Bible as opposed to its "spiritual" meaning. Instead, Paul is contrasting the Old Covenant's *external written code* ("the letter") with the New Covenant's *inward principle of life* ("the Spirit"). The Old Covenant, as an embodiment of the principle of *works*, was a "ministry of condemnation and death." By contrast, the New Covenant, as an embodiment of the principle of *grace*, is a "ministry of righteousness and the Spirit."

LETTER VS. SPIRIT

Over and over in the New Testament, this contrast between *letter* and *Spirit* is maintained. The difference between them is the difference between externals and internals, bondage and liberty, oldness and newness, slavery and sonship, death and life.

> For he is not a Jew who is one outwardly; neither is circumcision that which is *outward in the flesh*. But he is a Jew who is one inwardly; and circumcision is that which is *of the heart, by the Spirit, not by the letter;* and his praise is not from men, but from God.   Romans 2:28-29

> But now we have been *released from the Law,* having died to that by which we were bound, so that we serve in *newness of the Spirit* and not in *oldness of the letter.*   Romans 7:6

> For *the law of the Spirit of life* in Christ Jesus has *set you free* from the *law of sin and of death.*   Romans 8:2

> For what the Law could not do, weak as it was through the flesh, God did... in order that the requirement of the Law might be fulfilled in us, who do not walk according to the flesh, but according to the Spirit."   Romans 8:3-4

> If *by the Spirit* you are putting to death the deeds of the body, you will live. For all who are being *led by the Spirit of God,* these are sons of God. For you have not received a

THE LAW OF CHRIST

spirit of *slavery leading to fear again,* but you have received *a spirit of adoption as sons* by which we cry out, "Abba! Father!" Romans 8:13-15

For the kingdom of God is not *eating and drinking,* but *righteousness and peace and joy in the Holy Spirit.*

Romans 14:17

Now the Lord is the Spirit; *and where the Spirit of the Lord is, there is liberty.* But we all, with unveiled face beholding as in a mirror the glory of the Lord, are being transformed into the same image from glory to glory, *just as from the Lord, the Spirit.* 2 Corinthians 3:17-18

This is the only thing I want to find out from you: *did you receive the Spirit by the works of the Law,* or by hearing with faith? Are you so foolish? *Having begun by the Spirit,* are you now being perfected by the flesh?

Galatians 3:2-3

Does He then, *who provides you with the Spirit* and works miracles among you, *do it by the works of the Law,* or by hearing with faith? Galatians 3:5

Christ redeemed us from *the curse of the Law*... so that we might receive *the promise of the Spirit* through faith.

Galatians 3:13-14

God sent forth His Son, born of a woman, *born under the Law, in order that He might redeem those who were under the Law,* that we might receive the adoption as sons. And because you are sons, God has sent forth *the Spirit of His Son into our hearts,* crying, "Abba! Father!"

Galatians 4:4-6

You have been severed from Christ, you who are seeking to be *justified by law;* you have fallen from grace. For we *through the Spirit,* by faith, are waiting for the hope of righteousness. Galatians 5:4-5

> But if you are *led by the Spirit*, you are *not under the Law*.
> Galatians 5:18
>
> But the *fruit of the Spirit* is love, joy, peace, patience, kindness, goodness, faithfulness, gentleness, self-control; *against such things there is no law.*   Galatians 5:22-23

THE MINISTRY OF THE SPIRIT

It is very clear from these verses that any teaching concerning the "law of Christ" must be centered in the mighty reality of the Holy Spirit's New Covenant ministry. For Paul the contrast between the Old and New Covenants is not primarily a contrast between two kinds of laws—the Law of Moses and the law of Christ. The contrast is rather between "serving in oldness of the letter" and "serving in newness of the Spirit." Paul does not view the Christian life as being law-centered in any way. Instead, he views the Christian life as being *Christ-centered* and *Spirit-empowered.* The Christian has "died to the Law" that he might be "joined to another, to Him who was raised from the dead, that we might bear fruit for God."[1] The Christian does not unconsciously "walk in the Spirit" by consciously attempting to fulfill the Law; rather, he unconsciously "fulfills the Law" as he consciously seeks to walk in the Spirit: "For the law of the Spirit of life in Christ Jesus has set you free from the law of sin and of death....in order that the requirement of the Law might be fulfilled in us, who do not walk according to the flesh, but according to the Spirit."[2] This "walk in the Spirit" involves, among other things, obeying the Spirit's restraints when we sense in our hearts that He is "grieved" by something we are about to do.[3] It also involves obeying the Spirit's promptings when He urges us to do something positive—to speak up for God, or witness, or pray.[4]

It is highly significant that in the New Testament, sin is not thought of primarily in terms of breaking a list of written

---

[1] Romans 7:4   [2] Romans 8:2, 4   [3] Ephesians 4:30   [4] 1 Thessalonians 5:19

prohibitions, but in terms of grieving, quenching, resisting,[1] lying to,[2] testing,[3] insulting,[4] blaspheming[5] and otherwise offending a living Person—the Holy Spirit. On the other hand, godly living is spoken of in terms of living in the Spirit,[6] walking in the Spirit,[7] being led by the Spirit,[8] bearing the fruit of the Spirit,[9] being filled with the Spirit,[10] sowing to the Spirit,[11] rejoicing in the Spirit,[12] abounding in hope by the power of the Spirit,[13] praying in the Spirit,[14] worshiping in the Spirit,[15] being in the Spirit,[16] speaking words taught by the Spirit,[17] obeying the restraints of the Spirit,[18] being comforted by the Spirit,[19] serving in newness of the Spirit,[20] setting our minds on the things of the Spirit,[21] putting to death the deeds of the body by the power of the Spirit,[22] being strengthened by the Spirit,[23] preserving the unity of the Spirit,[24] loving in the Spirit,[25] having the joy of the Spirit,[26] guarding through the Spirit the treasure that has been given to us,[27] preaching the gospel by the Spirit,[28] casting out demons by the Spirit,[29] and listening to what the Spirit says![30] To these verses, many others might be added. It is not surprising, therefore, that Paul in 2 Corinthians 3 refers to the entire New Covenant as "the ministry of the Spirit."[31]

THE FRUIT OF THE SPIRIT

According to the New Testament, then, the Christian life is not a massive endeavor to keep a list of rules, whether that list is the Law of Moses or a new one updated by Christ in the Sermon on the Mount and made a thousand times more difficult to obey than the old one was. Instead, the Christian life is viewed as a matter of "walking in the Spirit." Rather than striving in our own power to

---

[1] Acts 7:51 [2] Acts 5:3 [3] Acts 5:9 [4] Hebrews 10:29 [5] Matthew 12:31-32
[6] Galatians 5:25 [7] Galatians 5:25 [8] Romans 8:14 [9] Galatians 5:22
[10] Ephesians 5:18 [11] Galatians 6:8 [12] Luke 10:21 [13] Romans 15:13
[14] Ephesians 6:18 [15] Philippians 3:3 [16] Revelation 1:10; Luke 2:27 [17] Luke 12:12; Acts 6:10; 1 Corinthians 2:13 [18] Acts 16:6-7 [19] Acts 9:31 [20] Romans 7:6 [21] Romans 8:5 [22] Romans 8:13 [23] Ephesians 3:16 [24] Ephesians 4:3
[25] Colossians 1:8 [26] Acts 13:52; Romans 14:17; 1 Thessalonians 1:6
[27] 2 Timothy 1:14 [28] 1 Peter 1:12 [29] Matthew 12:28
[30] Revelation 2:7, 11, 17, 29; 3:6, 13, 22 [31] 2 Corinthians 3:8

attain the impossible standards of the law of Christ, we are to rely on the Holy Spirit to produce the character of Christ in us. Every Christlike quality in the life of the New Covenant believer is viewed in the New Testament as being the "fruit" (i.e., natural outgrowth) of the Holy Spirit's powerful presence and activity.

Some have mistakenly thought that by diligently striving to obey the exacting standards of the law of Christ they can obtain more of the influence of the Holy Spirit in their lives. Just the opposite is taught in the Bible: The fruit of Christlikeness is not more of the Holy Spirit; rather, the fruit of the Holy Spirit is more Christlikeness. "The fruit *of the Spirit* is love, joy, peace, patience, kindness, goodness, faithfulness, gentleness, and self-control." "The kingdom of God is not eating and drinking (i.e., meticulous attention to rules and regulations), *but righteousness and peace and joy in the Holy Spirit*." The Holy Spirit is "provided" and miracles are accomplished, not by *works* but by *faith*.[1]

Christian, it is neither expected nor possible for you to produce righteousness, peace, or joy by your own efforts. Only by your being rightly related to the Holy Spirit can these qualities spring up in your life! Something of how this works in practice is described by Mari Jones in one of her parables taken from Welsh farm life. Living in the mountains of Wales, far from normal sources of electricity, the local farmers had taken advantage of a stream flowing down the mountainside.

> A dam had been built across the stream to divert the course of water to the intake, which was covered by a grating. Through this ran the water, the full force of it directed to a pipe which led, through a drop of some five hundred feet, to the turbine. Channeling the water in this way gave it a great increase of pressure and power to drive the turbine, which turned the dynamo that generated our electricity.[2]

---

[1] Galatians 3:2, 5   [2] Mari Jones, *When Swallows Return* (Bryntirion: Evangelical Press of Wales, 1992) 74-5.

In spite of this convenient arrangement, John and Mari Jones occasionally found themselves in darkness or semi-darkness. Why? Not because the waters of the stream had failed, but because high up the mountainside the grate had been blocked by sticks and debris. In such situations, the process of blockage often begins with only one small stick, but soon other branches follow, and eventually the influx of power from above is stopped almost completely. Only when the rubbish is removed from the grate, will the water begin to flow through the channel again and the lights shine brightly.

So it is with the Christian life! As Christians, we are not called upon to produce the power and light of the life of Christ. But we *are* called upon to remove any sticks and debris that may be blocking the free influx of that life to and through us. In short, we are called upon to *repent* of anything in our lives that may be quenching or grieving the Holy Spirit and to *believe* the promises that have been given us in Christ. Only then can we "present ourselves to God as those alive from the dead," [1] and rise to "walk in newness of life." [2]

How many times has every Christian experienced this reality! Finding himself dull and dry, the believer falls upon his knees to confess and be cleansed of the sins that are "choking the channels" of grace in his life. He then consciously places his trust in the promises of God regarding what has been done for him in Christ and rises to find himself immediately filled with a fresh sense of God's presence and power! Hallelujah! The power and the life are not ours, but Christ's!

> *Emptied that Thou shouldest fill me,*
> *A clean vessel in Thy hand;*
> *With no power but as Thou givest,*
> *Graciously with each command.*
> *Channels only, blessed Master,*
> *But with all Thy wondrous power,*
> *Flowing through us, Thou canst use us*
> *Every day and every hour.*
>
> Mary Maxwell

---

[1] Romans 6:13   [2] Romans 6:4

Chapter Eighteen Review

It is highly significant that in the New Testament, sin is not thought of primarily in terms of breaking a list of written prohibitions, but in terms of offending a living Person—the Holy Spirit. Likewise, godly living is not spoken of in terms of following a written code, but of living and walking "in the Spirit." Christians serve in "newness of the Spirit" and not in "the oldness of the letter." According to Paul, the entire New Covenant can be characterized as "the ministry of the Spirit."

Every Christlike quality in the life of the New Covenant believer is viewed in the New Testament as being the "fruit" of the Holy Spirit's powerful presence and activity. Only by our being rightly related to the Holy Spirit can qualities of Christlikeness spring up in our lives. As Christians, we are not called upon to produce the power and light of the life of Christ, but we are called upon *to repent* of anything in our lives that may be quenching or grieving the Holy Spirit and *to believe* the promises that have been given us in Christ.

– Chapter Nineteen –

THE MINISTRY OF THE SPIRIT—PART II

> But the fruit of the Spirit is love, joy, peace, patience, kindness, goodness, faithfulness, gentleness, self-control....
> Galatians 5:22-23

> You are already clean because of the word which I have spoken to you. Abide in Me, and I in you. As the branch cannot bear fruit of itself, unless it abides in the vine, so neither can you, unless you abide in Me. I am the vine, you are the branches; he who abides in Me, and I in him, he bears much fruit; for apart from Me you can do nothing.
> John 15:3-5

In 2 Corinthians 3, Paul refers to the entire New Covenant as "the ministry of the Spirit." It is not surprising, then, that the Christian life can be lived only by way of a constant provision of the Holy Spirit's divine power. This reality is clearly seen, not only in Paul's emphasis on "the fruit of the Spirit," but in our Lord's teaching concerning the vine and the branches. According to the Lord Jesus, no "branch" is able to bear fruit "of itself": "I am the vine, you are the branches; he who abides in Me, and I in him, he bears much fruit; *for apart from Me you can do nothing.*"

THE VINE AND THE BRANCHES

If our Lord's metaphor of the vine and the branches is meant to teach us anything, surely it is meant to teach us this: that the life flowing in us as Christians is the very life of Christ! Christians are partakers of the "life of God in the soul of man." Branches cannot bear fruit "of themselves"; they only bear fruit as they receive an inflow of sap from the vine. "Abide in Me, and I in you. As the branch cannot bear fruit of itself, unless it abides in the vine, so neither can you, unless you abide in Me." Beloved Christian, we *cannot* produce fruit *of ourselves!* God has put His very life within us, and the way we "bear fruit," according to the Lord Jesus Christ, is by "abiding in the vine."

When we think of "abiding in Christ," we must always remember that the most basic meaning of the word "abide" is "to stay or remain." Too often Christians have viewed "abiding" as *a feat to be accomplished.* However, by using the word "abide" to describe our responsibility in fruit-bearing, our Lord places the emphasis, not on *attaining,* but on *remaining!* The call to "abide" is not so much a call to "do something," as it is a call to "live where we are"! The most important thing, therefore, that we can learn from the command to "abide" is the fact of *our present position* of union with Christ, as partakers of His very life.

In the natural realm, those who remain ("abide") long enough in one place are said to "dwell" there; that place becomes their "abode." So it is with Christ; those who abide in Christ, "dwell" in Him, and He in them.

> If anyone loves Me, he will keep My word; and My Father will love him, and We will come to him, and make Our abode [a *residence* or *abiding*] with him.   John 14:23

> He who eats My flesh and drinks My blood *abides in Me, and I in him.* As the living Father sent Me, and I live because of the Father, so he who eats Me, he also shall live because of Me.   John 6:56-57

It is clear from these verses that abiding in Christ has to do with loving Him, obeying Him, and drawing our life from Him by "eating His flesh and drinking His blood." These words are not, of course, to be taken literally, as they were by the Jews.[1] "It is the Spirit who gives life; the flesh profits nothing; the words that I have spoken to you are spirit and are life."[2] To eat Christ's flesh and drink His blood has to do with *coming* to Him and *believing* on Him, as the

---

[1] John 6:52   [2] John 6:63

preceding context makes clear.[1] This "coming" and "believing" is not a one-time thing, but involves a lifetime of intimate *fellowship, dependence,* and *appropriation*. The result of such "abiding" will be "fruit": "He who abides in Me, and I in him, he bears much fruit."[2]

BEHOLDING THE GLORY OF CHRIST

In spite of our Lord's teaching concerning the vine and the branches, many Christians still seem to think that they will bear fruit primarily by focusing their attention on the Law. Large volumes, hundreds of pages in length, have been written expositing the Ten Commandments in an attempt to help Christians grow in grace. Samuel Bolton, one of the Puritans, expressed his convictions like this: "While you are in the wilderness of this world, you must walk under the conduct of Moses.... The law sends us to the Gospel that we may be justified; and the Gospel sends us to the law again to inquire what is our duty as those who are justified."[3] It could perhaps be argued that Bolton meant something different than his words seem to imply, but his statements nevertheless point us in the wrong direction. Christ does not need to send us back to Moses for our rule of duty; His own example in word and deed is more than sufficient! Neither does He need to focus our attention on Moses for growth in grace; to gaze upon His own glorious Person is more than adequate to transform us into His image.

The way for us to grow as Christians is not to constantly center our attention on "law and duty," even New Testament law and duty; the way for us to grow as Christians is to center our attention on Christ! In the very passage where Paul characterizes the entire New Covenant as "the ministry of the Spirit," he describes the glorious transformation that takes place in all those who gaze on Christ. As we might expect from the context, this transformation takes place through the *Spirit's* power; it is "from the Lord, the Spirit": "Now the Lord is the Spirit; and where the Spirit of the Lord is, there is

---

[1] John 6:35, 47, 50-54 [2] John 15:5 [3] Samuel Bolton, *The True Bounds of Christian Freedom* (London: Banner of Truth, 1964) 76, 71.

liberty. But we all, with unveiled face *beholding as in a mirror the glory of the Lord, are being transformed into the same image from glory to glory*, just as *from* the Lord, *the Spirit*." [1]

These verses do not speak, in the first place, of striving to be like Christ, but of just "beholding" Him. Many zealous new Christians work themselves to exhaustion, yet fail utterly in their attempt to duplicate Christ's character in their own lives. They are so caught up in striving to be like Christ that they never take time for the one thing that will transform them into Christ's image—beholding Him!

Beloved Christian, behold Christ! For a few moments, stop striving to be like Him, and just behold Him in His glory and beauty! Meditate on His words and works recorded in the gospel records. Behold His awful majesty as He calms storms, raises the dead, and forgives sins. Think of His tender love and humility as He washes the disciples' feet, bears with their constant failings, and "loves them to the end." [2] See Him in the garden sweating drops of blood for you and on the cross dying under your curse. Behold Him seated at the right hand of the Father, crowned with all glory and honor, still loving you as a bridegroom loves his bride. Fall down before Him and worship Him. Tell Him how much you love Him, in spite of all your failings and shortcomings. Confess your sins to Him and acknowledge your utter dependence upon Him. Trust in the glorious reality of His love for you and your union with Him. In short, *cultivate a love relationship with Him*. The way of holiness is ultimately a love relationship with Christ, empowered by the Holy Spirit.

> *Jesus, I am resting, resting in the joy of what Thou art;*
> *I am finding out the greatness of Thy loving heart.*
> *Thou hast bid me gaze upon Thee, and Thy beauty fills my soul,*
> *For, by Thy transforming power, Thou hast made me whole.*
>
> Jean Sophia Pigott

---

[1] 2 Corinthians 3:17-18   [2] John 13:1

THE MINISTRY OF THE SPIRIT—PART II

Cultivating a Love Relationship

According to the Bible, the Christian's relationship to Christ is of the most intimate sort imaginable. It is described in Ephesians 5:22-32 as the *reality* of which the intimacy of human marriage is but a *shadow*. Christians have been "joined to Christ" in a living union that results in bearing fruit for God: "Therefore, my brethren, you also were made to die to the Law...that you might be joined to another, to Him who was raised from the dead, that we might bear fruit for God."[1]

The first and greatest calling of the Christian is to love God. As simple as it may seem, it still bears repeating that the Christian life is not a matter of keeping a list of rules, but of pursuing a love relationship with a living Person. What husband, returning from a long journey, would be pleased to find his wife greeting him in obedience to a list of rules? (1) Greet husband. (2) Hug husband. (3) Kiss husband. (4) Feed husband. Would not her concern to "check items off the list" actually be regarded as an insult to his person? Would he not much rather find her so thrilled by his return that she actually *neglects* to do some of the things that she should have done?

What a shame and a blot that we, as Christians, are so ready to forget our Heavenly Bridegroom and turn back to rule-keeping and routine in the Christian life! (1) Read Bible. (2) Say prayers. (3) Attend church. (4) Keep commandments! As fervent love for Christ wanes, legalism[2] invariably grows, and with it, an emphasis on externals. Outward conformity to a mental list of prescribed conduct becomes the yardstick by which men are measured, rather than the presence of inward life and love for God. Such a mindset always results in "biting and devouring"[3] one another and a loss of the "sense of blessing"[4] that we once had. Instead, we become "boastful, challenging one another, envying one another."[5]

A brand-new Christian, driving down the highway singing praises to God while he absent-mindedly breaks the speed limit, is

---

[1] Romans 7:4 [2] See Appendix F. [3] Galatians 5:15 [4] Galatians 4:15
[5] Galatians 5:26

far more pleasing to Christ than the most exacting "commandment-keeper" who has "left his first love."

> I know your deeds and your toil and perseverance, and that you cannot endure evil men, and you put to the test those who call themselves apostles, and they are not, and you found them to be false; and you have perseverance and have endured for My name's sake, and have not grown weary. *But I have this against you, that you have left your first love.* Revelation 2:2-4

According to these verses, the church at Ephesus had many commendable qualities. They had "toiled" and "persevered" and "endured" for "Christ's name's sake" and had "not grown weary." Yet, they had "left their first love." In the realm of human marriage, the marks of "first love" are well known. Every waking moment and every facet of life is affected by such love. Lovers think of one another constantly, long for each other's presence when separated, and delight in intimate conversation and expressions of love when together. They joyfully make great sacrifices in order to please one another in special ways. Even in the midst of other activities, the fragrance of their beloved one lingers in their memory, and when there is a leisure moment, their heart returns immediately to the object of its delight. Needless to say, no amount of "toil" and "perseverance" and "endurance" in the Christian life can make up for the lack of this "first love" in our relationship with Christ! On the other hand, if our hearts are overflowing with love for Him, we will certainly be enabled by that love to "toil and persevere."

"STRIVING"

The fact that Christians are not expected to bear fruit in their own strength, but by abiding in Christ and centering their affections upon Him, does not mean that the Christian life is painless and carefree. Both the Lord Jesus and His apostles speak of "striving" as a characteristic of believers.[1] Christians are called upon to pursue,[2] to run,[3] to fight,[4] to be diligent,[5] to be on guard,[6] to devote themselves,[7] and to cleanse themselves.[8] Often they must do this entirely "by faith," in spite of all "feelings" to the contrary. The call to love Christ with all our hearts is certainly not a call to ease, apathy, and self-indulgence. The Christian follows in the steps of his Master along a pathway that is often stained with tears, sweat, and blood. To love as Christ loved will cost us everything. "If anyone comes to Me, and does not hate his own father and mother and wife and children and brothers and sisters, yes, and even his own life, he cannot be My disciple. Whoever does not carry his own cross and come after Me cannot be My disciple."[9]

Love is the costliest of all endeavors.

> *Hast thou no scar?*
> *No hidden scar on foot, or side, or hand?*
> *I hear thee sung as mighty in the land;*
> *I hear them hail thy bright, ascendant star.*
> *Hast thou no scar?*
>
> *Hast thou no wound?*
> *Yet I was wounded by the archers; spent,*
> *Leaned Me against a tree to die; and rent*
> *By ravening beasts that compassed Me, I swooned;*
> *Hast thou no wound?*
>
> *No wound? No scar?*
> *Yet, as the Master shall the servant be,*
> *And piercèd are the feet that follow Me.*
> *But thine are whole; can he have followed far*
> *Who has nor wound nor scar?*
>
> Amy Carmichael

---

[1] Luke 13:24; Romans 15:30; Colossians 1:29; Hebrews 12:4 [2] 1 Timothy 6:11; 2 Timothy 2:22; Hebrews 12:14 [3] 1 Corinthians 9:24-27; Hebrews 12:1
[4] 1 Timothy 1:18; 6:12 [5] Hebrews 4:11; 6:11-12; 2 Peter 1:5, 10; 3:14
[6] Luke 21:34 [7] Colossians 4:2 [8] 2 Corinthians 7:1 [9] Luke 14:26-27

In this costly path of discipleship, nothing so motivates the believer to "follow hard" after his Lord as a burning sense of Christ's love to him "poured out"[1] in his heart by the Holy Spirit. Paul himself was "controlled"[2] by the love of Christ, and he prayed for the Ephesians that they, too, "being rooted and grounded in love," might come to "know the love of Christ which surpasses knowledge," that they might "be filled up to all the fulness of God."[3] Every glimpse of our Lord's unfathomable love for us melts the coldness of our hearts and fills them all the more with love for Him[4] and desire to please Him at any cost. This is well illustrated by the testimony of a young runner who, as the finish line drew closer, found himself far back in a field of superior athletes. It was *a glimpse of his father* standing near the finish line that drew from him his last burst of energy and caused him to pass one runner after another until he finally collapsed from exhaustion.

"According to His Power"

The mutual love between a believer and his Lord enables him to "bear and endure all things."[5] Yet this love relationship must be constantly sustained and renewed by the Holy Spirit. Christians must wait upon and draw their strength from the Lord. *"He gives strength to the weary, and to him who lacks might He increases power. Though youths grow weary and tired, and vigorous young men stumble badly, yet those who wait for the Lord will gain new strength; they will mount up with wings like eagles, they will run and not get tired, they will walk and not become weary."*[6] The Christian life involves endurance, warfare, suffering, self-denial, and costly obedience to Christ's commands. It involves "striving." But that striving is not a striving energized by our own flesh; it is a striving empowered by the Spirit. Paul knew this inner strengthening by the Holy Spirit as such a felt reality that it spontaneously came to his mind whenever the subjects of suffering or "laboring" arose:

---

[1] Romans 5:5   [2] 2 Corinthians 5:14-15   [3] Ephesians 3:14-19   [4] 1 John 4:19
[5] 1 Corinthians 13:7   [6] Isaiah 40:29-31

THE MINISTRY OF THE SPIRIT—PART II

- "And for this purpose also I labor, *striving according to His power, which mightily works within me*." [1]
- "Join with me in suffering for the gospel *according to the power of God*." [2]
- "But we have this treasure in earthen vessels, that *the surpassing greatness of the power* may be of God and not from ourselves; we are afflicted in every way, but not crushed; perplexed, but not despairing; persecuted, but not forsaken; struck down, but not destroyed; always carrying about in the body the dying of Jesus, *that the life of Jesus also may be manifested in our body*. For we who live are constantly being delivered over to death for Jesus' sake, *that the life of Jesus also may be manifested in our mortal flesh*." [3]
- "For this reason, I bow my knees before the Father... that He would grant you, according to the riches of His glory, to be *strengthened with power through His Spirit* in the inner man...." [4]
- "Be strong in the Lord and *in the strength of His might*." [5]

If all this seems foreign to us, it is because we know so little of the profusion and "outpouring" of the Holy Spirit that is evident in the New Testament. When the Holy Spirit is present in power, as in times of historic revival, these realities find their fullest and clearest manifestations. It is then that believers experience "joy inexpressible and full of glory" [6] and find themselves "continually filled with joy and with the Holy Spirit." [7] It is then that the love of God is "poured out within their hearts by the Holy Spirit" [8] and they find themselves agonizing in prayer with "groanings too deep for words." [9] It is then that they are filled with power to witness [10] and with overflowing love for their enemies. [11] These are the activities of the Spirit that Paul has in mind when he speaks of suffering for the gospel "according to the power of God."

---

[1] Colossians 1:29   [2] 2 Timothy 1:8   [3] 2 Corinthians 4:7-11
[4] Ephesians 3:14, 16   [5] Ephesians 6:10   [6] 1 Peter 1:8   [7] Acts 13:52
[8] Romans 5:5   [9] Romans 8:26   [10] Acts 4:31, 33   [11] Acts 7:55-60

Sarah Edwards

The testimony of Sarah Edwards (1710-1758) after an unusual outpouring of the Holy Spirit in her own life illustrates something of this reality:

> At the same time, my heart and soul all flowed out in love to Christ; so that there seemed to be a constant flowing and reflowing of heavenly and divine love, from Christ's heart to mine; and I appeared to myself to float or swim, in these bright, sweet beams of the love of Christ, like the motes swimming in the beams of the sun, or the streams of his light which come in at the window.... When I arose on the morning of the Sabbath, *I felt a love to all mankind, wholly peculiar in its strength and sweetness, far beyond all that I had ever felt before. The power of that love seemed to be inexpressible. I thought, if I were surrounded by enemies, who were venting their malice and cruelty upon me, in tormenting me, it would still be impossible that I should cherish any feelings towards them but those of love, and pity, and ardent desires for their happiness.*[1]

Dirk Willems

A further account from the life of Dirk Willems (died 1569) provides an example of this supernatural Christlike love for one's enemies as it is lived out under the most trying circumstances.

> Dirk Willems lived in Asperen in the Netherlands during the later years of the Catholic persecution under the rule of the Duke of Alva. In 1569, he was tried and convicted of being an Anabaptist. In his official sentence, Dirk was charged with such "crimes" as having been himself "rebaptized" in Rotterdam as a young man and as having "permitted several persons to be rebaptized in his aforesaid

---

[1] *The Works of Jonathan Edwards* (1834; reprint, Edinburgh: Banner of Truth, 1979) 1.lxv-lxvii.

house; all of which is contrary to our holy Christian faith." For this, the court sentenced him to "be executed with fire, until death ensues" and declared "all his property confiscated, for the benefit of his royal majesty."

The unusual part of Dirk's story begins when he managed to escape from the castle that served as his prison. He did this by letting himself out of a window on a rope made of knotted rags and dropping to the ice-covered moat below. A guard who saw him escaping pursued him. Because Dirk's weight had been reduced by eating only prison rations, he was able to cross the thin ice of a pond safely, but his pursuer, being heavier, broke through the ice. When Dirk heard the guard's cries for help and realized that his life was in danger, he returned to rescue him. After this act of mercy, he was seized once more by the guard and led back to prison.

This time, Dirk was placed in a small, heavily barred room at the top of a tall church tower. It was not long before he was brought forth to be burned at the stake. Witnesses of the execution said that he suffered excessive pain in his death because of the bungling of his executioners and the strong wind that blew the flames away from the upper half of his body.[1]

This account of one Christian's compassion for his enemies, in spite of their extreme wickedness and hardness of heart, still lives among the citizens of Asperen after more than four hundred years. In fact, they recently named one of their streets in his honor.[2] Who can tell how much glory God has received from this one man's actions or how many have been pointed to Christ as a result?

---

[1] Thieleman J. van Braght, *Martyrs Mirror* (1886; reprint, Scottdale, PA: Herald Press, 1985) 741-2. [2] John S. Oyer and Robert S. Kreider, *Mirror of the Martyrs* (Intercourse, PA: Good Books, 1990) 36-7.

HOWELL HARRIS

Howell Harris (1714-1773), who suffered much for the cause of Christ, provides a final example of the mighty empowering of the Holy Spirit for service, sacrifice, and love. As an open-air preacher and "exhorter" during the Evangelical Awakening of the eighteen century, he not only endured continual insults and threats of death, but also had rocks, dirt, and dead animals hurled at him while preaching to unruly mobs. In his diary, he tells the source of his great strength and perseverance:

> Were it not for that love I had experienced I would have drawn back, I would have given up. I could never have struggled against the flood. *Love fell in showers on my soul so that I could scarce contain and control myself.* I knew no fear and had no doubt whatsoever as to my salvation.[1]
>
> I felt I was all love—so full of it that I could not ask for more.... *the strength of the love I experienced enabled me to go through all oppositions that came up against me.* All fears vanished, and I was as one established upon a rock.... I was comfortably and powerfully led by perpetual outpourings of love into my soul almost every time I prayed. Such a coward was I by nature, and such power the Lord gave unto me![2]

Only this powerful New Covenant "ministry of the Spirit" is sufficient to enable us, in some small measure, to love as Christ loved and thus "fulfill the law of Christ." For this reason, all Christians should come repeatedly to their heavenly Father "asking, seeking, and knocking" for more of the Holy Spirit's presence and power in their lives. We have our Lord's assurance that, of all the possible prayers that we might pray, this is the one most certain to be in accordance with His will and most certain to be answered! It

---

[1] D. Martyn Lloyd-Jones, *The Sons of God* (Grand Rapids, MI: Zondervan, 1975) 349. [2] Richard Bennett, *Howell Harris and the Dawn of Revival* (Bryntirion, Bridgend: Evangelical Press of Wales, 1962) 31.

THE MINISTRY OF THE SPIRIT—PART II

is also the one that involves the bestowal of the greatest gift—the Holy Spirit Himself!

> *And I say to you, ask, and it shall be given to you; seek, and you shall find; knock, and it shall be opened to you. For everyone who asks, receives; and he who seeks, finds; and to him who knocks, it shall be opened.* Now suppose one of you fathers is asked by his son for a fish; he will not give him a snake instead of a fish, will he? Or if he is asked for an egg, he will not give him a scorpion, will he? If you then, being evil, know how to give good gifts to your children, *how much more shall your heavenly Father give the Holy Spirit to those who ask Him?* Luke 11:9-13

Let us cry to God continually for the gift of His Spirit. Oh, that we might know more of His mighty working in our daily lives!

> Now to Him who is *able to do exceeding abundantly beyond all that we ask or think, according to the power that works within us,* to Him be the glory in the church and in Christ Jesus to all generations forever and ever. Amen.
>
> Ephesians 3:20-21

Chapter Nineteen Review

According to the New Testament, the Christian life can be lived only by way of a constant influx of the Holy Spirit's divine power. This reality is clearly seen, not only in Paul's emphasis on "the fruit of the Spirit," but also in our Lord's teaching concerning the vine and the branches. No branch can bear fruit "of itself," but only as it "abides" in the vine.

This same truth is illustrated by Paul's teaching that Christian growth is a result of gazing upon the glory of Christ. It is by "beholding the glory of the Lord" that we "are being transformed into the same image from glory to glory, just as from the Lord, the Spirit."

Again, the New Testament speaks of Christian "fruitfulness" as being the result of a marriage union between Christ and the believer. We have "died to the Law ... that we might be joined to another, to Him who was raised from the dead, that we might bear fruit for God." The Christian life is a love relationship with a living Person.

The Christian life also involves "striving"; it is not a life of ease and self-indulgence. Love is the costliest of all endeavors. Nevertheless, this striving is not in our own strength, but "according to the Lord's power, which mightily works within us." It is when the Holy Spirit is present in power that Christians are filled with overflowing love for their enemies and enabled to persevere under the most trying circumstances. We must cry to God for more of the Spirit's presence and power in our lives!

Conclusion

As we look back over the preceding chapters, we see a magnificent picture emerging: The "Sunrise from on High" has visited us; *God* has come into this dark world in the Person of Jesus Christ to redeem His sinful creatures! Christ's glory is a unique glory—"glory as of the only begotten from the Father, full of grace and truth." All of human history prior to His coming was only a preparation for Him. He is the focal point of all history.

In preparation for Christ's coming, God established covenants with men. His promises to Abraham set forth His gracious, immutable, and sovereign purpose to save a multitude of fallen humanity, by grace alone, through faith alone. His covenant with Moses set forth the immutable principles of righteousness that must be met in order for that salvation to be accomplished. By fulfilling in every way the just requirements of the Law, the Lord Jesus Christ also made possible the fulfillment of God's promise to Abraham that "all the nations of the earth" would be "blessed" in him.[1]

Christ saves His people by taking them into union with Himself. If we "belong to Christ, then we are Abraham's offspring, heirs according to promise."[2] All the blessings of salvation promised to Abraham's "seed" are ours "in Christ"; none of them come to us "on their own" or apart from Him.

In Christ, we are new creatures, with new hearts. We live in a new realm, the realm of grace, under a new covenant—a covenant in which every participant, "from the least to the greatest," knows God personally. God's law—the law of love—has been written within us. And that law is fulfilled, not by obedience to an external code, but by the outworking of an inward power—the very life of Christ in us.

Our standard is Christ. He is the ultimate and final revelation of the invisible God and His will for us. Christ lives in us by His Spirit to guide us into all truth and to reproduce His character in our

---

[1] Genesis 18:18   [2] Galatians 3:29

lives. We serve in "newness of the Spirit" and not in the "oldness of the letter." Our goal is that we might "know Christ, and the power of His resurrection and the fellowship of His sufferings."[1]

Love is at the very heart and center of the Christian life. Our *reason for existence* is that we might *love God* with all our heart, soul, mind, and strength, and *our neighbor* as ourselves. It is in this way that we will both glorify God and enjoy Him forever.

Such a salvation is glorious beyond imagination. *Nothing* could be more wonderful than to be a redeemed man or woman "in Christ"—"flesh of His flesh and bone of His bones"![2] Hallelujah!

> *Were the whole realm of nature mine,*
> *That were an offering far too small;*
> *Love so amazing, so divine,*
> *Demands my soul, my life, my all.*
>
> *But drops of grief can ne'er repay*
> *The debt of love I owe;*
> *Here, Lord, I give myself away;*
> *'Tis all that I can do.*
>
> Isaac Watts

---

[1] Philippians 3:10 [2] Genesis 2:23; Ephesians 5:28-32

I. LOVE

"On these two commandments hang the whole Law and the Prophets."

II. LOVE

Part Four

Appendices

Appendix A

Key Concepts

The Flow of Redemptive History

- God's saving purpose in Christ is the unifying principle that underlies and ties together all of God's dealings in human history, including the various covenants He has made at specific times with specific people.
- *Christ* is the focal point and goal of the entire Bible.
- The Abrahamic Covenant is based on *promise*, and is therefore *unconditional*, *immutable*, and *certain*.
- The Mosaic Covenant (Law) is characterized by the principle that *life* is contingent on *doing*, and therefore represents a *covenant of works*.
- In the New Covenant, promise is swallowed up as *anticipation* gives way to *realization*, and Law is swallowed up as *demand* gives way to *satisfaction*.

Freedom from the Law

- Christians have been released from the curse of the Law, they have been released from the Law as a requirement for obtaining favor and life, they have been released from the Law as an external rule that contradicts their real nature, and they have been released from the Law as a realm of demand as opposed to a realm of supply. They have also been released from the Law (and all of its 613 commandments) as a covenant rule of duty.
- The Lord Jesus Christ has swallowed up and replaced Moses as Prophet, just as He swallowed up and replaced Aaron as Priest and David as King.

- The law of Christ surpasses the Law of Moses as far as *sonship* surpasses *slavery*.
- *None* of the commandments of the Old Covenant bind us directly as covenant law, but *every one* of them has indirect relevance to us as part of God's revelation in Scripture.
- The way in which we can be certain to "keep and teach" every commandment of the Old Testament—whether "weighty" or "least"—is not only *by reverencing the Old Testament as the Word of God*, but *by believing on and following closely our Lord and Master*, who in His Person and teachings is the "fulfillment" of the "smallest letter and stroke" of the Law.
- Christians do not keep and teach the least commandments of the Law and prophets *by codifying a new "list of rules"* from the (spiritually interpreted) laws of the Old Testament, but *by walking in love by the power of the Spirit*.

The Law of Christ

- The one "new commandment" that Christ gave His disciples in the Upper Room is "new" because it is associated with a *new covenant*, because it imparts an entirely *new depth of meaning* to the word "love," and because it is given to those who belong to *a new realm* where "the darkness is passing away, and the true light is already shining."
- *Love* is the very heart and essence of the Law!
- The two great commandments are the unchanging moral obligation resting upon all men in all places throughout all time and eternity.
- The *essence* of the law never changes, but the *revelation* of law takes on clearer and clearer expression, until it finds its culmination in Christ.
- Love does more than impel me to keep the law; love *is* itself "the fulfillment of the law."
- *Love is man's supreme duty.* Law, in its essence, is nothing more than *the obligation to love.* And *love*—acting according to its own nature in the created order where God has placed it —is *the fulfillment of the law.*

KEY CONCEPTS

- We are to love one another "as Christ has loved us." *Christ Himself* is our "law"—our highest example and standard.

- The commandment to "love one another" has very real and practical applications that are spelled out in the many "one another" exhortations of the New Testament.

- The law of Christ is as inexhaustible as the Person of Christ Himself!

- The emphasis of the New Testament is, therefore, not on any codified list of commandments and prohibitions as our standard of conduct, but on *Christlike love* that is empowered and directed by *Christ Himself* through the Holy Spirit.

- To the degree Christ's life is manifested in us, to that degree the superiority of the "law of Christ" to every other "law" will also be manifested.

- It is highly significant that in the New Testament, sin is thought of primarily in terms of offending a living Person—the Holy Spirit. Likewise, godly living is spoken of in terms of living "in the Spirit," walking "in the Spirit," and bearing the "fruit of the Spirit."

- As Christians, we are not called upon to produce the power and light of the life of Christ ourselves, but we are called upon *to repent* of anything in our lives that may be quenching or grieving the Holy Spirit and *to believe* the promises that have been given us in Christ. We will then be enabled to "present ourselves to God as those alive from the dead," and to rise to "walk in newness of life."

- The Christian life involves endurance, warfare, suffering, self-denial, and costly obedience to Christ's commands. It involves "striving." This striving, however, is not meant to be done in our *own* strength, but "according to the *Lord's* power, which mightily works within us."

- Only the powerful New Covenant "ministry of the Spirit" is sufficient to enable us, in some small measure, to love as Christ loved and thus "fulfill the law of Christ." For this reason, all Christians should come repeatedly to their heavenly Father "asking, seeking, and knocking" for more of the Holy Spirit's presence and power in their lives.

Appendix B

"God is Love"

> The one who does not love does not know God, for *God is love*. 1 John 4:8

> *God is love*, and the one who abides in love abides in God, and God abides in him. 1 John 4:16

John's declaration that "God is love" is one of the most simple and profound statements of the entire Bible. The authors of Scripture often say that God is merciful, or faithful, or just, but never do they say that He is mercy, or faithfulness, or justice. Yet, here John asserts not only that God is *loving*, but that *God is love!* This led Jonathan Edwards to affirm that "the Godhead or the divine nature and essence does subsist in love." And Octavius Winslow, in his sermon on "The God of Love" (1870), maintains:

> Love is not so much an attribute of God as it is His very essence. It is not so much a moral perfection of His being as it is His being itself. He would not be God were He not love.... Love is so completely the essence of God that it shines out in every perfection of His nature, and is exhibited in every act of His administration.... He is nothing, and can do nothing in which His love is not an essential quality.... omnipotence is the power of love; omniscience is the eye of love; omnipresence is the atmosphere of love; holiness is the purity of love; justice is the fire of love.... God is essential love.

Though some of these statements may go beyond what is certainly implied by the fact that "God is love," they surely come closer to reality than many (more carefully worded) systematic theology texts. Often in those texts, the love of God is relegated to a minor *subheading* under the general topic of God's "goodness"!

The fact that "God is love" does not mean that we can logically reduce all His other attributes to love. Nevertheless, it surely does mean that love is the *central and essential* moral characteristic of His being. When God promises to show Moses "His glory" and "make all His goodness" pass before him, it is His *love* that is preeminent: "The LORD, the LORD God, compassionate and gracious, slow to anger, and abounding in lovingkindness and truth; who keeps lovingkindness for thousands, who forgives iniquity, transgression and sin."[1]

This does not mean that God will "by any means leave the guilty unpunished,"[2] but it does mean that He "does not *afflict willingly* or grieve the sons of men."[3] Rather, God has "*no* pleasure in the death of *anyone* who dies."[4]

Even John's statement that "God is light"[5] has a direct moral connection with the fact that "God is love": "The one who *loves* his brother abides in the *light*... the one who *hates* his brother is in the *darkness*."[6] This direct connection between *love* and *light* is not surprising, since the Bible associates "light" with life,[7] spiritual understanding,[8] disclosure,[9] and goodness,[10] whereas "darkness" has to do with death,[11] spiritual blindness,[12] things hidden because of shame,[12] and evil.[14]

---

[1] Exodus 34:6-7; see also Psalm 103:7-18. [2] Exodus 34:7 [3] Lamentations 3:31-33 [4] Ezekiel 18:31-32; 33:11 [5] 1 John 1:5 [6] 1 John 2:8-11 [7] John 1:4; 8:12 [8] 2 Corinthians 4:6; Luke 2:32 [9] Ephesians 5:13; John 3:21 [10] Matthew 5:16; 2 Corinthians 6:14; Ephesians 5:8-9 [11] Matthew 4:16 [12] 2 Corinthians 4:4; Matthew 6:23 [13] 2 Corinthians 4:2; John 3:20; Ephesians 5:11-12
[14] Isaiah 5:20; Luke 22:53; Acts 26:18

Appendix C

"CIVIL, CEREMONIAL, AND MORAL"

It has been customary for Reformed theologians to follow Aquinas (1225-1274) in dividing the laws of the Old Covenant into three categories: civil, ceremonial, and moral. *Civil* laws were those laws that related specifically to the governing of the theocracy and included such things as the procedures to be followed in cases of manslaughter,[1] the specific penalty for adultery,[2] and other concerns of social justice. *Ceremonial* laws, on the other hand, concerned matters like circumcision, ritual washings,[3] and the offering of sacrifices.[4] *Moral* laws were those laws that related directly to the character of God, such as the commandments not to murder or bear false witness against our neighbor.

The fact that the Bible does not specifically use terms such as "civil, ceremonial, and moral" does not mean that these concepts are inherently unbiblical. They are easy to grasp and, in some ways, helpful in understanding the laws of the Old Covenant. Most Christians (because of their New Covenant perspective) can recognize fairly quickly the more obvious examples of civil, ceremonial, and moral laws within the Mosaic legislation. Nevertheless, this mental division of the Mosaic Law into "categories" has led to much confusion and misunderstanding in the interpretation of Scripture.

THE LAW—A UNIT

The first problem (and it is a major one) arises from the fact that the New Testament everywhere views the Law of Moses as a unit. When Paul says that Christians are "no longer under a

---

[1] Exodus 21:12-14   [2] Leviticus 20:10   [3] Exodus 30:18-21   [4] Exodus 29:36-42

tutor," [1] he is speaking of the entire Mosaic economy, not just one part of it. Likewise, when he says that we have been "released from the Law, having died to that by which we were bound, so that we serve in newness of the Spirit and not in oldness of the letter," [2] he is speaking of release from the Law *as a whole*. Christians have moved out of the whole "realm" of law; they are "not under law, but under grace." [3] To put ourselves under any *part* of the Law is, therefore, to put ourselves under *all* of it.[4]

The Lord Jesus Christ had a similar mindset concerning the unity of the Law. When He drew examples from the Mosaic Law in order to set forth (by contrast) the laws of His kingdom,[5] He did not make a distinction between (for example) the Ten Commandments and the other commandments. Instead, He took illustrations from throughout the Law, including those commands that concerned oaths, divorce, civil justice ("an eye for an eye"), and treatment of enemies.

In the vast majority of cases in the New Testament, the word "Law" is thus a reference to the Mosaic Law as a covenantal unit. If we unconsciously impose our own "civil, ceremonial, and moral" categories upon verses that speak about the Law, we will therefore certainly misunderstand them. For example, when Paul says that we are not "under law" in Romans 6:14, many automatically read into these words the thought that we are "not under the condemnation of the law" or "not under the ceremonial law," but are "still under the moral law." But if this were Paul's meaning, he would never have anticipated the objection that immediately follows: "What then? Shall we *sin* because we are not under law but under grace?"

The same is true of Galatians 5:13. "For you were called to freedom, brethren; only do not turn your freedom into an opportunity for the flesh, but through love serve one another." If Paul had been teaching the Galatians that they were "freed" only from the "ceremonial law," but not the Law as a whole, he would never have anticipated the possibility that they might be tempted

---

[1] Galatians 3:25   [2] Romans 7:6   [3] Romans 6:14   [4] Galatians 5:3
[5] Matthew 5:20f

to "turn their freedom into an opportunity for the flesh." The fact is that Paul was teaching the Galatians that Christians have been "released" from the Law in its entirety. Christians are not "under the Law"! Even in matters that related to holy living, Paul was not *Law-centered* (not even "moral law as-it-is-found-in-the-Mosaic-legislation" centered) but *Christ-centered*. For Paul, holy living is secured in believers, not by their concentrating on the Law, but by the reality of their having died to sin (and Law!) in Christ and having been raised up with Him "to walk in newness of life"[1] by the power of the Holy Spirit.[2] Those who walk in *love* by the power of the *Spirit* will unconsciously "fulfill" the Law *as a by-product* of the Spirit's promptings and "fruit."[3]

CIVIL, OR CEREMONIAL, OR MORAL?

But there is a second problem with the "civil, ceremonial, moral" division. Who is qualified to decide which commandments of the Mosaic Law are moral, which are civil, and which are ceremonial? Who has the authority to tell us which commandments are "light" and which are "weighty"? Often a single commandment of the Old Covenant will seemingly include more than one category,[4] and the greatest commandments are sometimes "mixed in" with the most apparently insignificant.[5] Who is to decide "which is which"?

The answer to this question is that *no one is qualified to decide these matters except the inspired writers of Scripture*. While the Old Testament points us in the right direction,[6] it still leaves the majority of such matters unanswered. No Jew, for example, would have ever considered circumcision to be a "light" commandment; after all, Moses nearly lost his life because of it! It is not until we come to the *New Testament* that we learn that circumcision is "nothing"![7] And it is not until we come to the New Testament that we learn that *the second greatest commandment in the Law* actually appears in the

---

[1] Romans 6:1-6 [2] Romans 7:4-6; see Chapters 18-19. [3] Galatians 5:13-25; Romans 8:4 [4] Exodus 22:25 [5] Leviticus 19:18-19 [6] Micah 6:6-8; Hosea 6:6; Psalm 51:16-17; Proverbs 21:3 [7] 1 Corinthians 7:19; Galatians 5:6; 6:15

Old Covenant *immediately* next to a commandment not to "breed together two kinds of cattle"![1]

We are dependent, then, upon the teachings of the New Testament for an authoritative answer as to which commandments are "weighty"[2] and which are "nothing." The problem is that the New Testament (just like the Old) never gives us a detailed list of everything that is "moral" in the Mosaic Law. Instead, it only gives us "pointers" as to which things are most important. For example, it tells us that "love" is at the center of the Law, that circumcision is "nothing," and that the sacrifices of the Old Covenant are now fulfilled and ended in Christ. It is only because of these "pointers" that the "civil, ceremonial, and moral" categories work as well as they do. Christians, *because of their New Covenant perspective,* can recognize easily the more obvious examples of "ceremonial" and "civil" laws. Nevertheless, when it comes to less obvious matters that are not spelled out in the New Testament, there are a great many areas where these distinctions are blurred and many harmful disagreements arise. This is only to be expected, *since the Bible itself never divides the Law into categories.*

"The Unchanging Moral Law"

The third problem with the "civil, ceremonial, and moral" categories arises from the fact that many in the Reformed tradition have proceeded to equate the "moral law" with the Ten Commandments. As we have seen, the Bible itself does not even speak of "the moral law"; much less does it equate "the moral law" with the Decalogue! Those who do equate the two face many difficulties.

Polygamy

For example, most Christians would surely maintain that for a New Covenant believer to knowingly enter into a polygamous relationship would be an act of adultery.[3] Yet under the Old Covenant (which was summarized by "the words of the covenant,

---

[1] Leviticus 19:18-19   [2] Matthew 23:23   [3] Romans 7:3; 1 Corinthians 7:2

the Ten Commandments,"[1] including the Seventh Commandment against adultery), polygamy was not only permitted, but laws were given concerning who could become a second wife, how the various wives were to be treated, etc.[2] When David married multiple wives, God showed no open displeasure,[3] but when he committed adultery with Bathsheba, He chastened him severely.[4]

In addition to polygamy, we must face the issue of "concubines," which were also permitted under the Ten Commandments. Even the most gifted theologians seem unable to explain to their young children (or their teenagers, for that matter) *exactly what a concubine was* and why God allowed men like David and Solomon to have them! If the Decalogue is indeed the "unchanging moral law of God," are we willing to accept its definition of "adultery," which allows both multiple wives and concubines within its boundaries?

The permission of polygamy under the Old Covenant has often been compared to the permission of divorce, which was, according to the Lord Jesus, a concession to men's "hardness of heart."[5] This is surely true, and the laws related to polygamy should not be taken as endorsements of the practice, but as regulations to protect women. This observation, however, does not really touch on the issue at hand. If one of the Ten Commandments had been, "You shall not divorce your wife," and yet God had permitted divorce, *then* the situation would have been parallel. As it is, God said, "You shall not commit adultery," and yet permitted polygamy and concubines. We can agree that polygamy was a concession to the hardness of men's hearts in a particular cultural setting. We can also agree that its practice by men like David and Solomon constituted a transgression of perfect love and of God's original intention for marriage.[6] But we cannot agree that polygamy constituted an act of *adultery* on their part, because it is clear from the Old Testament narrative that it did not. Clearly, the definition of "adultery" has changed between that of the Seventh Commandment and that of the New Testament.

---

[1] Exodus 34:28; Deuteronomy 4:13   [2] Deuteronomy 21:15-17; Leviticus 18:18; Exodus 21:10-11   [3] 2 Samuel 3:2-5   [4] 2 Samuel 12:10-12   [5] Matthew 19:8
[6] Genesis 2:18, 24

Slavery

Another moral dilemma arises with regard to *slavery.* Slavery is mentioned without condemnation in both the Fourth and Tenth Commandments of the Decalogue.[1] In fact, slavery was accepted throughout the Mosaic legislation,[2] and prior to the American Civil War its recognition in the Ten Commandments was argued by some in defense of its continued practice. If we inquire as to *what exactly was involved in the slavery recognized by the Fourth and Tenth Commandments,* we find the answer to our question by examining the details of the slavery laws given by God to Moses. When we do so, we discover that although the Mosaic Law was much superior to other ancient law codes (e.g., the Code of Hammurabi) with regard to the treatment of slaves, it nevertheless fell far short of setting forth the epitome of God's will regarding such matters. For example, according to Mosaic Law a man was not to be punished for *killing* "his male or female slave with a rod," provided the slave "survives a day or two...for he is his property."[3] Like the laws concerning divorce, enactments of this sort must surely be understood, not as expressions of divine approval, but as evils permitted and regulated in order to prevent even greater evil. Nevertheless, such things *were* permitted by the Law of Moses, as summarized in the Decalogue. If the Ten Commandments are God's "unchanging moral law," are we willing to accept the type of slavery that is recognized by them?

The Sabbath

A final moral dilemma arises with regard to the Sabbath. Under the Fourth Commandment ("remember the Sabbath day to keep it holy"), men were enjoined to observe "complete rest" on the seventh day of the week. "Whoever does *any work* on the Sabbath day shall surely be put to death."[4] "In it you shall not do *any work.*"[5] If we ask what exactly God meant in the Fourth Commandment when

---

[1] Exodus 20:10, 17 [Note: the word translated "servant" here (Heb. *ebed*) is uniformly translated "slave" in the verses below.]   [2] E.g., Exodus 12:44; 21:26-27, 32; Leviticus 25:44-46; Deuteronomy 23:15   [3] Exodus 21:20-21
[4] Exodus 31:15   [5] Exodus 20:10

He forbade "any work," we find that "work" was defined *by God* as including such things as lighting a fire in one's dwelling,[1] preparing food,[2] and buying or selling.[3] Is this commandment part of God's "unchanging moral law"?[4] If so, exactly how are Christians to observe it? Is it permissible to turn on the electric lights in our homes on "the Sabbath" or use a bus to get to the morning worship service? (Both of these activities involve a violation of the Fourth Commandment, since they necessitate buying and also require others to work on the "Sabbath.") Who decides what is permissible on the Sabbath and what is not? Assuming that we are able to decide what is and is not permissible on the Sabbath, shouldn't we exercise church discipline toward those who continually do what is not permissible? If Sabbath breaking required the death penalty under the Old Covenant and is grouped together with murder, stealing, and adultery as one of the essential requirements of God's "unchanging moral law," surely it should entail the same disciplinary measures under the New Covenant as those sins do.

"But I Say Unto You"

Aside from these dilemmas, there is a further harmful consequence of identifying the Ten Commandments with "the unchanging moral law of God." *If the Ten Commandments are the consummate revelation of God's will for humanity, then it follows inevitably that the "law of Christ" can add nothing to them.* The most that Christ can do is exposit the "real meaning" of the Ten Commandments; He cannot set forth any higher standard of conduct than the one they already reveal. Historically, this has focused attention more on the Decalogue than on the manifold and rich imperatives of the New Testament. The commandments of Christ and His apostles become mere footnotes to the Ten, and many clever attempts are made to show that they were actually included in the "real meaning" of the Decalogue from the very beginning. Such an approach leads inevitably to a diminishing of the distinctive glories of the New Covenant.

---

[1] Exodus 35:3   [2] Exodus 16:23-24   [3] Nehemiah 10:31; 13:15-22
[4] See Appendix E, Q. 2.

These distinctive glories are manifested, not only by the matchless standards of the law of Christ itself, but also by the context in which those standards are set forth. The imperatives of the New Testament are always set forth in the context of a new age that has dawned among men: "The darkness is passing away, and the true light is already shining."[1] Christians have "tasted the powers of the age to come."[2] The kingdom of God is "in their midst."[3] They have been "raised up with Christ and seated with Him in the heavenly places."[4] They "have died and their lives are hidden with Christ in God."[5]

It is in this setting that husbands (for example) are exhorted to love their wives "just as Christ also loved the church." Not only does the superlative love of Christ for His bride set the highest standard imaginable for Christian husbands, but that standard is given to those who have themselves "been crucified with Christ" and who "no longer live, but Christ lives in them."[6] To give this exhortation a Mosaic flavor by implying that it takes us no further than the Seventh Commandment ("you shall not commit adultery") is inexcusable. "The Law was given through Moses; grace and truth were realized through Jesus Christ!"

Conclusion

Though the "civil, ceremonial, and moral" categories are not completely invalid, they nevertheless introduce much confusion and misunderstanding into any New Testament study of the Mosaic Law. This is particularly true when "the moral law" is identified with the Decalogue. Though the Lord and His apostles sometimes[7] refer to parts of the Ten Commandments in the New Testament, this is easily understandable in terms of their central position as "the words of the [Old] covenant."[8] It does not mean that they were given as an unchanging and comprehensive summary of all moral

---

[1] 1 John 2:8 [2] Hebrews 6:5 [3] Luke 17:21 [4] Ephesians 2:6 [5] Colossians 3:3
[6] Galatians 2:20 [7] Seven occasions: Matthew 5:21, 27; 15:4; 19:18-19; Romans 7:7; 13:9; Ephesians 6:2-3; James 2:11 [8] Exodus 34:28; Deuteronomy 4:13

duty for all men for all time. When asked by the "rich young ruler" which commandments must be kept in order to "obtain eternal life," Jesus could easily have said, "The Ten"! Instead, He quoted five commandments from the second table of the Decalogue along with a commandment not to "defraud" and the commandment to love our neighbors as ourselves.[1] When Paul says that "to those who are without law" he became "as without law," he does not proceed to say, "though not being without the law of God *but under the Ten Commandments*." Paul's focus for godly living was Christ, not the Decalogue. When Paul does quote at any length from the Decalogue, it is only to demonstrate its natural fulfillment by those who walk in love.[2] Paul's exhortation to Christians is that they "walk according to the Spirit," not that they "keep the Ten Commandments." The inevitable *result* of walking according to the Spirit is that "the requirement of the Law is fulfilled in us,"[3] but this is a *statement of fact*, not an exhortation to be obeyed.

In summary, if we are seeking for a *Biblical* distinction between the various commandments of the Law (as to which of them are unchanging and eternal) we do *not* find it in any supposed division between "civil, ceremonial, and moral" precepts. We find it, instead, in our Lord's statement that "the whole Law and the Prophets" *hang* on "the two great commandments."[4]

---

[1] Matthew 19:18-19; Mark 10:19   [3] Romans 13:8-10; Galatians 5:13-14
[3] Romans 8:4   [4] Matthew 22:34-40

Appendix D

THE LAWFUL USE OF THE LAW

As I urged you upon my departure for Macedonia, remain on at Ephesus, in order that you may instruct certain men not to teach strange doctrines, nor to pay attention to myths and endless genealogies, which give rise to mere speculation rather than *furthering the administration of God which is by faith.* But *the goal of our instruction is love from a pure heart and a good conscience and a sincere faith.* For some men, *straying from these things,* have turned aside to fruitless discussion, wanting to be teachers of the Law, even though they do not understand either what they are saying or the matters about which they make confident assertions.

But we know that *the Law is good, if one uses it lawfully,* realizing the fact that *law is not made for a righteous man,* but for those who are lawless and rebellious, for the ungodly and sinners, for the unholy and profane, for those who kill their fathers or mothers, for murderers and immoral men and homosexuals and kidnappers and liars and perjurers, *and whatever else is contrary to sound teaching, according to the glorious gospel of the blessed God,* with which I have been entrusted. 1 Timothy 1:3-11

LOVE IS THE GOAL

Paul says here that "the (Mosaic) Law is good," even in a New Covenant setting, but only *if* one "uses it lawfully." Something of what he means by this statement can be seen in the immediate context. The false teachers were using the Law in a way that led to "mere speculation" and "fruitless discussion." Instead, they should have used the Law to "further the administration of God which is by faith." In other words, they should have used the Law to promote the gospel. According to Paul, *"love" is the supreme goal of all Christian instruction*—whether that instruction comes from the Old Testament or the New. Such love flows only from *an inward renewal* (pure heart, good conscience, sincere faith) *that the Law itself is unable to give*. Any "use" of the Law, therefore, that is not centered on *love* as its supreme goal and outcome is a *misuse* of the Law! Any use of the Law that causes Christians to "bite and devour one another,"[1] to "judge"[2] and slander one another, to center their attention on "rules" and externals,[3] or in any way to become "subject again to a yoke of slavery,"[4] is a misuse of the Law.

How then can the Law be rightly used in a New Covenant setting? In what ways can it be "used lawfully" to point men to Christ and to *love* as the ultimate "goal of our instruction"? Paul's immediate answer to this question is found in verses 9-11. After saying that "the Law is good if one uses it lawfully," he immediately goes on to say that in order to do this, one must first "realize the fact that law is not made for a righteous man." Instead, law is made "for those who are lawless and rebellious, for the ungodly and sinners, for the unholy and profane, for those who kill their fathers or mothers, for murderers and immoral men and homosexuals and kidnappers and liars and perjurers, and whatever else is contrary to sound teaching, according to the glorious gospel of the blessed God." *In other words, the particular "use of the Law" that Paul has in mind in these verses is something essentially negative.* The law is not made for a righteous man, but for those who are lawless and rebellious. Its negations and prohibitions were not designed primarily to edify the saints, but to restrain and convict the wicked. (This accounts for the fact that Paul centers his teaching to Christians, not on the negations of the Law, but on the Person of Christ and the glorious redemption accomplished by Him.)

TO CONVICT THE JEWS OF SIN

In Paul's epistle to the Romans, we see him "using the Law" in this essentially negative fashion in *order to convict the Jews of sin*.

---

[1] Galatians 5:15 [2] Romans 14:3-4 [3] Romans 14:17; Hebrews 13:9
[4] Galatians 5:1

After establishing the condemnation of the Gentiles in Romans 1 (because of their sins against natural revelation), Paul goes on in Romans 2 to establish the condemnation of the Jews (because of their sins against special revelation—i.e., the Law). He uses the Law's prohibitions against such things as stealing, adultery, and sacrilege to convict the Jews of their sinful state[1] and ends by concluding that "both Jews and Greeks are all under sin."[2] The ultimate goal in view is to cause the Jews to see their need for Christ and His gospel.

Concerning this use of the Mosaic Law to convict of sin, it should be pointed out that, not only in Romans 2, but also in the case of the "rich young ruler" and in the case of Paul's own experience,[3] the Law of Moses was being applied *in an Old Covenant setting* to those who were, in fact, *Jews,* and therefore "under the Law." There is no example in Scripture of the Ten Commandments (as such) being preached to Gentiles in order to convict them of sin. (Most Gentiles had never even heard of the Ten Commandments.) Instead, the inescapable knowledge of God manifested in the created order and within the human conscience (the law written on the heart) was pressed upon them,[4] as well as the resurrection and Person of Christ and the coming judgment through Him.[5]

Paul's use of the Mosaic Law to convict the Jews of their sinfulness and need for Christ is clearly one way in which the Law can be "lawfully used" to promote the gospel. It is this use of the Law that Paul specifically has in mind in 1 Timothy 1:8-11. If we examine his practice and teaching in the rest of the New Testament, however, we can discover at least two other ways in which he used the Mosaic Law to "further the administration of God which is by faith" and to point men to "love" as the supreme goal of all Christian instruction.

To Testify of Christ

One of these additional "lawful uses of the Law" is seen in the Book of Acts. There we learn that it was Paul's "custom" when

---

[1] Romans 2:21-24 [2] Romans 3:9 [3] Romans 7 [4] Acts 17:16-34; Acts 14:11-18; Romans 1:14-32; 2:14-16 [5] Acts 17:30-31

witnessing in synagogues to "reason" with his Jewish listeners from the Old Testament Scriptures. This involved "explaining and giving evidence that the Christ had to suffer and rise again from the dead, and saying, 'This Jesus whom I am proclaiming to you is the Christ.'"[1] The second "lawful use of the Law" in a New Covenant setting, then, is to "preach Jesus"[2] from the Old Testament Scriptures. Though this applies primarily to the "Law" in its broader sense (either the Pentateuch or the Old Testament as a whole), it is also true of the Law in its narrower sense (the Mosaic legislation as such). Many of the commandments of the Mosaic Law (especially those pertaining to the temple service and sacrifices) pointed directly to the coming of the "Lamb of God" who would one day "take away the sins of the world." This preaching of Christ from the pages of the Old Testament, in conjunction with the eyewitness testimony of the apostles, was powerfully used by the Holy Spirit to convict those of Jewish background of their sins. *It is evident from the Book of Acts that this was by far the predominant "use of the Law" in apostolic preaching.* (The characteristics of apostolic preaching are discussed more fully in Chapter 17.) In this way, the Law was used to lead men directly to Christ and to "love from a pure heart and a good conscience and a sincere faith."

To Instruct Believers

A third "lawful use of the Law" is found scattered throughout the epistles of Paul. As we have seen in a previous chapter,[3] Paul views the whole Old Testament as still being "profitable" to New Testament believers "for teaching, for reproof, for correction, for training in righteousness."[4] He therefore quotes often from the Old Testament, since *"whatever was written in earlier times was written for our instruction,* that through *perseverance* and the *encouragement* of the Scriptures we might have *hope."*[5] Again, this applies not only to the prophetic and narrative portions of the Old Testament, but also to the commandments of the Law itself, as illustrations of

---

[1] Acts 17:1-3 [2] Acts 8:35 [3] Chapter 9 [4] 2 Timothy 3:16 [5] Romans 15:4

God's unchanging character and ways. Although the vast majority of Paul's references to the Old Testament do not involve the Mosaic commandments as such, he does occasionally quote from them in order to demonstrate their fulfillment by those who walk in love[1] or to reinforce Christian behavior.[2] Paul clearly believes, for example, that it is "lawful" to use the principles underlying the Law's prohibition of "muzzling the ox" to support the right of gospel laborers to be fed by those whom they serve. It is also lawful to use the Law's prohibition of plowing with an ox and a donkey together to illustrate the folly of Christians being "unequally yoked" with unbelievers.[3] *In such cases, the Law is being used to direct us to the true meaning and proper outworking of love in the Christian life.* Under the guidance of the Holy Spirit, Christians may find in the Mosaic Covenant many such profitable applications of the spiritual principles of *love* underlying[4] the Old Testament as a whole. We must be very careful when doing this, however, to ensure that our "applications" do not *contradict the clear teaching and emphasis of the New Testament.*

It is apparent from each of the three examples above that Paul actually "practiced what he preached" with regard to the "lawful use of the Law." In 1 Timothy 1, Paul says that *the Law should be used only to further the gospel* ("the administration of God which is by faith") *and Christian love* (love that flows "from a pure heart and a good conscience and a sincere faith"). We have found that this is exactly what Paul did! He used the Law to convict his fellow Jews of sin and to testify to them of Christ, and he used the spiritual principles underlying the Law to point Christians to the proper outworkings of *love* in their daily walk.

---

[1] Romans 13:8-10   [2] E.g., 1 Corinthians 9:8-10   [3] 2 Corinthians 6:14
[4] Matthew 7:12

Using the Law Today

The Mosaic Law (in conjunction with the preaching of Christ) was used in the New Testament primarily to convict Jews of sin, whereas natural revelation (in conjunction with the preaching of Christ) was used to convict Gentiles of sin. This does not mean, however, that we can never quote from the Mosaic Law or the Old Testament when preaching to Gentiles. God's word carries its own authority, and (since the whole Bible is a revelation of God's character) we may rightly use both the New Testament and the Old to preach Christ and to convict men of sin.

John the Baptist did not hesitate to reprove Herod for *marrying the wife of his brother Philip*, telling him that it was *"not lawful"*[1] for him to have his brother's wife. He also did not hesitate to reprove him for all the other "wicked things which he had done."[2] The result was that "Herod was afraid of John, knowing that he was a righteous and holy man."[3] In the same way, Christians should not hesitate to quote passages like Leviticus 18:22-23 and 20:13 to reinforce the innate knowledge[4] men have that homosexuality and bestiality are a perversion and "abomination" to the Lord.

Immediately a question arises as to which Old Covenant prohibitions may still be applied to men in our day. Homosexual behavior was punishable by death under the Law, but the eating of certain "unclean" animals was also said to be "detestable" to God and an "abomination" that resulted in the offender being "cut off" from Israel.[5] Yet we know from the New Testament that "nothing is unclean in itself"[6] and that to violate these food laws is no longer sinful. If God no longer considers the eating of pork to be detestable, how are we to know what actions He *does* still consider detestable? Paul gives us the answer in 1 Timothy 1, at the conclusion of verse 11. In addition to the sins and crimes that he specifically enumerates, Paul includes "whatever else is contrary to sound teaching, according to the glorious gospel of the blessed

---

[1] Mark 6:17-18; cf. Leviticus 20:21   [2] Luke 3:19   [3] Mark 6:20
[4] Genesis 19:7   [5] Leviticus 7:21; 17:10; Deuteronomy 14:3   [6] Romans 14:14

God, with which I have been entrusted." In other words, we see once again that it is the *New Testament* (the "sound teaching" of the "glorious gospel") that gives us the pattern for understanding and applying the *Old Testament* in our day. The principles underlying "the glorious gospel" tell us which Mosaic prohibitions we can rightly use in our present situation to reprove wicked men and point them to their need for Christ. This does not mean that every valid use of the Old Testament is *specifically* spelled out in the New,[1] but that Christians should always interpret and apply the Old Testament according to the example set for us by Christ and His apostles.

THE TEN COMMANDMENTS

Some evangelists and theologians maintain that conviction of sin can only take place when the Law (in the specific form of the Ten Commandments) is preached prior to the preaching of the gospel (the glorious Person, claims, death and resurrection of Christ). It is clear from the examples of apostolic preaching explored in Chapter 17 that this is not the case. It should also be noted that those who do employ the Ten Commandments in this way usually do not use them as they appeared in the Law of Moses. Instead, they "spiritualize" the Sabbath commandment (if they mention it at all) and fill the other commandments with the content of Christ's teachings in the Sermon on the Mount. The commandment not to commit adultery, for example, is presented as a commandment not to look lustfully on a woman, whereas the commandment not to murder is interpreted as a commandment not to hate. To do this is really to use a form of the "law of Christ" for conviction of sin.

As noted above, the fact that the Ten Commandments are part of the Mosaic Law does not mean that they can never be quoted when preaching to Gentiles or that they have no point of contact with the consciences of lost men in our day. Many people in Western cultures have some vague knowledge of the Ten Commandments as being a law from God, and even in cultures where no such

---

[1] Leviticus 18:23 is one example.

knowledge exists, men *already know* that it is wrong to murder, steal, commit adultery, etc.[1] We must always bear in mind, however, that the Decalogue is *not* the highest expression of God's law ever given to man, nor was the preaching of the Ten Commandments the method of evangelism used by the apostles. Furthermore, any method that follows a fixed "1, 2, 3" or "one size fits all" approach to witnessing is contrary to the New Covenant's emphasis on the guidance and "ministry" of the Spirit.

---

[1] Romans 1:32

– APPENDIX E –

FREQUENTLY ASKED QUESTIONS

1. Are Christians obligated to obey the Fourth Commandment to "remember the Sabbath and keep it holy"?

According to Matthew 5:19, Christians are to "keep and teach" (whether by inward reality or by outward action) even the *least* commandments of the Mosaic Law.[1] The Sabbath commandment is certainly included. If we attempt, with the help of the Holy Spirit, to view this Old Covenant commandment "through the lens of the New Testament," several interpretations as to *how* it is to be "kept" are possible. Some feel that, according to Hebrews 4, the Sabbath is to be kept by "resting from our own works"[2] and putting our trust in Christ for salvation. They view the Sabbath as a foreshadowing of the "rest" involved in justification by faith, which culminates ultimately in the "rest"[3] of heaven. Others see in the Old Testament Sabbath a profitable and abiding principle of needed weekly physical rest for both men and animals.[4] Still others believe that our obligation to keep the Sabbath (Saturday) has been transferred to the Lord's Day (Sunday) and that Christians should cease from ordinary labor and gather for worship on that day. All of these (and many more) are possible interpretations of the Biblical data and have been held by sincere and godly Christians down through the ages. We must remember, however, that *since Christ and His apostles have given us no authoritative application of this Old Covenant commandment*, we have no right to impose *our interpretation* of that commandment on the consciences of other Christians.

As mentioned above, some Christians understand the Sabbath to be fulfilled by "resting in Christ" for salvation. In good

---

[1] See Chapter 9.   [2] Hebrews 4:1-11   [3] Revelation 14:13   [4] Exodus 23:12

conscience before God, they have searched the Scriptures with earnest prayer and have come to this conclusion. On the other hand, some Christians believe that the Sabbath is to be kept as a literal day of physical rest. In good conscience before God, they also have searched the Scriptures with earnest prayer and have come to this conclusion. It is a *grievous sin* for the first group to slander their fellow believers in the second group as "legalists" because they seek to the best of their ability to follow God in this matter. On the other hand, it is also a *grievous sin* for the second group to slander their fellow believers in the first group as "antinomians" because *they* seek to the best of their ability to follow God in this matter. To call a man a *legalist* is to associate him by implication with lost religious people (like the Pharisees) who look to their own good works for salvation, and to call a man an *antinomian* is to associate him by implication with lost religious people who "turn the grace of God into licentiousness" and throw off the restraints of godly living. Those who would hurl either term of abuse at their fellow Christians are guilty of trampling underfoot our Lord's one "new commandment," at the very moment they think they are contending for what is pleasing to God.

2. How are Christians to observe the Lord's Day?

As stated above, many sincere and godly Christians believe that the Lord's Day was intended by God to replace the Old Testament Sabbath as a day of rest. They have found great blessing in setting aside this day exclusively for worship and meditation on the things of God. We must remember that, according to Paul, "He who observes the day, observes it for the Lord." [1] It is not our place to "regard with contempt" [2] anyone who does so. "To his own master he stands or falls; and stand he will, for the Lord is able to make him stand." [3] There are, however, several Biblical and historical reasons for rejecting the view that Christians are obligated to "keep the Sabbath" on the Lord's Day. To state these reasons at length

---

[1] Romans 14:6 [2] Romans 14:3 [3] Romans 14:4

would take us far beyond the scope of this book, but a few general observations may be helpful.

1. In Colossians 2:16-17, Paul clearly groups the Sabbath with other Old Testament regulations concerning "food, drink, festivals, and new moons."

> Therefore *let no one act as your judge* in regard to *food* or *drink* or in respect to a *festival* or a *new moon* or a *Sabbath day*—things which are *a mere shadow* of what is to come; but the *substance* belongs to Christ.

Here Paul commands us not to let anyone "act as our judge" in regard to these matters, since they are only "shadows" of the reality ("substance") that is found in Christ. There is no question whether or not it is the weekly Sabbath that is in view in these verses, since Paul follows the same grouping here (yearly festivals, monthly new moons, and weekly Sabbaths) as is found in several places in the Old Testament.[1]

Concerning its "shadowy" nature, the Sabbath is similar to circumcision. Even though physical circumcision was only a temporary commandment symbolizing a deeper spiritual reality,[2] it had a very prominent place in the Abrahamic Covenant because it was the "sign" of that covenant and was therefore identified with the covenant itself.[3]

> *This is My covenant*, which you shall keep, between Me and you and your descendants after you: *every male among you shall be circumcised*. And you shall be circumcised in the flesh of your foreskin; *and it shall be the sign of the covenant between Me and you*....thus shall *My covenant be in your flesh* for an everlasting covenant. But an uncircumcised male who is *not circumcised* in the flesh of his foreskin, that person shall be cut off from his people; *he has broken My covenant.* Genesis 17:10-14

---

[1] 1 Chronicles 23:31; 2 Chronicles 2:4; 8:12-13; 31:3; Ezekiel 45:17
[2] Romans 2:28-29   [3] Acts 7:8 "the covenant of circumcision"

Just as circumcision was the sign of the Abrahamic Covenant, so the Sabbath was the sign of the Mosaic Covenant:

> You shall surely observe My Sabbaths, *for this is a sign between Me and you* throughout your generations.... So the sons of Israel shall observe the Sabbath, *to celebrate the Sabbath* throughout their generations *as a perpetual covenant.* It is *a sign between Me and the sons of Israel* forever.... Exodus 31:13, 16-17

> And also *I gave them My Sabbaths to be a sign between Me and them*, that they might know that I am the Lord who sanctifies them.... *My Sabbaths ... shall be a sign between Me and you.* Ezekiel 20:12, 20

> And you shall remember that you were a slave in the land of Egypt, and the Lord your God brought you out of there by a mighty hand and by an outstretched arm; *therefore the Lord your God commanded you to observe the Sabbath day.*
> Deuteronomy 5:15

> Then You came down on Mount Sinai, and spoke with them from heaven; You gave them just ordinances and true laws, good statutes and commandments. *So You made known to them Your holy sabbath*, and laid down for them commandments, statutes and law, through Your servant Moses. Nehemiah 9:13-14 (NAS95)

The fact that the Sabbath was "given" to Israel as a sign of the Mosaic Covenant explains its place of prominence among "the words of the covenant, the Ten Commandments."[1] There is a sense in which the Sabbath's place in the Mosaic Covenant is similar to a wedding ring's place in the marriage covenant. Just as a wife's taking off her wedding ring and throwing it at her husband has a far deeper significance than the outward action itself might seem to imply, even so, any Jew's deliberate breaking of the Sabbath

---

[1] Exodus 34:28

Day was considered by God to be a very grave offense, punishable by death.

> Whoever does *any work* on the Sabbath day *shall surely be put to death.* So *the sons of Israel* shall observe the Sabbath, *to celebrate the Sabbath* throughout their generations *as a perpetual covenant. It is a sign between Me and the sons of Israel forever....* Exodus 31:15-17

The Sabbath was "a sign" of the covenant "between God and the sons of Israel." As such, it was extremely important in the Old Covenant setting but, like circumcision, now survives only as it has become a "reality" in Christ. According to Paul, Christ Himself is the "substance" of the Sabbath. Those who "rest from their own works" and put their trust in Christ alone for salvation enter into the reality that the Sabbath foreshadowed and should therefore "let no one act as their judge" in regard to the Sabbath day.

2. Observance of the Lord's Day as the "Christian Sabbath" is based on the theory that the Ten Commandments are God's "unchanging moral law"[1] and that the first day (Sunday) has replaced the seventh day (Saturday) as the day on which the Fourth Commandment enjoins men to rest. Yet, nowhere in the New Testament is there any teaching concerning such a change in the Ten Commandments. Neither is there any commandment telling us to observe the Fourth Commandment on a different day than the one God originally "blessed" and "sanctified." We are explicitly told in Genesis 2:3 that "God blessed the *seventh* day and sanctified *it.*" We are *not* told anywhere in the Bible that God has now blessed the *first* day and sanctified *it* instead of the seventh. Are we to believe that this change took place *in one of the Ten Commandments* without any trace of apostolic injunction or Jewish protest being recorded in the New Testament?

3. Those who believe that Christians are obligated to observe the Lord's Day as a "Christian Sabbath" also hold that Sabbath

---

[1] See Appendix C.

observance is a "creation ordinance" and that all men everywhere have been under obligation to keep the Sabbath since the beginning of time. If we look at the Scriptural evidence for this, however, we find it to be a theological conjecture rather than an explicit teaching of the Bible.

First, we find that God gave *no* commandment to mankind to keep the Sabbath, either in the book of Genesis or elsewhere in the Old Testament prior to the Exodus. This is in stark contrast with the institution of marriage (for instance), where God made His expectations of humanity clear and explicit from the beginning.[1] Neither do we find *any* reference to *anyone* keeping the Sabbath prior to the giving of the Law (though we do find, for example, *many* references to the offering of sacrifices[2] and even recognition of "clean" and "unclean" animals[3]). Nor do we *ever* find *any* time when Gentiles are reproved for not keeping the Sabbath, though they *are* reproved for many other sins.[4]

Second, as noted above,[5] the Old Testament represents the Sabbath as having been "made known"[6] and "given" to Israel *at the time of the Exodus*, as a "sign of the covenant between God and the sons of Israel." "*I gave them* My statutes and *informed them* of My ordinances....*also I gave them* My Sabbaths to be a sign between Me and them."[7] According to Deuteronomy 5:12-15, such Sabbath observance served as a reminder and commemoration of Israel's rest and deliverance from the labors of Egyptian slavery. "In it you shall not do any work, you or your son or your daughter or your male servant or your female servant or your ox or your donkey or any of your cattle or your sojourner who stays with you, *so that your male servant and your female servant may rest as well as you.* And you shall *remember that you were a slave* in the land of Egypt, and the LORD your God brought you out of there by a mighty hand and

---

[1] Genesis 2:18-24; 1:26-28; Matthew 19:3-5 [2] E.g., Genesis 8:20; 22:7-8; 31:54; 46:1 [3] Genesis 7:2, 8; 8:20 [4] E.g., Daniel 5:22-23; Jonah 1:2; Luke 3:19; Acts 24:25 [5] pp. 268-269 [6] Nehemiah 9:13-14; see also Exodus 16:4-5, 22-30, where Sabbath observance is first introduced and explained. [7] Ezekiel 20:11-12

FREQUENTLY ASKED QUESTIONS

by an outstretched arm; *therefore the* LORD *your God commanded you to observe the Sabbath day.*"

In addition to this, we learn from Exodus 20:8-12 that Sabbath observance was reminiscent of "God's rest" during the creation week. Both *the creation rest* and the *land of Canaan* are referred to in Scripture as "God's rest"[1] and are interpreted in the New Testament as types and shadows of one abiding spiritual reality—the "rest" that God's people must strive to enter.

> There remains therefore a Sabbath rest for the people of God. For the one who has entered His rest has himself also rested from his works, as God did from His. Let us therefore be diligent to enter that rest, lest anyone fall through following the same example of disobedience.
>
> Hebrews 4:9-11

It is clear from these verses that both God's rest in creation and the rest of Canaan were important, not because they represented part of "God's unchanging moral law," but because they foreshadowed the reality of "resting from our own works." This rest takes place initially in justification by faith[2] and finds its culmination in heaven.[3] Just like circumcision, the Sabbath was "made for man"[4] as a testimony of invisible realities that are relevant to all men, but because it was a "mere shadow of things to come," its "substance belongs to Christ."[5]

4. From the scant evidence that we have in the New Testament,[6] it seems that the first day of the week came to be known in the early church as "the Lord's Day" because it was on that day that Jesus rose from the dead, repeatedly appeared to His disciples,[7] and poured out the Holy Spirit.[8] The practice of Christian assembly on this day seems to have arisen *spontaneously*, not by commandment, and it was associated from its very beginning with *worship*, not cessation

---

[1] Psalm 95:8-11; Hebrews 3:11, 18; 4:1, 3, 5, 10   [2] Hebrews 3:18-19; 4:2-3, 10-11; 6:1; 9:14   [3] Revelation 14:13   [4] Mark 2:27-28   [5] Colossians 2:16-17
[6] Acts 20:7; 1 Corinthians 16:2; Revelation 1:10   [7] Luke 24:1-36; John 20:19, 26
[8] Acts 2:1-2

from labor. The early church viewed the Lord's Day as a *festival*, to be "celebrated" as a "day of joy." They repeatedly maintained, however, that they did not "keep the Sabbath."[1]

5. It is a matter of history that the early church did *not* observe the Lord's Day (Sunday) as a day of rest or "Christian Sabbath." Gentile converts met early Sunday morning for worship, then proceeded to *go to work* all day as on any other day of the week. It was not until the time of Constantine (AD 321) that Sunday was made a legal holiday. Even after AD 321, however, Christians continued to maintain the essential difference between the Lord's Day and the Sabbath.

A truly Sabbatarian view of the Lord's Day did not develop until the medieval period. By the late Middle Ages, the idea that Christians were obligated *because of the Fourth Commandment* to rest on Sunday had become an accepted part of Roman Catholic dogma. In America, most of our thinking regarding Sunday as the "Christian Sabbath" has been inherited directly from seventeenth-century Scottish and English Puritanism, a very late development in church history.

6. No one actually "keeps the Sabbath" in our day, even when allowance is made for observing it on the first day of the week instead of the seventh. In fact, it is questionable whether keeping the Sabbath is even possible in modern society. Everything from electric lights to telephone access requires someone to work on the "Sabbath" (whichever day of the week we consider it to be). Even the steel used in automobile manufacturing often comes from forges that run nonstop. By using these items, we are either breaking the Sabbath ourselves or supporting others in doing so.

7. If we do not accept God's standards for Sabbath observance set forth in the Old Testament,[2] what standards are we to use? Since the New Testament is silent regarding such changes, who is

---

[1] For these, and other matters of general history set forth below, see D. A. Carson, ed. *From Sabbath to Lord's Day* (1982; reprint, Eugene: Wipf and Stock Publishers, 1999), as well as most standard Bible encyclopedias under articles entitled "Sabbath" or "Lord's Day." [2] See Appendix C

qualified to make clear for us just how the Sabbath is now to be "remembered" or what actions are still forbidden on the Lord's Day? Is it permissible to use a cell phone on the Sabbath, play a game of tennis, or go to a restaurant? This is a serious matter if the "breaking" of the Sabbath is actually on par with sins like adultery and murder.

8. We must constantly bear in mind that if the Ten Commandments are the "unchanging moral law of God," then the Fourth Commandment is *one of the ten greatest moral requirements* resting on humanity. Failing to strictly observe the Lord's Day is *a grave moral offense*, parallel with such sins as idolatry, adultery, and murder. If this is actually the case, then nonobservance of the Lord's Day *cannot* be viewed as a matter of "Christian liberty," and those who do not keep the Sabbath *must* be disciplined by the church.[1] This means that they must also be considered to be non-Christians, just as those who persist in stealing, murder, or adultery must be considered to be non-Christians.[2] But how can this be, if we cannot even determine from the Bible what constitutes "Sabbath breaking" in a New Covenant setting?

For all of these reasons and many others, we must reject the idea that Christians are obligated by the Fourth Commandment to observe the Lord's Day as a "Christian Sabbath." But if the Lord's Day is not to be observed in this way, how is it to be observed? As noted above, it seems that the Lord's Day was the spontaneous day of worship for the early church, arising from the fact that Christ rose from the grave on the first day of the week. Since it has been known as *the Lord's Day* from apostolic times, it is altogether fitting for Christians to meet together on that day for joyful celebration, along with their fellow believers throughout the world. Whenever possible, it is certainly a great blessing to devote the whole day to rest, worship, and fellowship. However, the only New Testament absolute we have in this matter is that Christians are not to "forsake"

---

[1] Matthew 18:15-18; 1 Corinthians 5:9-13 [2] 1 Corinthians 6:9-11; Galatians 5:19-21

their "own assembling together."[1] Fellowship with other believers in a local church for worship, instruction, and mutual edification is a matter of utmost importance for every Christian.

3. In Deuteronomy 30:11-14, God tells the people of Israel that His Law is "not too difficult" for them to obey. How are we to understand this? Is it really possible for fallen men, whether unregenerate or regenerate, to keep the law of God perfectly?

As noted in Chapter 8, the Law of Moses served as *a civil law for a physical nation* of mostly unregenerate people. As such, it was analogous to the laws of other nations that existed at that time,[2] and many of its commandments dealt more with outward behavior than with inward motives.[3] The Mosaic Law was characterized by shadows and external ceremonies,[4] prohibitions of criminal behavior,[5] and even allowances at times for the hardness of men's hearts.[6] *On this level, the commandments were not too difficult to obey.* The Apostle Paul's "blameless" law keeping *prior* to his conversion provides a good example of such obedience:

> If anyone else has a mind to put confidence in the flesh, I far more: circumcised the eighth day, of the nation of Israel, of the tribe of Benjamin, a Hebrew of Hebrews; as to the Law, a Pharisee; as to zeal, a persecutor of the church; *as to the righteousness which is in the Law, found blameless.*
>
> Philippians 3:4-6

When Israel observed the Law's commandments and requirements (by keeping its dietary code, bringing the prescribed sacrifices at the proper time, not worshiping idols, not committing adultery, etc.), it experienced the blessing of God. This blessing took the form of "life and prosperity in the land" and is specifically mentioned in the verses that immediately follow verses Deuteronomy 30:11-14:

---

[1] Hebrews 10:25 [2] Cf. Deuteronomy 4:8 [3] See "Civil Nation vs. Spiritual Nation," p. 100. [4] Hebrews 9:8-14 [5] 1 Timothy 1:9-10 [6] Matthew 19:3-9; Mark 10:2-12

> See, I have set before you today *life and prosperity*, and death and adversity; in that I command you today to love the Lord your God, to walk in His ways and to keep His commandments and His statutes and His judgments, that you may *live and multiply*, and that the Lord your God may *bless you in the land where you are entering to possess it.*
>
> Deuteronomy 30:15-16

It is highly significant that even though the blessing of "life in the land" was not impossible to obtain and the Law in its civil applications was not "too difficult to obey," the nation of Israel still utterly failed to obey it! This led to God's "wrath" upon the nation and Israel's eventual expulsion from the land of Canaan. The moral inability[1] of the Jews to keep the Law is thus a fitting emblem of the moral inability of mankind in general to live up to God's standards, however reasonable and just those standards may be.

We must also constantly bear in mind that, according to both Jesus and Paul, the Law's promise of "life for obedience" represented something more than *just* the promise of "life in the land." On its deepest level, it embodied the promise of *"eternal life for perfect obedience."*[2] Viewed from this perspective, the Law required nothing less than *perfect* love for God (with *all* of one's heart, soul, mind, and strength) and *perfect* love for our fellow men. Such perfect love has indeed proved to be "too difficult" for anyone but Christ to fulfill, even though it asks nothing of men but that which is reasonable, natural, and good.[3]

4. In speaking of the Mosaic Law, Paul says that "law is not made for a righteous man." Would he say the same about the exhortations and commandments of the New Testament?

This question is helpful because it brings into focus a common misuse of the term "law." Many people use the word "law" to describe every imperative or "demand" of the Bible, including the

---

[1] Joshua 24:19-20; Deuteronomy 31:16-18, 20-21   [2] See "Blessings and Curses," p. 52.   [3] Jeremiah 2:32; Isaiah 1:3; Romans 7:12

New Testament's exhortations to believers to live holy lives. This is not what Paul means by the term "Law." When Paul speaks of "the Law," he is referring to the *Mosaic Covenant*.[1] This covenant was made with a specific people (the Jews) for a specific period of time (from Moses until Christ[2]) and represented a covenant of works[3] and "ministry of condemnation."[4] Since it served as a civil law for a physical nation, the Law of Moses was analogous to the laws of other nations that existed at that time. In this context, Paul views the Law as primarily negative, given to restrain and condemn the crimes of unregenerate men: "Law is not made for a righteous man, but for those who are lawless and rebellious, for the ungodly and sinners, for the unholy and profane, for those who kill their fathers or mothers, for murderers and immoral men and homosexuals and kidnappers and liars and perjurers...."[5]

Paul does not view the Christian life as "Law-centered" in any way. In fact, it is precisely because Christians have "died to the Law" that they can now bear fruit for God: "Therefore, my brethren, you also were made to die to the Law through the body of Christ, that you might be joined to another, to Him who was raised from the dead, that we might bear fruit for God. For while we were in the flesh, the sinful passions, which were aroused by the Law, were at work in the members of our body to bear fruit for death."[6] It is highly significant that the man described in Romans 7:14 as being "of flesh, sold into bondage to sin," is a man whose life is centered completely on the (Mosaic) Law: "The Law is holy.... the Law is spiritual.... I agree with the Law.... I joyfully concur with the law.... I myself with my mind am serving the law...."[7] Contrary to what many have supposed, the "man of Romans 7" is not a Christian striving to please the Lord Jesus Christ by following His teachings in the New Testament. Instead, he is a man whose sole focus is the Law of Moses. As one who serves in "oldness of the letter," he constantly strives to obey the Law, but in the end only

---

[1] Romans 5:14, 20; Galatians 3:17 [2] Galatians 3:19 [3] Galatians 3:12
[4] 2 Corinthians 3:9 [5] 1 Timothy 1:9-10 [6] Romans 7:4-5 [7] Romans 7:12, 14, 16, 22, 25

"bears fruit for death." Such Law-centered obedience is in complete contrast with Paul's view of the Christian life. As Christians, we "have been released from the Law, having died to that by which we were bound, so that we serve in newness of the Spirit and not in oldness of the letter."[1]

The exhortations and imperatives of the New Testament (in contrast to the Law) are not a "legal corpus"—a covenant of works, complete with blessings and curses. Instead they are gracious guideposts for godly living, given to believers to help them work out the glorious implications of what has already been done for them in Christ: "If then you have been raised up with Christ, keep seeking the things above, where Christ is, seated at the right hand of God. Set your mind on the things above, not on the things that are on earth. For you have died and your life is hidden with Christ in God."[2] The *imperatives* of the New Testament ("keep seeking the things above"; "set your mind on things above") are simply the logical outworkings of the great *indicatives* of the gospel ("you have been raised up with Christ"). These imperatives are given to those who are themselves new creatures in Christ—"alive from the dead"[3] and raised up to "walk in newness of life."[4]

5. **If the Law of Moses itself commanded that we should "love God with all our heart, soul, mind, and strength, and our neighbor as ourselves," how could the law of Christ hold forth a "higher" standard than the Law of Moses?**

As stated above, the Mosaic Law served as a civil law for a physical nation and, as such, dealt more with outward behavior than with inward motives. From this standpoint, the law of Christ does indeed present a higher standard than the one presented in the Law of Moses. To love God with "all" one's heart in the Mosaic setting did not imply sinless perfection, but simply wholehearted devotion to Jehovah. Those kings (for instance) who sought diligently to please God in all that He had commanded were said

---

[1] Romans 7:6   [2] Colossians 3:1-3   [3] Romans 6:13   [4] Romans 6:4

to have followed Him with "all their hearts." Josiah is one example of such a king. Because he thoroughly purged Judah of idolatry and reinstituted the Passover,[1] he is commended for having "turned to the LORD with all his heart and with all his soul and with all his might, according to all the law of Moses."[2]

As we have seen, however, the Law's promise of "life for obedience" represented, on its deepest level, the promise of "eternal life for perfect obedience." Such "perfect obedience" involves nothing less than *perfectly* loving both God and our fellow men. There can be no standard higher than this! The keeping of the two great commandments, *when they are considered in terms of their fullest and deepest meaning*, is thus sufficient of itself to merit eternal life.[3] These are the two commandments that Christ, as the last Adam, perfectly fulfilled for His people in order to obtain *righteousness* and *life* for them.[4] Viewed on this level, the law of Christ is not a higher *standard* than the two great commandments (an impossibility), but a clearer and higher *revelation* of what is involved in fulfilling that standard.

6. Was the Abrahamic Covenant conditional or unconditional? Or, were there two covenants with Abraham, one conditional and the other unconditional?

Throughout the Bible, God's covenant with Abraham is always spoken of as one covenant. The various provisions of this one covenant are reiterated and expanded several times during Abraham's lifetime[5] and repeated to Isaac[6] and Jacob,[7] but the covenant itself is always viewed as a unit.[8]

If we let Paul's clear teachings in the New Testament[9] govern our view of the Abrahamic Covenant, we will find that it is a covenant of *promise*, in which *blessings* are received by *grace* through *faith*. We

---

[1] 2 Kings 23:1-24 [2] 2 Kings 23:25; cf. 2 Chronicles 15:12-15; 16:9; ct. 1 Kings 11:4 [3] Luke 10:25-28 [4] Romans 5:17-18, 21 [5] Genesis 12:1-3, 7; 13:14-17; 15:1-21; 17:1-27; 18:17-19; 22:15-18 [6] Genesis 26:2-5 [7] Genesis 28:3-4, 13-15; 32:12 [8] E.g., Luke 1:72-73 (cf. vv. 54-55); Galatians 3:15-18 [9] Romans 4; Galatians 3-4; Romans 9

will also find that the Abrahamic Covenant is directly linked to the New Covenant, while it is contrasted with the Mosaic Covenant. In both the Abrahamic and the New Covenants, *blessing* is received by *grace* through *faith*.[1] In the Mosaic Covenant, by contrast, *blessing* is conditioned upon *obedience* and is not received by *grace* through *faith*. It is in this sense that the Abrahamic Covenant is "unconditional."

When we read the Old Testament accounts of God's dealings with Abraham in this light, we cannot help but be struck by the sovereign and gracious character of the promises made to him, and the stark contrast they present to the legal and conditional blessings and curses of the Mosaic Covenant. (Compare Genesis 12:7; 13:14-17; 15:1-21; 18:17-19 with Deuteronomy 28:1-68; Leviticus 26:3-39.)

This does not mean that Abraham's obedience was non-existent or irrelevant in the Abrahamic Covenant,[2] any more than a Christian's obedience is non-existent or irrelevant in the New Covenant.[3] It does mean, however, that both covenants are certain of fulfillment because their realization does not depend *ultimately* upon man's obedience, but upon God's faithfulness and sovereign[4] grace. Just as God's gracious work in every believer's heart ensures[5] that he will remain faithful in the New Covenant, so God's gracious work in the heart of Abraham ensured that he would remain faithful in the Abrahamic Covenant.

Because Abraham's obedience depended ultimately upon God's own faithfulness and grace, God could speak of the Abrahamic promises as *certain of fulfillment*, while at the same time speaking of *the necessity of Abraham's obedience*.

> The Lord said, "Shall I hide from Abraham what I am about to do, seeing that *Abraham shall surely become a great and mighty nation, and all the nations of the earth shall be blessed in him?* For I have chosen him, that he may command his children and his household after him to keep the way of

---

[1] Galatians 3:9; Romans 4:16 [2] Genesis 12:1, 4; 17:1-2, 9-14; 22:18; 26:5; Hebrews 6:15 [3] Matthew 7:21-23; Romans 6:17-18; 11:22; Hebrews 6:11-12; 12:14 [4] Romans 9:6-13; Galatians 4:23-31 [5] Jeremiah 32:40

the Lord by doing righteousness and justice, *so that the Lord may bring to Abraham what he has promised him.*"

Genesis 18:17-19

We see from these verses that there was no question as to whether or not Abraham would actually "become a great and mighty nation" and "all the nations of the earth" be "blessed in him." This was an absolute certainty. At the same time, there was also no question as to whether or not Abraham would obey God and "command his children and his household after him to keep the way of the LORD." God's sovereign "choice" of Abraham ensured that he *would* obey God and that the Lord *would* "bring to Abraham what He had promised him"!

Passages like Genesis 22:15-18 (sometimes quoted to show the conditionality of the Abrahamic Covenant) should be read with these realities in view.

> Then the angel of the Lord called to Abraham a second time from heaven, and said, "By Myself I have sworn, declares the Lord, *because you have done this thing*, and have not withheld your son, your only son, indeed I will greatly bless you, and I will greatly multiply your seed as the stars of the heavens, and as the sand which is on the seashore; and your seed shall possess the gate of their enemies. And in your seed all the nations of the earth shall be blessed, *because you have obeyed My voice.*"

The word "because" in these verses should not be understood as if Abraham's obedience is somehow meritorious. Neither is God saying that Abraham has now passed a new milestone of consecration that will entitle him to receive blessings that are not already his. On the contrary, God had *promised* Abraham many years before that He would "bless" him and "multiply his seed as the stars of the heavens," and Abraham had *believed* God's promise to him at that time. (See Genesis 12:2-3; 15:5-6.) In other words, *these blessings had already belonged to Abraham* for many years before his act of obedience in offering Isaac.

It is clear, then, that we should understand Genesis 22:15-18 in the same way that we understand similar verses in the New Testament. When Jesus says that in the final judgment "the King will say to those on His right, 'Come, you who are blessed of My Father, inherit the kingdom prepared for you from the foundation of the world. *For I was hungry, and you gave Me something to eat; I was thirsty, and you gave Me drink, etc.*,' "[1] no one supposes that He is teaching salvation by works. Rather, He is teaching that works are the *evidence* of true conversion and the inevitable *consequence* of saving faith. Even so, what God is saying in Genesis 22:15-18 is that Abraham's obedience *confirmed the reality* of the faith that he *already possessed*. Abraham had "believed God" and it had been "reckoned to him as righteousness" some thirty years before this, but as James says, this act of obedience confirmed the reality of his faith, and *"the Scripture was fulfilled* which says, 'And Abraham believed God, and it was reckoned to him as righteousness,' and he was called the friend of God."[2]

7. Wasn't the Old Covenant actually a covenant of grace, since it provided for sacrifices to be made as a means of forgiveness for those who had sinned?

Throughout the Bible, God's giving of the Law to Israel is always viewed as an act of great kindness and blessing. "He declares His words to Jacob, His statutes and His ordinances to Israel. He has not dealt thus with any nation; and as for His ordinances, they have not known them. Praise the LORD!"[3] When Paul asks what advantage the Jews had over the Gentiles, his answer is, "Great in every respect. First of all, that they were entrusted with the oracles of God."[4]

God's giving of the Law was gracious in that it revealed to Israel, far more clearly than to any other people in history, God's character and ways. The Jews had in the Law "the embodiment

---

[1] Matthew 25:34-36, 41-43 [2] James 2:21-23 [3] Psalm 147:19-20; cf. Deuteronomy 4:6-8; Psalm 119; etc. [4] Romans 3:1-2

of knowledge and of the truth."[1] On the one hand, God revealed Himself as *perfectly holy and righteous*: sinful men cannot approach Him on their own merits without certain death. On the other hand, He revealed Himself as *kind and merciful*: He is slow to anger and willing to forgive. At the same time, He revealed Himself as *perfectly just*: sin cannot be forgiven without the death of a sacrifice. In all these ways and more, God's giving of the Law to Israel was a gracious act on His part.

It is true, also, that the provision of sacrifices for sin in the Old Covenant was an act of grace. God was under no obligation to provide *any* means by which transgressions of the covenant could be removed; that He did so was a matter of sheer mercy: "For the life of the flesh is in the blood, and *I have given it to you* on the altar to make atonement for your souls; for it is the blood by reason of the life that makes atonement."[2] The sacrifices made it (temporarily) possible for God to continue to dwell with and bless His Old Covenant people, in spite of their shortcomings. They also served as a constant reminder that salvation could never be obtained on the basis of human merit. Moreover, they foreshadowed Christ's sacrifice yet to come, which would one day actually "take away" sin.

In light of these things, every Jew should have realized: (1) that God is holy and just, (2) that man is sinful and in need of forgiveness, and (3) that salvation can never be merited, but must come through the death of a sacrificial lamb. Some did realize this and experienced the reality of sins forgiven *by looking beyond the Law to the Promise*—thereby "following in the steps of the *faith* of their father Abraham."[3] Others, however, looked to their own meticulous *law keeping* for righteousness in the sight of God.[4] They even viewed their careful observance of the Law's sacrificial requirements as something meritorious. Those who did this perished, in spite of the gracious revelation they had received in the Law concerning God's character, man's sin, and the true way of salvation.

To say all this is not the same, however, as to say that the Old Covenant itself was based on the principle of grace. The Law was

---

[1] Romans 2:20   [2] Leviticus 17:11   [3] Romans 4:12   [4] Romans 9:30-10:11

gracious *as a revelation* of God's character and ways, but it was not gracious *as a covenant*. We must constantly bear in mind that the commandments of the Law were not merely wise and good guidelines for godly living, but were *conditions* for obtaining *life*[1] and *blessing*[2] "in the land." The Mosaic Covenant was thus characterized by the principle that *life* is contingent on *doing*—a principle which, according to both Jesus and Paul, could be applied on a deeper level to eternal life.[3] Because its blessings were contingent on man's obedience, the Old Covenant stands in sharp contrast with the New Covenant, where all who *believe* "receive *the abundance of grace* and of *the gift of righteousness*"[4] and therefore "reign in life" because of what *Christ* has done for them. There are indeed commandments and exhortations to obey in the New Covenant, but they cannot be characterized as a "ministry of death" or a "ministry of condemnation," as the commandments of the Old Covenant in "letters engraved on stones"[5] can be!

It is sometimes said that the Mosaic Covenant must be viewed as gracious because it set forth both a *standard of conduct* and a provision of *sacrifices* for those who transgressed that standard. This statement is somewhat misleading. It implies that the commanding aspect of the Law (its "standard of conduct") was one thing and the sacrifices were another. This was clearly not the case. The offering of sacrifices was *part* of the "standard of conduct" set forth by the Law; many of the Law's six hundred and thirteen commandments were actually *duties* relating to the sacrificial system.

Furthermore, this statement is misleading if we take it to mean that the Law's "standard of conduct" was exclusively a "moral" standard, and that the sacrifices were graciously provided for transgressions of that moral standard. In reality, the Law's standard of conduct related to *all kinds* of "righteousness"—civil, ceremonial, and moral—and the sacrifices that *were* provided to remove

---

[1] Leviticus 18:5; 25:18-19; 26:3-5; Deuteronomy 4:1, 40; 5:33; 8:1; 30:15-20
[2] Deuteronomy 28:1-14; ct. 29:21 "all the curses of the covenant"   [3] Luke 10:25-28; Romans 10:5; Galatians 3:12   [4] Romans 5:17   [5] 2 Corinthians 3:7

ceremonial unrighteousness, often *were not* provided to remove *moral* and *civil* unrighteousness. (See below.)

To say all this is just to say (once again) that *the Law is a unit.* It cannot be neatly divided into mental categories, whatever those categories might be. Paul never makes an explicit distinction between the Old Covenant's standard of righteousness and its sacrificial system. He also never says that because the Old Covenant made provision for sacrifices, it was based on the principle of grace, or that the reason the Law cannot save us now is that its sacrifices have been abolished in Christ. Instead, he seems to equate the entire Old Covenant with the commanding aspect of the Law. It seems that for Paul "the Old Covenant" equals "the Law" equals command, and "cursed is everyone who does not abide by all things written in the book of the Law [including the commandments relating to sacrifices], to perform them."[1]

We see this emphasis repeatedly in Paul's actual statements concerning the Law. For example, when he says that "the Law" came in "that the transgression might increase," it is clear from the context[2] that he is speaking of the *entire Mosaic economy* (including its sacrificial system), not just the "moral" aspects of the Law. It is this same Mosaic economy *in its entirety* that Paul refers to as a strict disciplinarian who kept the Jews in "bondage" and treated them like "slaves"[3] until the time of Christ's coming. Likewise, it is the *covenant* "proceeding from Mount Sinai" that "bears children who are to be slaves."[4] And again, it is the *Old Covenant itself* that Paul considers to be a "ministry of condemnation and death."[5]

Several considerations are summarized below that may help us to understand why Paul viewed the Old Covenant in this light, even though it made provision for the (ceremonial[6]) removal of sin:

1. It is a serious misconception to think that the Old Covenant graciously provided sacrifices for every transgression of the Law. This was not true even of the Ten Commandments, which comprised

---

[1] Galatians 3:10   [2] Romans 5:13-14, 20   [3] Galatians 3:17-4:5
[4] Galatians 4:24   [5] 2 Corinthians 3:5-18   [6] Hebrews 9:9-10, 13-14

FREQUENTLY ASKED QUESTIONS

the very "words of the covenant."[1] The penalty for idolatry,[2] Sabbath breaking,[3] murder,[4] and adultery[5] was *death*, not sacrifice! The same was true of blasphemy,[6] sodomy,[7] bestiality,[8] necromancy,[9] cursing of parents,[10] and other such sins. Sacrifices were provided mainly for unintentional sins.[11] In most cases, there was no sacrifice for deliberate sin, but judgment.[12] The principle of "life for obedience" and "death for disobedience" thus still held true *in the midst of the sacrificial system* and characterized the Mosaic Covenant as a whole.

2. As stated above, many of the six hundred and thirteen commandments of the Law were themselves actually *duties relating to the sacrificial system*. Three things characterized the commandments regarding sacrifices. First, they were *mandatory,* not optional, and thus represented further obligations placed upon the Jews. Those who did not offer the required sacrifices were condemned by the Law and under its curse; forgiveness *required* atonement.[13] Second, not only were the sacrifices mandatory, the regulations surrounding them were *rigorous* and *exacting*.[14] God would not accept the sacrifices of those who did not follow these regulations meticulously. Third, sacrifices were *expensive*. As the word "sacrifice" itself implies, they involved significant forfeiture on the part of those who offered them. For example, the sacrifice required for *unintentional* sin was "a ram without defect from the flock,"[15] whereas the sacrifice required from one *cleansed of leprosy* was "two male lambs without defect, and a yearling ewe lamb without defect, and three-tenths of an ephah of fine flour mixed with oil for a grain offering, and one log of oil." Though the Law made provision for the poor, even then the expense of sacrificing was considerable: "But if he is poor, and his means are insufficient, then he is to take one male lamb for a guilt offering as a wave offering to make atonement for him, and one-tenth of an

---

[1] Exodus 34:28 [2] Deuteronomy 13:1-11 [3] Exodus 31:15 [4] Deuteronomy 19:11-13; Leviticus 24:17 [5] Leviticus 20:10 [6] Leviticus 24:10-16
[7] Leviticus 20:13 [8] Leviticus 20:15-16 [9] Leviticus 20:27 [10] Leviticus 20:9
[11] Leviticus 5:17-19; Numbers 15:22-26; see also Leviticus 4:2, 22, 27; 5:15, etc. [12] Numbers 15:30-31; contrast, however, Leviticus 5:1-6; 6:1-7.
[13] Leviticus 4:31, 35 [14] E.g., Leviticus 14:1-32 [15] Leviticus 5:17-19

THE LAW OF CHRIST

ephah of fine flour mixed with oil for a grain offering, and a log of oil, and two turtledoves or two young pigeons which are within his means."[1] Sacrifices were obviously costly and often stretched finances to the limit!

From this standpoint, therefore, the sacrificial system represented *obligation, rigor,* and *expense,* not grace. These three factors together caused even the sacrificial provisions of the Law to be *part* of the heavy "yoke" which none of the Jews were "able to bear."[2] In saying this, we must always bear in mind that the requirements of the Law were "heavy" *only because of man's sin.* "The Law is holy, and the commandment is holy and righteous and good."[3] God required nothing of man but that which was reasonable, natural, good, and right.[4] Nevertheless, for fallen men the Law represents a "yoke of slavery."[5]

3. When we say that the Mosaic Covenant made a provision of forgiveness for those who "transgressed the Law," we must be clear what we are saying. *Many* transgressions of the Law involved ritual "uncleanness." These transgressions were "sins" and required sacrifices for their forgiveness, even though they did not relate in any direct way to the character of God or to "right and wrong" as we would now know it.

> If a person touches any unclean thing, whether a carcass of an unclean beast, or the carcass of unclean cattle, or a carcass of unclean swarming things.... Or if he touches human uncleanness, of whatever sort his uncleanness may be with which he becomes unclean, *and it is hidden from him, and then he comes to know it, he will be guilty....* So it shall be when he becomes guilty in one of these, that he shall *confess* that in which he has *sinned.* He shall also bring his *guilt offering* to the Lord for his *sin which he has committed,* a female from the flock, a lamb or a goat as a *sin offering.* So the priest shall *make atonement* on his behalf for his *sin.*
> Leviticus 5:2-3, 5-6

---

[1] Leviticus 14:10, 21-22   [2] Acts 15:10   [3] Romans 7:12   [4] Jeremiah 2:32; Isaiah 1:3   [5] Galatians 5:1

Here we learn that anyone who *inadvertently* touched the carcass of an unclean animal had to sacrifice a *lamb* or *goat* in order to be forgiven for this "sin"! Again, we see that in these cases the sacrifices of the Law represented an additional *burden* upon the Jews, not a gracious *provision* for their moral lapses, as we might at first suppose. These sacrifices were gracious in their *intended purpose* (to remove ceremonial uncleanness, to teach Israel something of the awful holiness ["separateness"] of God, and to provide types and shadows of spiritual realities), but they were not gracious *in and of themselves*.

4. Finally, and perhaps most importantly, the continual offering of sacrifices under the Old Covenant, instead of assuring the Jews of forgiveness, actually only reminded them of the fact that their sins had never really been put away. "But in those sacrifices there is a reminder of sins year by year. For it is impossible for the blood of bulls and goats to take away sins."[1] Again, viewed from this perspective, the sacrifices did not represent "grace," but "law"! The sacrifices of the Old Covenant were, in fact, ineffectual in actually accomplishing *anyone's* justification in the sight of God. It is only in Christ that "everyone who believes is *freed* (Gk. *justified*) *from all things, from which they could not be freed through the Law of Moses*."[2]

In light of these considerations, it is not hard to understand why Paul would characterize the Old Covenant in its entirety as a "ministry of condemnation and death" and as a strict disciplinarian who kept his subjects in "bondage" as "slaves."

8. Is the Law a "tutor" to Gentiles as well as Jews and to individuals as well as nations?

When Paul says in Galatians 3:24 that the Law "was our guardian until Christ came,"[3] he is referring to the period of redemptive history that lasted from the time of the Exodus "until" the coming of Christ. During that period, the Mosaic Covenant had a temporary role as "guardian" or "child-conductor" to the

---

[1] Hebrews 10:3-4 [2] Acts 13:38-39; Hebrews 9:15 [3] ESV

THE LAW OF CHRIST

nation of Israel as a whole. When Christ came, that period ended. "Now that faith has come, we are no longer under a guardian (the Mosaic Covenant)."

In addition to this, several English translations reflect the fuller concept that the Law was not only a "guardian *until* Christ came" but also a "*tutor* to *lead us* to Christ." "Therefore the Law has become our tutor to lead us to Christ, that we may be justified by faith."[1] (The words "to lead us" or "to bring us" are not expressed in the Greek, but may be implied.) This "fuller" translation of Galatians 3:24 seems to be a valid understanding of Paul's words, since he says in the immediate context that the Law was "added because of transgressions." What he means by this statement can be seen by comparing this passage to his other writings, where the work of the Law as a "tutor" is more prominent.[2] The Law was intended to "lead" the Jews to Christ by showing them their sinfulness, the power of sin, their need of a Savior, etc. "But the Scripture has shut up all men under sin, that the promise by faith in Jesus Christ might be given to those who believe."[3]

Though Paul is speaking in Galatians 3 of the Mosaic Law as it related specifically to the Jews, he seems to view that Law as representative of the legal principles under which Gentiles also are condemned and enslaved. We see this in verses 22-23, where Paul maintains that *all* men (both Jew and Gentile) have been "shut up under sin," as well as in verses 13-14, where he identifies the curse from which Christ has delivered both Jewish and Gentile believers as being "the curse *of the Law*." Furthermore, Paul asks those *Gentiles* who want to put themselves under the rules and regulations of the *Law of Moses* how it is that they "desire to be enslaved *all over again*" to "the weak and worthless elemental things" of their past life.[4]

From all this it should be clear that, regardless of how we translate Galatians 3:24, the *principle* that God uses law to lead men to Christ *is a Biblical one*. Sin has no meaning apart from a standard

---

[1] NAS [2] Romans 5:20; 7:7-25; 1 Corinthians 15:56; etc.; see "Why the Law Then?" p. 57. [3] Galatians 3:22 [4] Galatians 4:9

FREQUENTLY ASKED QUESTIONS

of some sort. All men stand condemned by whatever law they are "under." For Gentiles, this is the law of conscience; for Jews, it is the Law of Moses; and for those who have heard the message of the New Testament, it is the law of Christ.

9. Should we teach our children the Ten Commandments?

We should certainly teach our children the Ten Commandments. They show us the things that God considered to be of utmost importance in the conduct of His Old Covenant people. Honoring one's parents, for example, is seen to be of parallel importance with not murdering one's neighbor or committing adultery with his wife. We should be careful, of course, when teaching the Ten Commandments, to make clear their present-day application and overall place in Biblical revelation. And we should always bear in mind that it is far more important to teach our children the words and deeds of the Lord Jesus Christ than even the Ten Commandments. To focus on the Ten Commandments as our standard of righteousness, while the full blaze of Christ's own glory shines before us, is like turning away from the sun to gaze at a candle.

10. If the Old Covenant has been abolished and the Ten Commandments are not the rule of duty for Christians, what is the definition of sin?

Paul makes it clear that in the New Testament, "the law of God" is defined, not by reference to the *Ten Commandments*, but by reference to *the law of Christ*: "though not being without *the law of God* but under *the law of Christ*."[1] As long as we keep this fact in mind, the classic definition of sin given by the Westminster Shorter Catechism is a valid one: "Sin is any want of conformity unto, or transgression of, the law of God." A more obviously Christ-centered definition might be this: "Sin is any want of Christlikeness or failure to love as Christ would love." This is just another way of saying

---

[1] 1 Corinthians 9:21

that sin is any failure to love God with all our heart, soul, mind, and strength, or to love our neighbor as ourselves.

John's reference to sin as "lawlessness" (Gk. *anomia*) in 1 John 3:4 has often been quoted to prove that sin must be defined in terms of the Law of Moses. It is clear, however, that John's statement is not intended as a textbook definition of sin. Neither is John thinking of "lawlessness" only in terms of the Ten Commandments, as is evident from the context.[1] This becomes even clearer when we consider Jesus' use of the same word ("lawlessness") in the Sermon on the Mount.

> Not everyone who says to Me, "Lord, Lord," will enter the kingdom of heaven; but he who does *the will of My Father* who is in heaven. Many will say to Me on that day, "Lord, Lord, did we not prophesy in Your name, and in Your name cast out demons, and in Your name perform many miracles?" And then I will declare to them, "I never knew you; depart from Me, you who practice *lawlessness*." Therefore everyone who hears *these words of Mine*, and acts upon them, may be compared to a wise man, who built his house upon the rock.　　　　　　Matthew 7:21-24

In these verses, the practice of *lawlessness* is directly paralleled, both with failing to do *the will of the Father* and with failing to act on *the words of Christ*. In other words, *God's will* is that we obey *Christ's words*: "This is My beloved Son, *listen to Him!*" As Christians, we are to "observe all that *Christ* commanded us."[2] *Lawlessness* in a New Testament context has to do with failing to act on the words of *Christ*, not with failing to observe the Ten Commandments.

11. Paul says that Gentiles "show the work of the Law written in their hearts." How is this different from God's promise in the New Covenant to "write His laws upon the hearts"[3] of Christians?

---

[1] E.g., 1 John 2:3, 6, 7-10; 3:22-24　　[2] Matthew 28:20　　[3] Hebrews 8:10

Sometimes the Bible uses the same (or similar) terminology to describe two differing realities. When Paul speaks of the work of the Law having been "written in the hearts" of Gentiles, he is referring to the inescapable knowledge of right and wrong that the Gentiles possess *in their consciences*: "they show the work of the Law written in their hearts, their conscience bearing witness, and their thoughts alternately accusing or else defending them."[1] The conscience of an unregenerate man stands against the sin that *the man himself desires to commit* and condemns him when he commits it.

By contrast, when God promises to write His law "on the hearts" of Christians, He is speaking of *regeneration*—the giving of "a new heart" that actually *delights* to do what the law commands (and what the conscience tells us is right). For the Christian, law is no longer an "external" rule that contradicts his true nature and desires, but part of the internal makeup of his "heart."

12. Were true believers in Old Testament times "born again" (regenerate)?

According to the Bible, all men are "by nature children of wrath... dead in trespasses and sins... walking according to the prince of the power of the air... indulging the desires of the flesh and of the mind."[2] "A natural man does not accept the things of the Spirit of God; for they are foolishness to him, and he cannot understand them, because they are spiritually appraised."[3] Instead, man's natural mind is "hostile toward God; for it does not subject itself to the law of God, for it is not even able to do so; and those who are in the flesh cannot please God."[4] All these considerations make it clear that *without regeneration* no man can either *believe God* or *love His law*. When we read, then, of Old Testament saints who *did* believe God and *did* love His law,[5] we must conclude that they were regenerate. This explains why Christians through the centuries have found the Psalms (for example) to be such fitting

---

[1] Romans 2:15 [2] Ephesians 2:1-3 [3] 1 Corinthians 2:14 [4] Romans 8:7-8
[5] Genesis 15:6; Hebrews 11; Psalm 119:97, 113, 163

expressions for certain aspects of their own prayer and worship: regenerate men wrote them.

One of the promises of the New Covenant given through Jeremiah is that God's people "shall not teach again, each man his neighbor and each man his brother, saying, 'Know the LORD,' for they shall all know Me, from the least of them to the greatest of them." [1] This promise envisions a day when *all* of God's people, "from the least to the greatest of them," will know the Lord personally. It does not imply, however, that *no one* "knew the Lord" under the Old Covenant. In fact, it specifically says that *some* of God's Old Covenant people *did* "know the Lord," and that those who *did* were in the habit of exhorting their "neighbors and brothers" to know the Lord also.

In the same way, Ezekiel 36:26-27 speaks of a day coming when God will give His people "a new heart and a new spirit." This promise envisions a time yet future when God's people *as a whole* will be regenerate (i.e., the time of the New Covenant). Again, it does not imply that *no one* had "a new heart and a new spirit" at the time the promise was made. In fact, God commanded the wicked of Ezekiel's day to "cast away from them all their transgressions which they had committed, and make themselves a new heart and a new spirit!" [2]

Similarly, God promised in Deuteronomy that there was a day coming when He would circumcise the hearts of His people *corporately*: "Moreover the LORD your God will circumcise your heart and the heart of your descendants, to love the LORD your God with all your heart and with all your soul, in order that you may live." [3] Again, this promise of future blessing does not imply that *no one* had a "circumcised heart" until the coming of the New Covenant. In fact, God commanded the people at that very time to "circumcise their hearts, and stiffen their necks no more." [4] (Commandments such as those in Ezekiel 18:31 and Deuteronomy 10:16 refer to the whole scope of regeneration and conversion, not

---

[1] Jeremiah 31:31-34 [2] Ezekiel 18:31 [3] Deuteronomy 30:6; ct. 29:2-4
[4] Deuteronomy 10:16; Jeremiah 4:4

just to regeneration proper, which is a sovereign work of the Holy Spirit.[1]) It is in light of such passages that the Lord Jesus marvels that Nicodemus could be an *Old* Covenant "teacher of Israel," yet not understand matters relating to the new birth.[2] For all these reasons, we must maintain that true believers in Old Testament times *were* regenerate. Having said this, however, we must also immediately emphasize and maintain the vast differences between the privileges experienced by the saints of the Old Testament and those of the New. These privileges relate not only to knowledge,[3] but also to the work of the Holy Spirit in individual believers.[4] It is in this sense that "he who is *least* in the kingdom of heaven is *greater* than" John the Baptist![5]

13. Why is the term "in-lawed to Christ" (Gk. *ennomos Christou*) that Paul uses in 1 Corinthians 9:21 significant?

Throughout his writings, Paul uses the term "under" with the connotation of *subjection to a ruling power*. He thus says not just that "both Jews and Greeks *have sinned*," but that "both Jews and Greeks are all *under sin*"[6] and that "Scripture has shut up all men *under sin*."[7] All men are said to be "under sin" because they are subject to sin as a ruling power. Sin "reigns"[8] over them, making them its slaves[9] and leading them to destruction. The phrase "under law"[10] has similar connotations, and when used with reference to fallen humanity, always implies something negative. Those who are "under law" are subject to law as a ruling power—they are "under" its condemnation and curse, under its ability to "stir up" sin, under its "yoke of slavery,"[11] etc. Thus, it is significant that when Paul speaks of Christians, he does not actually say that they are "*under* the law of Christ," but rather that they are "in-lawed to Christ." In Paul's thinking, *union with Christ* is central. Christians have been "made to die to the Law" so that they "might be *joined*

---

[1] John 3:8 [2] John 3:10 [3] Matthew 13:16-17 [4] John 7:37-39; Acts 2:14-18; Galatians 4:4-7 [5] Matthew 11:11; Luke 16:16 [6] Romans 3:9 [7] Galatians 3:22 [8] Romans 5:21 [9] John 8:34 [10] Romans 2:12; 3:19; 6:14-15; 1 Corinthians 9:20; Galatians 3:23, 25; 4:2-5, 21; 5:18 [11] Galatians 5:1

to another, to Him who was raised from the dead, that we might bear fruit for God."[1] The law of Christ is not an external standard that we are "under," but an inward reality written on our hearts and empowered by Christ's life within us. "It is no longer we who live, but Christ lives in us."[2] "Christ... is our life."[3]

14. What does Paul mean when he says in Romans 7:14 that "the Law is spiritual"?

When Paul says that "the Law is *spiritual;* but I am of *flesh,* sold into bondage to sin," he is making the same contrast between the "realms" of "flesh" and "Spirit" as elsewhere in Romans[4] and in his other writings.[5] *The Law is said to be "Spiritual" because it can only be fulfilled by those who are "in the Spirit."* For those who are "in the flesh," the Law actually serves to "arouse sinful passions in their members."[6] These truths are summed up in Romans 8:3-4. "For what the Law could not do, *weak as it was through the flesh,* God did... in order that *the requirement of the Law might be fulfilled in us,* who do not walk according to the *flesh,* but according to the *Spirit.*"

15. Why would any Jew think that Jesus had come to "abolish the Law or the Prophets"?[7]

If "to abolish the Law or the prophets" means "to destroy the Old Testament Scriptures," it is difficult to imagine how any Jew could have thought that Jesus had come to do this. Over and over, He makes it clear that He accepts the Old Testament Scriptures as the very word of God—authoritative[8] and unbreakable.[9] He repeatedly represents His own life and ministry in terms of their prophecies and foreshadowings.[10]

When it comes to the *ethical* or commanding aspect of the Old Testament, however, the Jews might have gotten a different

---

[1] Romans 7:4 [2] Galatians 2:20 [3] Colossians 3:4 [4] Romans 7:5-6; 8:6-9; see Chapter 11 of my book, *Justification and Regeneration.* [5] E.g., 1 Corinthians 2:12-3:3 [6] Romans 7:5 [7] Matthew 5:17 [8] E.g., Matthew 21:42; 22:29; 26:54, 56; John 7:38; 13:18 [9] John 10:35 [10] E.g., Matthew 26:24; Luke 4:21; 24:27; John 5:39

impression. Throughout His public ministry, the Lord Jesus Christ said and did things in relation to the Law of Moses that would have been shocking to any devout Jew. On some occasions, He seemed to ignore the prohibitions of the Law altogether. For example, when Jesus was approached by a leper, He reached out and *touched* him,[1] in apparent disregard of Leviticus 5:2-6 and the "sin" normally incurred by such contact. Jesus then told the leper, "Go and show yourself to the priest, and make an offering for your cleansing, just as Moses commanded...." This in itself would not have been notable, but the *reason* He gave for making this offering was *not* that Moses had commanded it, but *"for a testimony to them"*![2]

On another occasion, when Jesus paid the temple tax for Peter and Himself, He made it clear that He did not do this out of obligation: as the Son of God, He was "exempt"[3] from such requirements. Instead, He paid the temple tax as an act of gracious condescension: "lest we give them [the Jews] offense"! And when the Pharisees condemned His disciples for "doing what is *not lawful* on the Sabbath," He appealed to the *majesty of His own Person* to justify their law breaking: The priests in the temple "*break the Sabbath*, and are innocent" because they serve *the temple*. How much more, then, can His disciples break the Sabbath and yet remain innocent, since they serve One who is infinitely *"greater than the temple"*?[4] "For the Son of Man is Lord [even][5] of the Sabbath."[6]

In light of such examples, it is not surprising that in the Sermon on the Mount Jesus would warn His hearers against the mistaken idea that He had come to "abolish" the Law and the Prophets. Not only might His public ministry in general have given this impression; His ethical teaching in particular might do so. Jesus wants to make it clear that the various "you have heard / but I say to you" contrasts of Matthew 5 do not abolish the imperatives of the Old Testament, but instead bring them to their intended goal and "fulfillment." In the same way that the types and shadows of

---

[1] Luke 5:12-13; see also Luke 8:43-44 and Leviticus 15:25.   [2] Luke 5:14
[3] Matthew 17:24-27   [4] Matthew 12:5-6; compare John 5:18.   [5] Mark 2:28
[6] Matthew 12:8

the sacrificial system are "swallowed up" in the reality of Christ's death on the cross, so the commandments of the Law of Moses are swallowed up in the fulness of Christ's ethical teachings!

This reality is illustrated in the account of the woman taken in adultery. For the reasons stated above, Jesus' enemies imagined a conflict between His teachings and those of Moses. Wanting to capitalize on this conflict, they quickly seized an opportunity to trap Him by bringing to Him a woman "caught in adultery, in the very act."[1] Their attempt to pit Jesus against Moses ended in dismal failure, however. In a display of transcendent wisdom and goodness, He upheld both perfect righteousness and perfect love—not only in relation to the woman herself, but also in relation to her accusers. Moreover, He did this, not by setting Himself against the ethical requirements of the Law of Moses, but by "fulfilling" them!

16. Some say that in Matthew 5:20-48 Christ is not advancing beyond the Law of Moses, but only correcting Jewish distortions of it and bringing out its true intent. Why is this view insufficient?

Though the essence of the Mosaic Law is love to God and man, the national and temporal setting of that law required an expression that is far below New Covenant standards. What Christ set forth in the Sermon on the Mount was a higher expression of the one unchanging law of God. In doing this, He did far more than just comment on the "true meaning" of the individual commandments in the Mosaic code.

This becomes obvious when the various "you have heard / but I say to you" contrasts are considered individually; several of them do not fit the "true intent" pattern of interpretation at all. For example, in His teaching concerning vows, Jesus does indeed correct Jewish abuses of the system of vows established in the Old Testament, but He then goes beyond this by setting aside that system altogether. The same is true of His replacement of the Law's "eye for an eye"

---

[1] John 8:4

precept with the commandment that we should "not resist him who is evil" but "turn the other cheek" and even allow the one who wants to sue us for our shirt to "have our coat also."

If we are looking for a common pattern in Jesus' antitheses, the one thing that *is* most prominent in every one of them is His magisterial "but I say to you." As the long-awaited "prophet like Moses," He sets forth with unquestioned authority the standards by which those in "the kingdom of heaven" will live. In doing this, He does not overthrow the Law of Moses, but neither does He gain His authority from it or limit Himself to it. Rather, His teachings swallow it up and "fulfill" it.

17. How can love, by its very nature, tell us that things such as homosexuality are wrong?

Paul's teaching that "love is the fulfillment of the Law" must be understood in the total context of man's existence as one who has been created in the "image of God."[1] Love can tell me not to murder my neighbor only in a setting where my neighbor has value as God's image bearer.[2] Love can tell me that homosexual acts toward my neighbor are "degrading" only in a world where such acts are "unnatural" and therefore not "proper."[3] Love can tell me not to steal my neighbor's car only in a setting where private property exists.[4]

Just as the fact that "God is love" does not mean that all His other attributes can be logically deduced from or reduced to love, even so, the fact that love is the essence of the law does not mean that love can tell men what to do apart from the total created order in which they exist. Because we are made in the image of God, all of us have an inescapable knowledge that we are persons (not mere animals or machines). We also know inescapably that to help an old woman across the street is a "higher" course of action than to murder her. Furthermore, we know that we are under *moral obligation* to follow this higher course of action. In short, we know

---

[1] Genesis 1:26-27   [2] Genesis 9:6   [3] Romans 1:26-28   [4] Acts 5:4

that we *ought* to help her and that to murder her would be "wrong." Because we are created in the image of God, we also know there is such a thing as justice or equity, that circles cannot be squares, that sunsets are "beautiful," that life must have meaning, etc. It is only in this total context of man's creation in the image of God that love can properly direct our behavior.

18. Why did the Jerusalem Council instruct Gentile converts to "abstain from things sacrificed to idols and from blood and from things strangled and from fornication"?[1] Is it wrong for Christians to eat foods containing blood?

Paul makes it very clear in his epistles[2] that there is nothing inherently wrong with eating "things sacrificed to idols." Such eating *becomes* wrong, however, if it causes fellow believers to "stumble," for it then involves breaking the law of Christ: "For if because of food your brother is hurt, you are no longer *walking according to love.*"[3] The same holds true for other Old Testament food laws, such as "abstaining from blood and from things strangled." The Jerusalem Council did not forbid these things because they were inherently sinful, but because such practices among Gentile converts would unnecessarily offend the Jews. The Christian's duty in such cases is summed up by Paul: "Give no offense either to Jews or to Greeks or to the church of God."[4]

Note: "Abstaining from fornication" (in the sense of extramarital immorality) would have already been part of the basic apostolic teaching to these Gentile converts. It is possible that it is included here because fornication was such a common practice among the Gentiles. (It was even incorporated into their idolatrous "worship" services!) On the other hand, some scholars believe that the term "fornication" is used here in the more technical sense of "marriage between those who, according to Mosaic Law, are too closely related." Such marriages among the Gentiles would have been

---

[1] Acts 15:28-29   [2] 1 Corinthians 8; Romans 14   [3] Romans 14:15
[4] 1 Corinthians 10:32

considered by the Jews to be fornication. For Gentile Christians to avoid *this kind* of "fornication" would thus be another example of not unnecessarily offending those of Jewish background.

19. Is it wrong for Christians to get tattoos?

This question is perhaps worthy of consideration, not only because tattoos are advocated in our day as a "witnessing tool," but also because it provides an opportunity to explore some overarching New Testament principles that apply to questions of this sort. Tattoos are forbidden in Leviticus 19:27-28, along with "harming the edges of the beard": "You shall not round off the side-growth of your heads, nor harm the edges of your beard. You shall not make any cuts in your body for the dead, nor make any tattoo marks on yourselves: I am the LORD."

Some Bible students believe that both of these verses apply to pagan religious customs or mourning rites in honor of various deities. If so, they would have present-day application only in cultures where tattoos have negative religious connotations. On the other hand, this interpretation is not certain. Some believe that God forbade tattoos because they involved a voluntary and permanent disfigurement of the human body as God's creation. It is obvious that in order to make a decision about the rightness or wrongness of getting a tattoo, Christians will have to turn to the higher considerations and principles given in the New Testament. We will consider seven of these that may be helpful in making a decision of this sort.

1. Will my getting a tattoo dishonor or deeply wound those who love me most? To "treat others as we want them to treat us" is the New Covenant's "Golden Rule" by which Christians are to live.[1] This consideration alone can sometimes show us the right course of action when there are no other clear guidelines to follow in making a decision.

---

[1] Matthew 7:12; Luke 6:31

2. *Would I have to go against my own conscience to get a tattoo?* Do I have any doubts or uneasiness about doing this? Is it right to do something *permanent* and *irreversible* to my body, when I may later regret it? Could it be that tattoos *were* forbidden by God because they voluntarily disfigure His creation? Do I sense that I will grieve the Holy Spirit if I follow this course of action? Can I do this in complete confidence?

These questions flow from the general principle that it is wrong to do anything against one's own conscience, even in matters that may be indifferent in themselves. "But he who doubts is condemned if he eats, because his eating is not from faith; and whatever is not from faith is sin."[1]

3. *Will it hinder my ministry if I do not get the tattoo?* Are tattoos such an integral part of the group I am trying to reach that my not having a tattoo will hinder my witness to them? In other words, is this a situation where I should become "like" those I am seeking to reach in order not to give unnecessary offense in my presentation of the truths of the gospel to them? "Paul wanted this man to go with him; and he took him and circumcised him because of the Jews who were in those parts, for they all knew that his father was a Greek."[2]

4. *If my tattoo enhances my ministry to this group, would it hinder my ministry to another group if God later called me to go elsewhere?* Should I do something permanent to my body, if it rules out the possibility of ministering to certain people in the future? In other words, should I put myself in a position where it is no longer possible for me to "become all things to *all* men"?[3]

5. *Will my tattoo embolden some weaker brother (who sees my example) to go against his own conscience by getting a tattoo himself?* "For if someone sees you, who have knowledge, dining in an idol's temple, will not his conscience, if he is weak, be strengthened to eat things sacrificed to idols? *For through your knowledge he who is weak is ruined, the brother for whose sake Christ died.*"[4] "It is good not to eat meat or to drink wine, or to do anything by which my brother

---

[1] 2 Romans 14:23; cf. v. 14 [2] Acts 16:3 [3] 1 Corinthians 9:19-23
[4] 1 Corinthians 8:10-11

stumbles."[1] "For if because of food my brother is hurt, I am no longer walking according to love."[2]

6. Am I mastered by this desire, or am I completely neutral in it, wanting only God's perfect will in this matter? "All things are lawful for me, but not all things are profitable. All things are lawful for me, *but I will not be mastered by anything.*"[3]

7. Have I humbled myself and sought counsel from those who are older, wiser, and godlier than I am? "You younger men, likewise, be subject to your elders; and all of you, clothe yourselves with humility toward one another, for God is opposed to the proud, but gives grace to the humble."[4]

None of these considerations gives us a clear-cut "Yes or No" answer to the question before us, and answers may vary depending on individuals and circumstances. This is why Paul tells us to "present our bodies as a living and holy sacrifice" to God. We must "not be *conformed to this world,* but be *transformed* by the renewing of our mind, *that we may prove what the will of God is,* that which is good and acceptable and perfect."[5] God is faithful to guide those who truly want to know His will.

20. How does the nature of the New Covenant relate to the practice of infant baptism?

The Old Covenant was made with the physical nation of Israel, which consisted of all the natural descendants of Abraham, Isaac, and Jacob. The only thing necessary for a person to be considered a "Jew" was for him to be born of Jewish parents. Every newborn Jewish baby (through no choice of his own) would grow up directly "under" the Law of Moses. In other words, individuals became *actual participants* in the Old Covenant *by physical birth.* For this reason, it was entirely logical and appropriate for God to command that Jewish infants be circumcised as a sign of their natural descent from the Patriarchs and (hence) their participation in the Old Covenant.

---

[1] Romans 14:21   [2] Romans 14:15   [3] 1 Corinthians 6:12   [4] 1 Peter 5:5
[5] Romans 12:1-2

THE LAW OF CHRIST

As long as such physical Jews outwardly kept the precepts of the Law and did not commit offences that required them to be "cut off" from the people of Israel, they remained "in good standing" as members of the Old Covenant. Most of them did not have a personal knowledge of the Lord. Therefore, it was necessary for those in the Old Covenant who *did* know the Lord to "teach everyone his fellow citizen, and everyone his brother, saying, 'Know the Lord.'" [1]

With the arrival of the New Covenant, this situation changed dramatically. Men and women enter the New Covenant, not by physical birth, but by spiritual rebirth.[2] *Everyone* in the New Covenant, "from the least to the greatest of them," knows the Lord personally.[3] *Everyone* in the New Covenant is both justified[4] and regenerate.[5] *No one* is a Christian (i.e., a participant in the New Covenant) just because he or she has been born of Christian parents. For this reason, baptism rightly belongs only to those who give evidence of *spiritual rebirth* and not to those who are merely the physical infants of Christian parents.

To say this another way, the New Covenant belongs only to those who are the *true* (spiritual) *children of Abraham*. One becomes a true child of Abraham, not by physical birth, but by faith in Christ. ("Therefore, be sure that it is *those who are of faith* who are sons of Abraham."[6]) For this reason, baptism rightly belongs only to those who give evidence of having exercised faith in Christ.

Historically, infant baptism has repeatedly been linked with regeneration (in one way or another) by those who practice it. This has been true, not only of Roman Catholicism, but of "Protestant" denominations as well. In the Anglican Church, for example, upon baptizing an infant, ministers are required to say, "Seeing now dearly beloved brethren that this child is regenerate and grafted into the body of Christ's Church...." They are then supposed to thank God "that it hath pleased thee to regenerate this infant with thy Holy Spirit, to receive him for thine own child by adoption and to incorporate him into thy Holy Church" (Book of Common Prayer).

---

[1] Hebrews 8:11 [2] John 3:3-8 [3] Hebrews 8:11; John 6:45 [4] Hebrews 8:12
[5] Hebrews 8:10 [6] Galatians 3:7

Again, in Luther's Shorter Catechism we read the following: "Q. What gifts or benefits does Baptism bestow? A. It effects forgiveness of sins, delivers from death and the devil, and grants eternal salvation to all who believe, as the Word and promise of God declare." Even the great Princeton theologian, Charles Hodge, had this to say about infant baptism: "Those parents sin grievously against the souls of their children who neglect to consecrate them to God in the ordinance of baptism. Do let the little ones have their names written in the Lamb's book of life, even if they afterwards choose to erase them." [1]

Such statements by those who advocate infant baptism often stand in direct contradiction to their own teachings elsewhere. When this is the case, it only serves to illustrate how much confusion can be caused by a failure to distinguish properly between the Old and New Covenants.

21. What is the relationship between the church and Old Testament Israel?

1. Covenant Theology has tended to view the church as basically identical with Old Testament Israel, hence B. B. Warfield's statement that "God established His Church in the days of Abraham and put children [i.e., infants] into it." "They must remain there until He puts them out. He has nowhere put them out. They are still then members of His Church and as such entitled to its ordinances." [2] When Martyn Lloyd-Jones, in 1966, called true Christians to come out of apostate religious bodies (such as Anglicanism), John Stott responded in a similar vein as Warfield by saying, "I believe history is against what Dr. Lloyd-Jones has said.... Scripture is against him, the remnant was within the church not outside it." [3]

It is important to consider the concept of "the church" that lies behind statements of this sort. When the nation of Israel was in a

---

[1] Charles Hodge, *Systematic Theology* (Grand Rapids: Eerdmans, 1973) 3.588.
[2] B. B. Warfield, *Studies in Theology* (1932; reprint, Grand Rapids: Baker, 2003) 9.408.   [3] Iain Murray, *David Martyn Lloyd-Jones, The Fight of Faith* (Edinburgh: Banner of Truth, 1990) 525.

THE LAW OF CHRIST

state of general apostasy in the days of Elijah, God preserved for Himself "a remnant" of seven thousand men who had not "bowed the knee to Baal."[1] The remnant was thus "within" the nation of Israel, "not outside it." But when Paul speaks of "the remnant" in the New Testament, he is not speaking of a group *within the church;* he is speaking of those elect Jews who (along with believing Gentiles) make up *the church itself.*

> And Isaiah cries out concerning Israel, "Though the number of the sons of Israel be as the sand of the sea, it is *the remnant* that will be *saved.*" Romans 9:27
>
> In the same way then, there has also come to be at the present time *a remnant* according to *God's gracious choice.* But if it is by grace, it is no longer on the basis of works, otherwise grace is no longer grace. What then? That which Israel is seeking for, it has not obtained, but *those who were chosen obtained it*, and the rest were hardened....
> Romans 11:5-7

The church is itself "a remnant according to God's gracious choice." To say that the remnant is "within the church" is thus to confuse "the church" with the vast amalgam of apostate "Christendom" that goes under the guise of Christianity but "denies its power."[2] To argue that "the remnant" of evangelical Christians ought to stay "within the church" is to argue that evangelicals should not separate from apostate Christendom. The logical conclusion of this argument, of course, is that the Reformation itself was a mistake and "the remnant" in the days of Luther and Calvin should have stayed in "the church" (Roman Catholicism). Such conclusions only serve to illustrate the fact that the church of the New Testament should *not* be thought of as basically identical to physical Israel in the Old Testament.

2. In contrast with Covenant Theology, Classic Dispensationalism goes to the opposite extreme and views Israel and the church

---

[1] Romans 11:4   [2] 2 Timothy 3:5

as two entirely separate entities. According to this view, God has two distinct plans for physical Israel and the church. The church is viewed as a mere "parenthesis" in God's dealings with Israel. One day God will yet establish Israel *on the earth* as a physical nation with *earthly* blessings in fulfillment of Old Testament prophecy, whereas the church will be established *in heaven* as the subject of *heavenly* blessings. Although "Progressive" Dispensationalists have moved away from some of these views, they still maintain that Old Testament prophecies concerning "Israel" *are yet to be fulfilled* in a future "millennium" *by ethnic Jews.*

3. The position that has been set forth in this book is that the Biblical relationship between Israel and the church is one of type and antitype. The church is the *true* "Israel of God,"[1] made up of the *true* "children of Abraham"[2] who are the *true* "Jews."[3] It is the *true* "holy nation"[4]—a "kingdom of priests"[5] who offer "spiritual sacrifices"[6] after having been redeemed from "Egypt"[7] by the death of "Christ their Passover."[8] There is thus a very real difference between the New Testament church and Old Testament Israel. The church is not a physical nation, but a spiritual one—the very "body of Christ," of which each individual Christian is a "member."

Having said this, however, we must never lose sight of the fact that the relationship between the church and Israel is one of continuity as well as discontinuity. Christianity is, in fact, Jewish. The New Covenant is made with the renewed "house of Israel and house of Judah,"[9] which is composed of the "remnant" of believing Jews, along with believing Gentiles, who are now "partakers with them of the rich root of the [Jewish] olive tree."[10] These Gentiles were once "excluded from the commonwealth of Israel, and strangers to the covenants of promise," but have now been "brought near by the blood of Christ" and are "no longer strangers and aliens,

---

[1] Galatians 6:15-16; Romans 9:6 [2] Galatians 3:7, 29 [3] Romans 2:28-29; Philippians 3:3 [4] 1 Peter 2:9 [5] Revelation 5:9-10; cf. Exodus 19:6 [6] 1 Peter 2:5 [7] Revelation 11:8 [8] 1 Corinthians 5:7 [9] Jeremiah 31:31; Hebrews 8:6-13 [10] Romans 11:17

but ... are fellow citizens with the saints [Jewish believers], and are of God's household."[1]

In addition to this basic continuity between Judaism and Christianity, we must also remember that *all true "children of Abraham" through the centuries* (including those who lived in the midst of Old Testament Israel) *share an essential unity.* This unity arises from the fact that all who have ever been saved, have been saved by grace alone, through faith alone. The Lord Jesus speaks of this essential unity when He says that "many shall come from east and west [i.e., converted Gentiles], and recline at the table with *Abraham, and Isaac, and Jacob,* in the *kingdom of heaven;* but the sons of the kingdom [i.e., unconverted Jews] shall be cast out into the outer darkness."[2] Heaven is a place where all the regenerate—whether they were of Jewish or of Gentile background—will forever be "together with the Lord."

22. Should Christians have as many children as possible in order to "raise up a godly seed" that will outnumber the "ungodly seed" of unbelievers?

Children are a great blessing from God,[3] but our motive for having them should not be to increase the physical numbers of the "Christian" community. Thinking of this sort involves an essentially "Old Covenant" mentality whereby the children of believers are automatically considered to be "covenant children" by birth, and the children of unbelievers are considered to be "heathen." Apart from modern authors, this idea is put forth in the Westminster Confession of Faith (24:3), which teaches that one of the reasons for marriage is "for the increase ... of the Church with an holy seed." Some recent supporters of this view have even advocated letting the horrors of abortion go unchecked, since by it unbelievers are only decreasing the numbers of their own (ungodly) "seed."

Children's books written from this perspective often do not speak to children about their need for regeneration and conversion, but

---

[1] Ephesians 2:11-19   [2] Matthew 8:11-12   [3] Psalm 127:3-5

treat them as "little Christians" who "love God" from their earliest days. As a result, multitudes grow up thinking they are children of God simply because they have been baptized as infants, have been raised in a Christian family, have attended church faithfully, and have lived clean, moral lives. Sadly, they are often complete strangers to the miracle whereby men become "new creatures" in Christ and "all things become new."

23. Were the Old Testament "ceremonial" laws meant to give us a pattern for healthy eating, good hygiene, etc.?

It is true that God would never have given His people any laws that were *harmful* to their physical welfare. In the realm of diet, for example, we can be certain that eating "milk and honey" is not detrimental to good health! Neither is the eating of pork *essential* to good health, since pork was denied to the Jews. Likewise, circumcision must not be harmful to the health of infants, or God would not have commanded it, and ceremonial washings may well have prevented the spread of bacteria.[1]

Nevertheless, it is a mistake to think of the dietary laws as "health food laws from God" or of circumcision as a "healthy baby law from God." According to the Bible, these laws were given primarily to separate Israel from other nations[2] and to point to deeper spiritual realities.[3] Though some of them can now be seen as having hygienic benefits, most of them do not fit this pattern at all,[4] and none of them should be used as divine endorsements of our own personal dietary convictions (e.g., "the Bible says pork is not good for you").

Those who start following these laws as "God-given pointers toward good hygiene" invariably begin to subtly look down on those Christians who don't, viewing them as being less "Biblical" and less spiritual than themselves. We may circumcise our children and not

---

[1] E.g., Leviticus 15:2-11 [2] Leviticus 20:24-26; see also 15:31 and 16:16, where "dying in their uncleanness" had to do, not with *disease*, but with "defiling God's tabernacle" which was "among them." [3] Colossians 2:16-17
[4] E.g., Leviticus 12:2-5; 15:16-24; 16:23-24, 26, 28; etc.

eat pork, but that does not make us *any* more "Biblical" than those Christians who do *not* circumcise their children and *do* eat pork.

24. How does the "law of Christ" relate to the teachings of "theonomy"?

Theonomists believe that the civil aspects of the Mosaic Law were intended by God, not only to govern the theocracy (Old Testament Israel), but also to serve as a pattern for governments in our day. Thus, if Christians had the power to do so, they should pass laws reflecting the prohibitions and punishments that were in force during the Old Covenant. For example, the death penalty should be instituted for such things as adultery, homosexuality, heresy, and Sabbath breaking.

While it is true that the only basis for right and wrong (and thus for law of any kind) is God's character revealed in the heart of man and in Scripture, it is a mistake to conclude that the laws of the Mosaic theocracy should be applied directly to secular cultures. Those laws were given to Old Testament Israel specifically as a "child-conductor" to prepare the way for the coming of Christ and the New Covenant. In keeping with this goal, the theocracy was a sacralist society where only one religion was tolerated; those born within the pale of Judaism had no choice as to whether or not they wanted to be Jews. Christianity, by contrast, is a voluntary religion of personal decision and commitment. True faith cannot be forced. Men cannot be coerced into becoming Christians by being "baptized" in a river or ocean at sword point, as in the days of Constantine. The weapons of Christianity are spiritual; its only sword is the "sword of the Spirit." Any "Christianity" that must maintain and advance its cause through the use of an earthly sword is not Biblical Christianity.[1]

It is very significant that Christians do not have *any* direct commands in the New Testament to attempt to change, exert pressure upon, or gain control over existing political institutions. Instead, they are commanded to be in subjection to the government, pay their taxes,[2] and pray for those in authority.[3] The goal of such prayer

---

[1] John 18:36 [2] Romans 13:1-8 [3] 1 Timothy 2:1-2

is "that we may lead a tranquil and quiet life in all godliness and dignity." In societies where Christians have the right to vote or run for office, they should by all means try to pass laws that will preserve life, peace, and basic justice. As mature sons who "have the mind of Christ," they should study both the Old and New Testaments in an attempt to understand what laws would help to accomplish these goals. But, ultimately, they know that the battle they are fighting will not be won with carnal weapons. Laws that force stores to close on Sundays or forbid Mormons to knock on doors will only provide a temporary and external restraint of evil. Any real and lasting advancement of the kingdom of God in this world can only be accomplished through the preaching of the gospel and the spiritual weapons that accompany it.[1] Such "weapons" often go hand in hand, not with "dominion" over the church's earthly enemies, but with "afflictions, hardships, distresses, beatings, imprisonments, tumults, labors, sleeplessness, and hunger"[2] inflicted by those enemies. Christians should be under no delusion that they will advance the kingdom of God by gaining control of the state and coercing the ungodly to act like Christians. Historically, such thinking has inevitably led to the persecution, drowning, or burning of true Christians along with other "heretics" and "enemies of the state."

25. Is the present-day teaching of "patriarchy" a Biblical application of Old Testament principles to New Covenant believers?

The New Testament clearly instructs fathers to lead their families and bring their children up in the "discipline and instruction of the Lord."[3] The teaching of "patriarchy" seeks to supplement this New Testament instruction by an appeal to the role of patriarchs in the Old Testament. The word "patriarch" comes from a similar Greek word that occurs four times in the New Testament. It is applied to Abraham,[4] the twelve sons of Jacob,[5] and David.[6] In the Septuagint (the Greek translation of the Hebrew Old Testament), it is used with

---

[1] 2 Corinthians 10:3-5 [2] 2 Corinthians 6:4-10; note v. 7. [3] Ephesians 6:4
[4] Hebrews 7:4 [5] Acts 7:8-9 [6] Acts 2:29

reference to the head of a tribe or father's household.[1] A patriarch was thus a ruling ancestor—often the founding father of a family, clan, or nation. Not every man in the days of Abraham, Isaac, and Jacob was a patriarch! Patriarchs were essentially tribal chieftains who ruled over their relatives and descendants and passed on that rule to their firstborn sons. This is illustrated in the case of Jacob, who has a place among the "patriarchs" solely because he deceived his father and received the blessing intended for Esau.

> When Esau heard the words of his father, he cried out with an exceedingly great and bitter cry, and said to his father, "Bless me, even me also, O my father!"... But Isaac answered and said to Esau, "Behold, *I have made him your master, and all his relatives I have given to him as servants;* and with grain and new wine I have sustained him. Now as for you then, what can I do, my son?" Genesis 27:34, 37

An Old Testament "patriarch" was thus one who had the position of "father" and master over a whole clan, including his relatives and, in some cases, even his own brothers! Needless to say, it is quite a stretch to apply this ancient Eastern custom to the structuring of the Christian family! The ideas of the modern patriarchy movement may or may not be good in themselves, but, in any case, they should not claim to be derived from Scripture, nor should they be taught as Biblical absolutes. For example, the teaching that daughters should not go to college, but stay home and "pursue their father's vision," should be presented as a personal conviction, not as "the Biblical world view." The same holds true for the belief that only men should have the right to vote and other distinctive teachings of the patriarchy movement.

26. How does "the law of Christ" relate to "pacifism"?

Whereas Theonomy wants to make the Law of Moses the "law of the land," pacifism wants to apply the Sermon on the Mount in

---
[1] 1 Chronicles 24:31; 2 Chronicles 26:12

FREQUENTLY ASKED QUESTIONS

a similar fashion. Neither position is Biblical. As noted above, the Law of Moses was given to the theocracy (not all nations) in order to accomplish a particular purpose during a particular time. The Sermon on the Mount, on the other hand, is given to the church (not civil magistrates) and is intended to guide Christ's regenerate sheep in their journey through the labyrinth of this world, where (according to the Sermon itself) they will face persecution and abuse "on account of" Him.[1] Christ's command to "turn the other cheek" was thus intended for *Christians*, not for civil government, which is specifically "established by God" to maintain order and justice as a "minister of God" through the use of "the sword."[2]

27. Is it right for Christians to fight in "just" wars, serve as police officers, discipline their children, and otherwise use physical force in an attempt to secure righteousness?

The fact that God directly commanded His Old Covenant people to destroy other nations as a judgment upon their sins[3] proves that war, in and of itself, is not necessarily immoral. In the same way, the fact that God has directly established civil government to "bear the sword" as His "minister" proves that it cannot be morally wrong for representatives of the government to use physical force, if necessary, to prevent crime and maintain justice. This includes police officers and (ideally) soldiers fighting to maintain global justice and peace. Physical discipline of children (in the context of loving nurture) is also directly commanded by God in Scripture.[4] There is nothing inherently wrong, then, with Christians serving as police officers, fighting as soldiers, or using physical means to discipline their children, provided these things are done in submission to Scriptural guidelines.

Nevertheless, there are principles related to the law of Christ that need to be considered in this question, as in all other such questions. Governments, at best, have a *preservative* role in society. The most

---

[1] Matthew 5:8-10, 39-40 [2] Romans 13:1-4 [3] Deuteronomy 9:4-6; Leviticus 18:25 (vv. 21-24); Genesis 15:16 [4] Proverbs 19:18; 22:15; 23:13-14

that any government can do is preserve justice and maintain law and order. The church, on the other hand, has a *redemptive* role in society. Only the church can preach the gospel and see souls freed from sin and turned to righteousness.

For the Christian, the establishing or maintaining of mere *justice* should be the minimum goal of his actions. Justice is essential, but the Christian should desire something more. He should desire to be used in a *redemptive* capacity in the lives of others. Many non-Christians can apprehend criminals just as effectively as Christians can, but only Christians can preach the gospel to the prisoners on death row once they have been apprehended. Many non-Christians can "pull the trigger" and kill "enemy" soldiers just as well as (or better than) Christians can, but only Christians can save men's souls by witnessing to them about Christ. For this reason, many Christians have felt led to become conscientious objectors or chaplains or medics, and those believers who *have* felt led to serve in the difficult role of police officers or soldiers have often started Bible studies or used other means of evangelism to reach those around them.

Even in the matter of childrearing, Christian parents will not look upon corporal punishment as the ultimate solution to their children's needs. In raising their children, they will seek to go *beyond* the establishment of mere equity to the place of redemption.

– APPENDIX F –

LEGALISM VS. LAWLESSNESS

The term "legalism" does not appear in the Bible and is therefore difficult to define Biblically. For purposes of this study, however, legalism can be defined as *reliance on law keeping to secure salvation and sanctification*. The "laws" that the legalist seeks to keep may be either God-given commandments or man-made rules and regulations. According to this definition, a person is not necessarily a legalist merely because he has an overly sensitive conscience with regard to matters such as honesty or frugality. Neither are those who emphasize human responsibility as much as divine sovereignty legalists.[1] Nor is a person a legalist because he insists on the need for spiritual disciplines such as fasting and self-denial.

The term "lawlessness" *does* appear in the Bible, and its meaning is clear from the contexts in which it is found: "What partnership have *righteousness* and *lawlessness*, or what fellowship has *light* with *darkness*? Or what harmony has *Christ* with *Belial?*"[2] Here we see that lawlessness is the opposite of "righteousness" and is associated with "darkness" and "Belial." The Greek term "lawless" literally means "without law" (Gk. *anomos: a* = "without," *nomos* = "law"). The term "antinomian," which does *not* appear in the Bible, also comes from the Greek word for "law": anti = "against," *nomos* = "law." True antinomians are not only *without law*, but also *against law*.

OPPOSING ERRORS

Nothing is sufficient to secure true holiness of life except the regenerating and indwelling power of the Holy Spirit. It is not surprising, then, that false teachers (who are "devoid of the Spirit"[3]) have always tended toward either legalism or lawlessness in their

---

[1] Philippians 2:12-13   [2] 2 Corinthians 6:14-15; see also Matthew 7:23; 13:41; 23:28; 24:12.   [3] Jude 19

approach to "Christian" living. Those who are legalistic have substituted *law* for *grace*,[1] and those who are lawless have "turned the *grace* of our God into *licentiousness*."[2] Though we may be inclined to think of legalism as a particularly "Jewish" sin and lawlessness as a particularly "Gentile" sin, in reality both tendencies coexist in every natural man. The sinful heart that is legalistic in its thinking one day may be lawless in its actions the next. In fact, *external* legalism often coincides with *internal* lawlessness; the scribes and Pharisees are a primary example.[3]

No Christian can be a true legalist, since trust in law is mutually exclusive of trust in Christ.[4] In the same way, no Christian can be truly lawless, since Christ "never knew" those who "practice lawlessness."[5] Nevertheless, Christians can be adversely affected by both legalism (as the Galatians were) and lawlessness (as the Corinthians were). True Christians can become *legalistic in their mindset*, concentrating on obedience to a mental "list of duties" rather than their relationship to Christ, and seeking by their daily "performance" to maintain God's favor and smile. Likewise, true Christians can become *lawless in their mindset,* using "grace" as an excuse for a lazy and careless spiritual lifestyle, rather than "disciplining themselves for the purpose of godliness."[6] Every professing Christian should give heed to the warning signs of both legalism and lawlessness, since each dishonors God, and the Holy Spirit will never allow either of them to "reign" in the life of a true believer.

CHARACTERISTICS OF LEGALISM

1. The legalist centers his life around laws rather than God. The greatest sin of the legalist is that he does not really *love and worship God*. Instead, his "heart, soul, mind, and strength"—his affections, concerns, thoughts, and energies—are all centered on laws, rules, and regulations. This is particularly odious to God because it gives lost men the impression that true religion is

---

[1] Galatians 5:4 [2] Jude 4 [3] Matthew 23:28 [4] Galatians 5:4 [5] Matthew 7:23
[6] 1 Timothy 4:7

something ugly and impersonal—a matter of lifeless rule keeping, rather than a love relationship with a living God. The fact that such Pharisaic religion is "highly esteemed among men" makes it even more "detestable in the sight of God."[1] True Christian living, by contrast, is something joyful, free, and unconstrained. It glorifies God because it flows from a heart that delights in Him and loves Him supremely.

> And He said to him, "You shall love the Lord your God with all your heart, and with all your soul, and with all your mind. This is the great and foremost commandment."
>
> Matthew 22:37-38

> The kingdom of God is not eating and drinking, but righteousness and peace and joy in the Holy Spirit.
>
> Romans 14:17

2. The legalist is more concerned about rule keeping than the needs of his fellow men. The second greatest sin of the legalist is that he does not really *love others*. To the legalist, "rules" are more important than people, and "sacrifice" is more important than "compassion."[2] Legalism is insensitive to human need. It is law-centered, not love-centered. It cares more about the fine points of things like Sabbath observance than the sufferings of its fellow men.[3] The conscience of a legalist will not be troubled when it sends away a Judas to commit suicide, but it will be very concerned not to transgress some fine point of legal protocol.[4]

> The second [greatest commandment] is like it, "You shall love your neighbor as yourself." Matthew 22:39

> And He entered again into a synagogue; and a man was there with a withered hand. And they were watching Him to see if He would heal him on the Sabbath, in order that they might accuse Him. And He said to the man with the withered hand, "Rise and come forward!" And He said

---

[1] Luke 16:14-15 [2] Matthew 9:11-13 [3] Mark 3:1-6 [4] Matthew 27:3-6

to them, "Is it lawful on the Sabbath to do good or to do harm, to save a life or to kill?" But they kept silent. And after looking around at them with anger, grieved at their hardness of heart, He said to the man, "Stretch out your hand." And he stretched it out, and his hand was restored. And the Pharisees went out and immediately began taking counsel with the Herodians against Him, as to how they might destroy Him. Mark 3:1-6

And when the Pharisees saw this, they said to His disciples, "Why is your Teacher eating with the tax-gatherers and sinners?" But when He heard this, He said, "It is not those who are healthy who need a physician, but those who are sick. But go and learn what this means, 'I desire compassion, and not sacrifice,' for I did not come to call the righteous, but sinners." Matthew 9:11-13

At that time Jesus went on the Sabbath through the grain fields, and His disciples became hungry and began to pick the heads of grain and eat. But when the Pharisees saw it, they said to Him, "Behold, Your disciples do what is not lawful to do on a Sabbath." But He said to them, "Have you not read what David did, when he became hungry, he and his companions; how he entered the house of God, and they ate the consecrated bread, which was not lawful for him to eat, nor for those with him, but for the priests alone? Or have you not read in the Law, that on the Sabbath the priests in the temple break the Sabbath, and are innocent? But I say to you, that something greater than the temple is here. But if you had known what this means, 'I desire compassion, and not a sacrifice,' you would not have condemned the innocent. For the Son of Man is Lord of the Sabbath." Matthew 12:1-8

Then when Judas, who had betrayed Him, saw that He had been condemned, he felt remorse and returned the thirty pieces of silver to the chief priests and elders, saying, "I have sinned by betraying innocent blood." But they said,

> *"What is that to us? See to that yourself!"* And he threw the pieces of silver into the sanctuary and departed; and he went away and hanged himself. And the chief priests took the pieces of silver and said, *"It is not lawful to put them into the temple treasury, since it is the price of blood."*
>
> Matthew 27:3-6

3. Legalism emphasizes externals. The legalist views righteousness primarily in terms of external acts, rather than internal attitudes. He has a shallow view of sin and imagines that by keeping the law outwardly he is pleasing to God. He knows nothing of real heart righteousness. He "judges according to outward appearance,"[1] whereas God "looks at the heart."[2]

> Woe to you, scribes and Pharisees, hypocrites! For you clean the outside of the cup and of the dish, but inside they are full of robbery and self-indulgence. You blind Pharisee, first clean the inside of the cup and of the dish, so that the outside of it may become clean also. Woe to you, scribes and Pharisees, hypocrites! For you are like whitewashed tombs which on the outside appear beautiful, but inside they are full of dead men's bones and all uncleanness. Even so you too outwardly appear righteous to men, but inwardly you are full of hypocrisy and lawlessness.
>
> Matthew 23:25-28

> And when the Pharisee saw it, he was surprised that He had not first ceremonially washed before the meal. But the Lord said to him, "Now you Pharisees clean the outside of the cup and of the platter; but inside of you, you are full of robbery and wickedness. You foolish ones, did not He who made the outside make the inside also? But give that which is within as charity, and then all things are clean for you."
>
> Luke 11:38-41

---

[1] John 7:22-24   [2] 1 Samuel 16:7

Because of its emphasis on externals, legalism tends to promote outward conformity and uniformity, rather than true unity of spirit. Everyone looks alike, talks alike, dresses alike. Legalism stifles spontaneity, individuality, and freedom.

4. Legalism majors on minors. Since legalists are blind to the "weighty" matters of the law, they center their attention on fine points and neglect the things that are most important. They "strain out the gnat" by observing minor rules and regulations, but "swallow the camel" by failing to love God and others.

> Woe to you, scribes and Pharisees, hypocrites! For you tithe mint and dill and cumin, and have neglected the weightier provisions of the law: justice and mercy and faithfulness; but these are the things you should have done without neglecting the others. You blind guides, who strain out a gnat and swallow a camel! Matthew 23:23-24

5. Legalism develops into a religion of experts. Because the legalist has no living relationship with God as his teacher and guide, he must have a "rule" for every situation that may arise. A whole class of people ("lawyers") is needed, therefore, to interpret the fine points of the law and to "fill in the blanks" when they feel that God has not given sufficiently detailed revelation.

> And one of the lawyers said to Him in reply, "Teacher, when You say this, You insult us too." But He said, "Woe to you lawyers as well! For you weigh men down with burdens hard to bear, while you yourselves will not even touch the burdens with one of your fingers.... Woe to you lawyers! For you have taken away the key of knowledge; you did not enter in yourselves, and those who were entering in you hindered." Luke 11:45-46, 52

6. Legalism tends to make absolutes out of personal convictions or man-made traditions and then imposes these on others. As noted above, the legalist must have a rule for every situation. When these are not spelled out clearly in Scripture, they must be "deduced" using a mixture of human reasoning and personal opinion. Such human reasoning and personal opinion is soon accepted as "what the Bible teaches," and a new "absolute" is born! These unbiblical absolutes range literally all the way from the teaching that chrome bumpers on cars are "worldly" and must be painted black, to the idea that all Christians must homeschool their children and bake homemade bread!

> And the Pharisees and some of the scribes gathered together around Him when they had come from Jerusalem, and had seen that some of His disciples were eating their bread with impure hands, that is, unwashed. (For the Pharisees and all the Jews do not eat unless they carefully wash their hands, thus observing the traditions of the elders; and when they come from the market place, they do not eat unless they cleanse themselves; and there are many other things which they have received in order to observe, such as the washing of cups and pitchers and copper pots.) And the Pharisees and the scribes asked Him, "Why do Your disciples not walk according to the tradition of the elders, but eat their bread with impure hands?" And He said to them, "Rightly did Isaiah prophesy of you hypocrites, as it is written, 'This people honors Me with their lips, but their heart is far away from Me. But in vain do they worship me, teaching as doctrines the precepts of men.'"
>
> Mark 7:1-7

7. Legalism causes men to sin against others in the name of righteousness. When personal opinions and human traditions are elevated to the position of absolutes, the weighty matters of the law (such as love for God and love for others) are inevitably minimized and invalidated. In order to keep his traditions, the legalist will sin even against his own loved ones, all the while soothing his conscience with the idea that he is "only obeying God."

> Neglecting the commandment of God, you hold to the tradition of men.... You nicely set aside the commandment of God in order to keep your tradition. For Moses said,

"Honor your father and your mother"; and, "He who speaks evil of father or mother, let him be put to death"; but you say, "If a man says to his father or his mother, anything of mine you might have been helped by is Corban (that is to say, given to God)," you no longer permit him to do anything for his father or his mother; thus invalidating the word of God by your tradition which you have handed down; and you do many things such as that.

Mark 7:8-13

8. Legalism is characterized by self-centeredness, pride, judgmentalism, and contempt for others. Self, in one manifestation or another, is prominent in all forms of legalism.

> *I* thank You that *I* am not like other people.... *I* fast twice a week; *I* pay tithes of all that *I* get.
> Luke 18:11-12 (NAS95)

The legalist has no real comprehension of his own sinfulness or of God's holiness. He does not really believe that "there is none good but God,"[1] so he vainly imagines that he can "establish his own righteousness"[2] by keeping the law. *He is not cast upon God for mercy*, since he has no need of it. *He is not cast upon God for righteousness*, since he thinks he has his own righteousness. *He is not cast upon God for enablement to live a holy life*, since he views the law in terms of externals that he can keep in his own power. *He is not even cast upon God for guidance*, since he has his rulebook and his rules to apply to every situation. The legalist is thus *proud, self-righteous, and self-sufficient*.

Because he is proud and self-righteous, *the legalist views others with contempt*. He considers himself to be better than other men.

> And He also told this parable to some people who trusted in themselves that they were righteous, and viewed others with contempt: "Two men went up into the temple to pray,

---

[1] Matthew 19:16-22   [2] Romans 10:3

one a Pharisee and the other a tax collector. The Pharisee stood and was praying this to himself: 'God, I thank You that I am not like other people: swindlers, unjust, adulterers, or even like this tax collector....'"

Luke 18:9-11 (NAS95)

Furthermore, all legalists are *judgmental*; they sit above others and look down on them, paying close attention to their supposed faults. Legalists also take it upon themselves to judge the motives of other men's hearts.

> Do not judge lest you be judged. For in the way you judge, you will be judged; and by your standard of measure, it will be measured to you. And why do you look at the speck that is in your brother's eye, but do not notice the log that is in your own eye? Or how can you say to your brother, "Let me take the speck out of your eye," and behold, the log is in your own eye? You hypocrite, first take the log out of your own eye, and then you will see clearly to take the speck out of your brother's eye.   Matthew 7:1-5

> Let not him who does not eat judge him who eats, for God has accepted him. Who are you to judge the servant of another? To his own master he stands or falls; and stand he will, for the Lord is able to make him stand.
>
> Romans 14:3-4

In light of these things, it is not surprising that when true Christians move in the direction of legalism, they lose the "sense of blessing"[1] that they once had. They realize deep down that they can never "perform" well enough to maintain God's favor, and they find themselves in a state of misery and bondage. Rather than being filled with *love* for one another, they begin, instead, to "bite and devour one another."[2]

---

[1] Galatians 4:15   [2] Galatians 5:15

9. **Legalism is of no real value in mortifying sin.** Though it has an outward show of righteousness, legalism actually fosters sin, rather than destroying it. Either it stirs men to commit even worse sins than the ones they are trying to put to death, or it replaces outward and obvious sins with "religious" ones that are more hidden and deceitful.

> If you have died with Christ to the elementary principles of the world, why, as if you were living in the world, do you submit yourself to decrees, such as, "Do not handle, do not taste, do not touch!" (which all refer to things destined to perish with the using)—in accordance with the commandments and teachings of men? These are matters which have, to be sure, the appearance of wisdom in self-made religion and self-abasement and severe treatment of the body, but are of no value against fleshly indulgence.
> Colossians 2:20-23

CHARACTERISTICS OF LAWLESSNESS

1. **The lawless person centers his life around self and sin, rather than God and others.** "Self" is the real god of every lawless person. He cares more about his own will and desires than about pleasing or glorifying the Lord. His inner attitude is, "I do not want this Man [Christ] to reign over me."[1] The lawless person also cares more about his own will and desires than about what is best for his fellow men. Like the legalist, he utterly fails to keep the two great commandments.

> These men are those who are hidden reefs in your love feasts when they feast with you without fear, *caring for themselves;* clouds without water, carried along by winds; autumn trees without fruit, doubly dead, uprooted; wild waves of the sea, casting up their own shame like foam; wandering stars, for whom the black darkness has been reserved forever.
> Jude 12-13

---

[1] Luke 19:12-14

2. Lawlessness turns the grace of God into a license for sin. Lawlessness teaches that because we are saved by grace rather than works, it does not matter how we live. It says that Christians are free to sin because they are not under Law, and it encourages men to neglect or think lightly of Christ's commandments. Those who *are* careful to obey Christ are vilified as "legalists."

> For certain persons have crept in unnoticed, those who were long beforehand marked out for this condemnation, *ungodly persons who turn the grace of our God into licentiousness and deny our only Master and Lord, Jesus Christ.* Jude 4

> What then? Shall we sin because we are not under law but under grace? May it never be! Do you not know that when you present yourselves to someone as slaves for obedience, you are slaves of the one whom you obey, either of sin resulting in death, or of obedience resulting in righteousness? Romans 6:15-16

> Not everyone who says to Me, "Lord, Lord," will enter the kingdom of heaven; but he who does the will of My Father who is in heaven. Many will say to Me on that day, "Lord, Lord, did we not prophesy in Your name, and in Your name cast out demons, and in Your name perform many miracles?" And then I will declare to them, "I never knew you; depart from Me, you who practice lawlessness." Matthew 7:21-23

3. Lawlessness teaches that it is not necessary to be holy in order to be saved. Lawlessness implies or openly advocates the idea that those who are personally unrighteous *can* inherit the kingdom of God, saying that good works are *not* the test of true conversion, and sanctification is *not* a necessary evidence of justification. *Repentance* is viewed either as *not being part of the gospel message* or as *not involving any actual change of practice* with regard to sin. Faith can then be "without works" and yet still be true saving faith.

> Pursue peace with all men, and *the sanctification* [holiness] *without which no one will see the Lord.*   Hebrews 12:14

> Or do you not know that *the unrighteous shall not inherit the kingdom of God?* Do not be deceived; neither fornicators, nor idolaters, nor adulterers, nor effeminate, nor homosexuals, nor thieves, nor the covetous, nor drunkards, nor revilers, nor swindlers, shall inherit the kingdom of God.
> 1 Corinthians 6:9-10

> *You will know them by their fruits.* Grapes are not gathered from thorn bushes, nor figs from thistles, are they? Even so, every good tree bears good fruit; but the bad tree bears bad fruit. A good tree cannot produce bad fruit, nor can a bad tree produce good fruit. Every tree that does not bear good fruit is cut down and thrown into the fire. *So then, you will know them by their fruits.*   Matthew 7:16-20

> What use is it, my brethren, if a man says he has faith, but he has no works? Can that faith save him?... You believe that God is one. You do well; the demons also believe, and shudder. But are you willing to recognize, you foolish fellow, that faith without works is useless?
> James 2:14, 19-20

4. Lawlessness views the law of God with contempt. Those who are lawless are not afraid to treat God's commandments and requirements lightly and with disdain. By their attitudes and actions, they imply that the law itself is evil. Paul, on the other hand, extols the law as "holy, righteous, and good" and rejects as unthinkable any idea that the law is sin.

> What shall we say then? *Is the Law sin? May it never be!* On the contrary, I would not have come to know sin except through the Law....   Romans 7:7

> So then, the Law is holy, and the commandment is holy and righteous and good. *Therefore did that which is good become a cause of death for me? May it never be!* Rather it was

sin, in order that it might be shown to be sin by effecting my death through that which is good, that through the commandment sin might become utterly sinful.

Romans 7:12-13

5. Lawlessness dishonors God. Hypocrisy and lawlessness by those who claim to be Christians causes God's name to be blasphemed among unbelievers and His truth to be maligned.

Therefore, say to the house of Israel, "Thus says the Lord God, 'It is not for your sake, O house of Israel, that I am about to act, but for My holy name, which you have profaned among the nations where you went. And I will vindicate *the holiness of My great name which has been profaned* among the nations, which you have profaned in their midst. Then the nations will know that I am the Lord,' declares the Lord God, 'when I prove Myself holy among you in their sight.'" Ezekiel 36:22-23

You who boast in the Law, through your breaking the Law, do you dishonor God? For *"The name of God is blasphemed among the Gentiles because of you,"* just as it is written.

Romans 2:23-24

But false prophets also arose among the people, just as there will also be false teachers among you, who will secretly introduce destructive heresies, even denying the Master who bought them, bringing swift destruction upon themselves. And many will follow their sensuality, and *because of them the way of the truth will be maligned....*

2 Peter 2:1-2

Older women likewise are to be reverent in their behavior, not malicious gossips, nor enslaved to much wine, teaching what is good, that they may encourage the young women to love their husbands, to love their children, to be sensible, pure, workers at home, kind, being subject to their own husbands, *that the word of God may not be dishonored.*

Titus 2:3-5

APPENDIX G

LOVE IN THE NEW TESTAMENT

The New Testament has much to say about love. The fountain of love is God Himself—the "God of love."[1] His love is manifested between the Persons of the Trinity, toward all men,[2] and especially toward "His own."[3] Because of God's love for us, we love Him[4] and other Christians.[5] Love to God and love to our fellow men are inseparably tied together. It is impossible to truly love God without loving our fellow men[6] or to truly love our fellow men without loving God.[7] Most of the direct New Testament references to "love" are listed in this appendix. In some cases, verses have been listed more than once because it is not clear whether God's love for us or our love for Him or our love for others (or all three) is in view.

GOD'S LOVE

Matthew 5:44-46 "But I say to you, *love* your enemies, and pray for those who persecute you *in order that you may be sons of your Father who is in heaven; for He causes His sun to rise on the evil and the good, and sends rain on the righteous and the unrighteous.* For if you *love* those who love you, what reward have you?"

Mark 10:21 "And looking at him, *Jesus felt a love for him*, and said to him, 'One thing you lack: go and sell all you possess, and give to the poor, and you shall have treasure in heaven; and come, follow Me.'"

Luke 6:35 "But *love* your enemies, and do good, and lend, expecting nothing in return; and your reward will be great, and you will be sons of the Most High; *for He Himself is kind* to ungrateful and evil men."

---

[1] 2 Corinthians 13:11 [2] Matthew 5:44-48 [3] John 13:1 [4] 1 John 4:19
[5] 1 John 5:1 [6] 1 John 3:17; 4:20; John 21:15-17; cf. Leviticus 19:14, 32; 25:36, 43; Proverbs 14:31; Genesis 9:6; James 3:9 [7] 1 John 5:2

John 3:16 "For *God so loved the world*, that He gave His only begotten Son, that whoever believes in Him should not perish, but have eternal life."

John 3:35 "*The Father loves the Son*, and has given all things into His hand."

John 5:20 "For *the Father loves the Son*, and shows Him all things that He Himself is doing...."

John 10:17 "For this reason *the Father loves Me*, because I lay down My life that I may take it again."

John 11:3 "The sisters therefore sent to Him, saying, 'Lord, behold, he *whom You love* is sick.'"

John 11:5 "Now *Jesus loved* Martha, and her sister, and Lazarus."

John 11:36 "And so the Jews were saying, 'Behold *how He loved him!*'"

John 13:1 "Now before the Feast of the Passover, Jesus knowing that His hour had come that He should depart out of this world to the Father, *having loved His own* who were in the world, *He loved them* to the end."

John 13:23; 19:26; 20:2; 21:7, 20 "one of His disciples, *whom Jesus loved*...."

John 13:34 "A new commandment I give to you, that you love one another, even as *I have loved you*, that you also love one another."

John 14:21 "He who has My commandments and keeps them, he it is who loves Me; and he who loves Me shall be *loved by My Father*, and *I will love him*, and will disclose Myself to him."

John 14:23 "Jesus answered and said to him, 'If anyone loves Me, he will keep My word; and *My Father will love him*, and We will come to him, and make Our abode with him.'"

John 14:31 "But that the world may know that *I love the Father*, and as the Father gave Me commandment, even so I do."

John 15:9-10 "Just as *the Father has loved Me*, I have also *loved you*; abide in *My love*. If you keep My commandments, you will abide in *My love*; just as I have kept My Father's commandments, and abide in *His love*."

John 15:12-13 "This is My commandment, that you love one another, just as *I have loved you*. *Greater love has no one than this, that one lay down his life for his friends*."

John 16:27 "For the *Father Himself loves you*, because you have loved Me, and have believed that I came forth from the Father."

John 17:23-24 (NAS95) "I in them and You in Me, that they may be perfected in unity, so that the world may know that You sent Me, and *loved them*, even as *You have loved Me*. Father, I desire that they also, whom You have given Me, be with Me where I am, so that they may see My glory which You have given Me, for *You loved Me* before the foundation of the world."

John 17:26 (NAS95) "And I have made Your name known to them, and will make it known, so that the *love* with which *You loved Me* may be *in them*, and I in them."

Romans 5:5 "And hope does not disappoint, because the *love of God* has been poured out within our hearts through the Holy Spirit who was given to us."

Romans 5:8 "But God demonstrates *His own love toward us*, in that while we were yet sinners, Christ died for us."

Romans 8:35 "Who shall separate us from *the love of Christ?* Shall tribulation, or distress, or persecution, or famine, or nakedness, or peril, or sword?"

Romans 8:37 "But in all these things we overwhelmingly conquer through *Him who loved us*."

Romans 8:39 "Nor height, nor depth, nor any other created thing, shall be able to separate us from the *love of God*, which is in Christ Jesus our Lord."

Romans 9:13 "Just as it is written, *'Jacob I loved*, but Esau I hated.'"

2 Corinthians 5:14 "For the *love of Christ* controls us, having concluded this, that one died for all, therefore all died."

2 Corinthians 9:7 "Let each one do just as he has purposed in his heart; not grudgingly or under compulsion; for *God loves a cheerful giver.*"

2 Corinthians 13:11 "Finally, brethren, rejoice, be made complete, be comforted, be like-minded, live in peace; and the *God of love* and peace shall be with you."

2 Corinthians 13:14 "The grace of the Lord Jesus Christ, and *the love of God*, and the fellowship of the Holy Spirit, be with you all."

Galatians 2:20 "I have been crucified with Christ; and it is no longer I who live, but Christ lives in me; and the life which I now live in the flesh I live by faith in the Son of God, *who loved me*, and delivered Himself up for me."

Ephesians 1:4-5 "Just as He chose us in Him before the foundation of the world, that we should be holy and blameless before Him. *In love He predestined us* to adoption as sons through Jesus Christ to Himself, according to the kind intention of His will."

Ephesians 2:4 "But God, being rich in mercy, because of *His great love with which He loved us ....*"

Ephesians 3:19 "And to know *the love of Christ which surpasses knowledge*, that you may be filled up to all the fulness of God."

Ephesians 5:2 "And walk in love, just as *Christ also loved you*, and gave Himself up for us, an offering and a sacrifice to God as a fragrant aroma."

Ephesians 5:25 "Husbands, love your wives, just as *Christ also loved the church* and gave Himself up for her."

2 Thessalonians 2:16 "Now may our Lord Jesus Christ Himself and God our Father, *who has loved us* and given us eternal comfort and good hope by grace."

Titus 3:4 "But when the kindness of God our Savior and *His love for mankind* appeared...."

Hebrews 12:6 "For those *whom the Lord loves* He disciplines, and He scourges every son whom He receives."

1 John 3:1 "See *how great a love the Father has bestowed upon us*, that we should be called children of God; and such we are. For this reason the world does not know us, because it did not know Him."

1 John 3:16 "We know *love* by this, that *He laid down His life for us;* and we ought to lay down our lives for the brethren."

1 John 4:8 "The one who does not love does not know God, for *God is love.*"

1 John 4:9-10 "By this *the love of God* was manifested in us, that God has sent His only begotten Son into the world so that we might live through Him. In this is *love*, not that we loved God, but that *He loved us* and sent His Son to be the propitiation for our sins."

1 John 4:11-12 "Beloved, if *God so loved us*, we also ought to love one another. No one has beheld God at any time; if we love one another, God abides in us, and *His love* is perfected in us."

1 John 4:16 "And we have come to know and have believed *the love which God has for us. God is love*, and the one who abides in love abides in God, and God abides in him."

1 John 4:19 "We love, because *He first loved us.*"

Jude 1:21 "Keep yourselves in *the love of God*, waiting anxiously for the mercy of our Lord Jesus Christ to eternal life."

Revelation 1:5 "And from Jesus Christ, the faithful witness, the first-born of the dead, and the ruler of the kings of the earth. To *Him who loves us*, and released us from our sins by His blood."

Revelation 3:9 "Behold, I will cause those of the synagogue of Satan, who say that they are Jews, and are not, but lie—behold,

I will make them to come and bow down at your feet, and to know that *I have loved you*."

Revelation 3:19 "Those *whom I love*, I reprove and discipline; be zealous therefore, and repent."

Our Love for God

Matthew 6:24 "No one can serve two masters; for either he will hate the one and *love the other,* or he will hold to one and despise the other. You cannot serve God and mammon."

Matthew 10:37 "He who *loves* father or mother more than *Me* is not worthy of Me; and he who *loves* son or daughter more than *Me* is not worthy of Me."

Matthew 22:37 "And He said to him, 'You shall *love the Lord your God* with all your heart, and with all your soul, and with all your mind.'"

Matthew 24:12 "And because lawlessness is increased, *most people's love* will grow cold."

Mark 12:30 "And you shall *love the Lord your God* with all your heart, and with all your soul, and with all your mind, and with all your strength."

Mark 12:33 "And to *love Him* with all the heart and with all the understanding and with all the strength, and to love one's neighbor as himself, is much more than all burnt offerings and sacrifices."

Luke 7:42 "When they were unable to repay, he graciously forgave them both. Which of them therefore will *love him* more?"

Luke 7:47 "For this reason I say to you, her sins, which are many, have been forgiven, for *she loved much*; but he who is forgiven little, *loves little*."

Luke 10:27 "And he answered and said, 'You shall *love the Lord your God* with all your heart, and with all your soul, and with all your strength, and with all your mind; and your neighbor as yourself.'"

Luke 11:42 "But woe to you Pharisees! For you pay tithe of mint and rue and every kind of garden herb, and yet disregard justice and *the love of God*; but these are the things you should have done without neglecting the others."

Luke 16:13 "No servant can serve two masters; for either he will hate the one, and *love the other*, or else he will hold to one, and despise the other. You cannot serve God and mammon."

John 5:42 "But I know you, that you do not have the *love of God* in yourselves."

John 8:42 "Jesus said to them, 'If God were your Father, you would *love Me*; for I proceeded forth and have come from God, for I have not even come on My own initiative, but He sent Me.'"

John 14:15 "If *you love Me*, you will keep My commandments."

John 14:21 "He who has My commandments and keeps them, he it is *who loves Me*; and he *who loves Me* shall be loved by My Father, and I will love him, and will disclose Myself to him."

John 14:23-24 "Jesus answered and said to him, 'If *anyone loves Me*, he will keep My word; and My Father will love him, and We will come to him, and make Our abode with him.' He who does not *love Me* does not keep My words; and the word which you hear is not Mine, but the Father's who sent Me."

John 14:28 "You heard that I said to you, 'I go away, and I will come to you.' If *you loved Me*, you would have rejoiced, because I go to the Father; for the Father is greater than I."

John 16:27 "For the Father Himself loves you, because *you have loved Me*, and have believed that I came forth from the Father."

John 21:15-17 "So when they had finished breakfast, Jesus said to Simon Peter, 'Simon, son of John, *do you love Me* more than these?' He said to Him, 'Yes, Lord; You know that *I love You*.' He said to him, 'Tend My lambs.' He said to him again a second time, 'Simon, son of John, *do you love Me*?' He said to Him, 'Yes, Lord; You know that *I love You*.' He said to him, 'Shepherd My sheep.' He said to him the third time, 'Simon, son of John, *do you love Me?*' Peter was grieved because He said to him the third time, *'Do you love Me?'* And he said to Him, 'Lord, You know all things; You know that *I love You*.' Jesus said to him, 'Tend My sheep.' "

Romans 8:28 "And we know that God causes all things to work together for good to those *who love God*, to those who are called according to His purpose."

1 Corinthians 2:9 "But just as it is written, 'Things which eye has not seen and ear has not heard, and which have not entered the heart of man, all that God has prepared for *those who love Him*.' "

1 Corinthians 8:3 "But if anyone *loves God*, he is known by Him."

1 Corinthians 16:22 "If anyone does not *love the Lord*, let him be accursed. Maranatha."

Ephesians 3:17 "So that Christ may dwell in your hearts through faith; and that you, being rooted and grounded in *love*...."

Ephesians 6:24 "Grace be with all those who *love our Lord Jesus Christ with a love incorruptible.*"

1 Thessalonians 5:8 "But since we are of the day, let us be sober, having put on the breastplate of faith and *love*, and as a helmet, the hope of salvation."

2 Thessalonians 3:5 "And may the Lord direct your hearts into *the love of God* and into the steadfastness of Christ."

2 Timothy 3:4 "treacherous, reckless, conceited, lovers of pleasure rather than *lovers of God*...."

Hebrews 6:10 "For God is not unjust so as to forget your work and *the love which you have shown toward His name*, in having ministered and in still ministering to the saints."

James 1:12 "Blessed is a man who perseveres under trial; for once he has been approved, he will receive the crown of life, which the Lord has promised to those *who love Him*."

James 2:5 "Listen, my beloved brethren: did not God choose the poor of this world to be rich in faith and heirs of the kingdom which He promised to those *who love Him?*"

1 Peter 1:8 "And though you have not seen Him, *you love Him*, and though you do not see Him now, but believe in Him, you greatly rejoice with joy inexpressible and full of glory...."

1 John 2:5 "But whoever keeps His word, in him *the love of God* has truly been perfected. By this we know that we are in Him...."

1 John 2:15 "Do not love the world, nor the things in the world. If anyone loves the world, the *love of the Father* is not in him."

1 John 3:17 "But whoever has the world's goods, and beholds his brother in need and closes his heart against him, how does *the love of God* abide in him?"

1 John 4:17-21 "By this, *love* is perfected with us, that we may have confidence in the day of judgment; because as He is, so also are we in this world. There is *no fear in love; but perfect love casts out fear*, because fear involves punishment, and the one who fears is not *perfected in love*. *We love*, because He first loved us. If someone says, '*I love God*,' and hates his brother, he is a liar; for the one who does not love his brother whom he has seen, cannot *love God* whom he has not seen. And this commandment we have from Him, that the one *who loves God* should love his brother also."

1 John 5:1-3 "Whoever believes that Jesus is the Christ is born of God; and whoever *loves the Father* loves the child born of Him. By this we know that we love the children of God, when *we love God* and observe His commandments. For this is *the love of God*, that we keep His commandments; and His commandments are not burdensome."

2 John 1:3 "Grace, mercy and peace will be with us, from God the Father and from Jesus Christ, the Son of the Father, *in truth and love.*"

2 John 1:6 "And this is *love*, that we walk according to His commandments. This is the commandment, just as you have heard from the beginning, that you should walk in it."

Revelation 2:4 "But I have this against you, that you have left *your first love.*"

OUR LOVE FOR OTHERS

Matthew 5:43-44 "You have heard that it was said, 'You shall *love your neighbor*, and hate your enemy.' But I say to you, *love your enemies*, and pray for those who persecute you."

Matthew 5:46 "For if you *love those who love you*, what reward have you? Do not even the tax-gatherers do the same?"

Matthew 19:19 "Honor your father and mother; and you shall *love your neighbor* as yourself."

Matthew 22:39 "The second is like it, 'You shall *love your neighbor* as yourself.'"

Mark 12:31 "The second is this, 'You shall *love your neighbor* as yourself.' There is no other commandment greater than these."

Luke 6:27 "But I say to you who hear, *love your enemies*, do good to those who hate you."

Luke 6:32 "And if you *love those who love you*, what credit is that to you? For even sinners *love those who love them.*"

Luke 6:35 "But *love your enemies*, and do good, and lend, expecting nothing in return; and your reward will be great, and you will be sons of the Most High; for He Himself is kind to ungrateful and evil men."

John 13:34-35 "A new commandment I give to you, that you *love one another*, even as I have loved you, that you also *love one* *another.* By this all men will know that you are My disciples, if you have *love for one another.*"

John 15:12 "This is My commandment, that you *love one another,* just as I have loved you."

John 15:17 "This I command you, that you *love one another.*"

Romans 12:9-10 "Let *love* be without hypocrisy. Abhor what is evil; cling to what is good. *Be devoted to one another in brotherly love*; give preference to one another in honor."

Romans 13:8-10 "Owe nothing to anyone except to *love one another*; for he who *loves his neighbor* has fulfilled the law. For this, 'You shall not commit adultery, you shall not murder, you shall not steal, you shall not covet,' and if there is any other commandment, it is summed up in this saying, 'You shall *love your neighbor* as yourself.' *Love* does no wrong to a neighbor; *love* therefore is the fulfillment of the law."

Romans 14:15 "For if because of food your brother is hurt, you are no longer walking *according to love*. Do not destroy with your food him for whom Christ died."

Romans 15:30 "Now I urge you, brethren, by our Lord Jesus Christ and by the *love of the Spirit*, to strive together with me in your prayers to God for me."

1 Corinthians 4:21 "What do you desire? Shall I come to you with a rod or with *love* and a spirit of gentleness?"

1 Corinthians 8:1 "Now concerning things sacrificed to idols, we know that we all have knowledge. Knowledge makes arrogant, but *love edifies.*"

1 Corinthians 13:1-4 "If I speak with the tongues of men and of angels, but do not have *love*, I have become a noisy gong or a clanging cymbal. And if I have the gift of prophecy, and know all mysteries and all knowledge; and if I have all faith, so as to remove mountains, but do not have *love*, I am nothing. And if I give all my possessions to feed the poor, and if I deliver my body to be burned, but do not have *love*, it profits me nothing.

Love is patient, *love* is kind, and is not jealous; *love* does not brag and is not arrogant."

1 Corinthians 13:8 "*Love* never fails; but if there are gifts of prophecy, they will be done away; if there are tongues, they will cease; if there is knowledge, it will be done away."

1 Corinthians 13:13 "But now abide faith, hope, *love*, these three; but the greatest of these is *love*."

1 Corinthians 14:1 "Pursue *love*, yet desire earnestly spiritual gifts, but especially that you may prophesy."

1 Corinthians 16:14 "Let all that you do be done in *love*."

1 Corinthians 16:24 "My *love* be with you all in Christ Jesus. Amen."

2 Corinthians 2:4 "For out of much affliction and anguish of heart I wrote to you with many tears; not that you should be made sorrowful, but that you might know the *love* which I have especially for you."

2 Corinthians 2:8 "Wherefore I urge you to reaffirm your *love* for him."

2 Corinthians 6:6 "in purity, in knowledge, in patience, in kindness, in the Holy Spirit, in *genuine love*...."

2 Corinthians 8:7-8 "But just as you abound in everything, in faith and utterance and knowledge and in all earnestness and in the *love* we inspired in you, see that you abound in this gracious work also. I am not speaking this as a command, but as proving through the earnestness of others the sincerity of your *love* also."

2 Corinthians 8:24 "Therefore openly before the churches show them the proof of your *love* and of our reason for boasting about you."

2 Corinthians 11:11 "Why? Because I do not *love* you? God knows I do!"

2 Corinthians 12:15 "And I will most gladly spend and be expended for your souls. If I love you the more, am I to be *loved* the less?"

Galatians 5:6 "For in Christ Jesus neither circumcision nor uncircumcision means anything, but faith working through *love*."

Galatians 5:13-14 "For you were called to freedom, brethren; only do not turn your freedom into an opportunity for the flesh, but *through love serve* one another. For the whole Law is fulfilled in one word, in the statement, 'You shall *love your neighbor* as yourself.' "

Galatians 5:22 "But the fruit of the Spirit is *love*, joy, peace, patience, kindness, goodness, faithfulness."

Ephesians 1:15 "For this reason I too, having heard of the faith in the Lord Jesus which exists among you, and *your love for all the saints*...."

Ephesians 3:17 "So that Christ may dwell in your hearts through faith; and that you, being rooted and grounded in *love*...."

Ephesians 4:2 "With all humility and gentleness, with patience, showing forbearance to one another *in love*...."

Ephesians 4:15-16 "But *speaking the truth in love*, we are to grow up in all aspects into Him, who is the head, even Christ, from whom the whole body, being fitted and held together by that which every joint supplies, according to the proper working of each individual part, causes the growth of the body for *the building up of itself in love*."

Ephesians 5:2 "And *walk in love*, just as Christ also loved you, and gave Himself up for us, an offering and a sacrifice to God as a fragrant aroma."

Ephesians 5:25 "Husbands, *love your wives*, just as Christ also loved the church and gave Himself up for her."

Ephesians 5:28 "So husbands ought also to *love their own wives* as their own bodies. He who *loves his own wife* loves himself."

Ephesians 5:33 "Nevertheless let each individual among you also *love his own wife* even as himself; and let the wife see to it that she respect her husband."

Ephesians 6:23 "Peace be to the brethren, and *love with faith*, from God the Father and the Lord Jesus Christ."

Philippians 1:9 "And this I pray, that your *love may abound still more and more* in real knowledge and all discernment."

Philippians 1:16 "The latter do it out of *love*, knowing that I am appointed for the defense of the gospel."

Philippians 2:1-2 "If therefore there is any encouragement in Christ, if there is any *consolation of love*, if there is any fellowship of the Spirit, if any affection and compassion, make my joy complete by being of the same mind, maintaining the *same love*, united in spirit, intent on one purpose."

Colossians 1:4 "Since we heard of your faith in Christ Jesus and the *love which you have for all the saints*...."

Colossians 1:8 "And he also informed us of *your love in the Spirit*."

Colossians 2:2 "That their hearts may be encouraged, having been *knit together in love*, and attaining to all the wealth that comes from the full assurance of understanding, resulting in a true knowledge of God's mystery, that is, Christ Himself."

Colossians 3:14 "And beyond all these things *put on love*, which is the perfect bond of unity."

Colossians 3:19 "Husbands, *love your wives*, and do not be embittered against them."

1 Thessalonians 1:3 "Constantly bearing in mind your work of faith and *labor of love* and steadfastness of hope in our Lord Jesus Christ in the presence of our God and Father...."

1 Thessalonians 3:6 "But now that Timothy has come to us from you, and has brought us good news of your faith and *love*, and that you always think kindly of us, longing to see us just as we also long to see you."

1 Thessalonians 3:12 "And may the Lord cause you to increase and *abound in love for one another,* and for all men, just as we also do for you."

1 Thessalonians 4:9 "Now as to the *love of the brethren,* you have no need for anyone to write to you, for you yourselves are taught by God to *love one another.*"

1 Thessalonians 5:8 "But since we are of the day, let us be sober, having put on the breastplate of faith and *love,* and as a helmet, the hope of salvation."

1 Thessalonians 5:13 "And that you esteem them very highly *in love* because of their work. Live in peace with one another."

2 Thessalonians 1:3 "We ought always to give thanks to God for you, brethren, as is only fitting, because your faith is greatly enlarged, and the *love of each one of you toward one another* grows ever greater."

1 Timothy 1:5 "But the goal of our instruction is *love* from a pure heart and a good conscience and a sincere faith."

1 Timothy 1:14 "And the grace of our Lord was more than abundant, with the faith and *love* which are found in Christ Jesus."

1 Timothy 2:15 "But women shall be preserved through the bearing of children if they continue in faith and *love* and sanctity with self-restraint."

1 Timothy 4:12 "Let no one look down on your youthfulness, but rather in speech, conduct, *love,* faith and purity, show yourself an example of those who believe."

1 Timothy 6:11 "But flee from these things, you man of God; and pursue righteousness, godliness, faith, *love,* perseverance and gentleness."

2 Timothy 1:7 "For God has not given us a spirit of timidity, but of power and *love* and discipline."

2 Timothy 1:13 "Retain the standard of sound words which you have heard from me, in the faith and *love* which are in Christ Jesus."

2 Timothy 2:22 "Now flee from youthful lusts, and pursue righteousness, faith, *love* and peace, with those who call on the Lord from a pure heart."

2 Timothy 3:10 "But you followed my teaching, conduct, purpose, faith, patience, *love*, perseverance...."

Titus 2:2 "Older men are to be temperate, dignified, sensible, sound in faith, *in love*, in perseverance."

Titus 2:4 "That they may encourage the young women to *love their husbands*, to *love their children*...."

Titus 3:15 "All who are with me greet you. Greet those who *love* us in the faith. Grace be with you all."

Philemon 1:5 "Because I hear of your *love*, and of the faith which you have toward the Lord Jesus, and toward all the saints...."

Philemon 1:7 "For I have come to have much joy and comfort in your *love*, because the hearts of the saints have been refreshed through you, brother."

Philemon 1:9 "Yet for *love's* sake I rather appeal to you—since I am such a person as Paul, the aged, and now also a prisoner of Christ Jesus...."

Hebrews 10:24 "And let us consider how to stimulate one another *to love* and good deeds."

Hebrews 13:1 "Let *love of the brethren* continue."

James 2:8 "If, however, you are fulfilling the royal law, according to the Scripture, 'You shall *love your neighbor* as yourself,' you are doing well."

1 Peter 1:22 "Since you have in obedience to the truth purified your souls for a *sincere love of the brethren*, fervently love one another from the heart."

LOVE IN THE NEW TESTAMENT

1 Peter 2:17 "Honor all men; *love the brotherhood*, fear God, honor the king."

1 Peter 4:8 "Above all, *keep fervent in your love for one another*, because *love* covers a multitude of sins."

1 Peter 5:14 "Greet one another with a *kiss of love*. Peace be to you all who are in Christ."

2 Peter 1:7 "And in your godliness, brotherly kindness, and in your brotherly kindness, *love*."

1 John 2:10 "The one who *loves his brother* abides in the light and there is no cause for stumbling in him."

1 John 3:10-11 "By this the children of God and the children of the devil are obvious: anyone who does not practice righteousness is not of God, nor the one who does not *love his brother*. For this is the message which you have heard from the beginning, that we should *love one another*."

1 John 3:14 "We know that we have passed out of death into life, because we *love the brethren*. He who does not *love* abides in death."

1 John 3:18 "Little children, let us not *love* with word or with tongue, but in deed and truth."

1 John 3:23 "And this is His commandment, that we believe in the name of His Son Jesus Christ, and *love one another*, just as He commanded us."

1 John 4:7-8 "Beloved, let us *love one another*, for love is from God; and everyone who *loves* is born of God and knows God. The one who does not *love* does not know God, for God is love."

1 John 4:11-12 "Beloved, if God so loved us, we also ought to *love one another*. No one has beheld God at any time; if we *love one another*, God abides in us, and His love is perfected in us."

1 John 4:16 "And we have come to know and have believed the love which God has for us. God is love, and the one who *abides in love* abides in God, and God abides in him."

1 John 4:20-21 "If someone says, "I love God," and hates his brother, he is a liar; for the one who does not *love his brother* whom he has seen, cannot love God whom he has not seen. And this commandment we have from Him, that the one who loves God should *love his brother* also."

1 John 5:1-2 "Whoever believes that Jesus is the Christ is born of God; and whoever loves the Father *loves the child* born of Him. By this we know that we *love the children of God*, when we love God and observe His commandments."

2 John 1:1 "The elder to the chosen lady and her children, *whom I love* in truth; and not only I, but also all who know the truth…."

2 John 1:5 "And now I ask you, lady, not as writing to you a new commandment, but the one which we have had from the beginning, that we *love one another*."

3 John 1:1 "The elder to the beloved Gaius, *whom I love* in truth."

3 John 1:6 "And they bear witness to *your love* before the church; and you will do well to send them on their way in a manner worthy of God…."

Jude 1:2 "May mercy and peace and *love* be multiplied to you."

Jude 1:12 "These men are those who are hidden reefs in your *love feasts* when they feast with you without fear, caring for themselves; clouds without water, carried along by winds; autumn trees without fruit, doubly dead, uprooted…."

Revelation 2:19 "I know your deeds, and your *love* and faith and service and perseverance, and that your deeds of late are greater than at first."

Other Titles Available from Granted Ministries Press

Ever, *only*, ALL for *Thee*
Frances Ridley Havergal: Glimpses of
Her Life and Writings
— *Pamela Bugden*

Foundations for the Flock:
Truths About the Church for All the Saints
— *Conrad Mbewe*

The Hidden Life of Prayer
and The Prayer-Life of Our Lord
— *D. M. M'Intyre*

Justification and Regeneration
— *Charles Leiter*

The Person of Christ
The Perfection of His Humanity
Viewed as a Proof of His Divinity
— *Philip Schaff*

Pilgrim of the Heavenly Way
— *Daniel Smith*

Spiritual Depression
Its Causes and Cure
— *D. Martyn Lloyd-Jones*

Valuable Selections from the
Writings of Frances Ridley Havergal
— *Frances Ridley Havergal*

Valuable Selections from the
Writings of George Müller
— *George Müller*

— IN SPANISH —

Justificación and Regeneración
— *Charles Leiter*

WHAT YOU CAN AFFORD POLICY

As with all of the resources that we make available, this book is offered to any who believe they can benefit from it, whether they can pay for it or not. There is a cost for the book, but we do not want this to be an obstacle to anyone. If you cannot afford to purchase a copy, or if you can only afford a portion of the price, we ask that you write and give us the opportunity to serve God by providing for His people. Our only stipulation is that you not request the book unless you are certain to read it within six months. We do not want to generously enlarge your library, but to generously enlarge your spiritual condition.

GRANTED MINISTRIES PRESS
120 N. Third St.
Hannibal, MO 63401
www.grantedministries.org

Forthcoming Titles from Granted Ministries Press

Thoughts for Young Men   *J.C. Ryle*

The Selected Writings of   *D. M. M'Intyre*
D. M. M'Intyre

Thoughts on Religious Experience   *Archibald Alexander*

For a current list of projects, including status, cancellations, and projected release dates, visit: grantedministries.org/projects

That in all things He might have preeminence

Granted Ministries strives to make the very best Christian teaching available around the world. We do this primarily through our website and also through the printing of books and distribution of discs. We are a non-profit charity seeking to serve Christ faithfully by diligently helping His church to know Him more fully.

www.grantedministries.org

CLEAR ADVICE

EASY NAVIGATION

MINISTRY PRICES

TRUSTED CONTENT.